MUSLIM KINGDOMS OF SOUTH

Encyclopaedia of Indian History Series

MUSLIM KINGDOMS OF SOUTH

Anil Saxena

ANMOL PUBLICATIONS PVT. LTD.
NEW DELHI - 110 002 (INDIA)

ANMOL PUBLICATIONS PVT. LTD.
H.O.: 4374/4B, Ansari Road, Darya Ganj,
New Delhi-110 002 (India)
Ph.: 23278000, 23261597
B.O.: No. 1015, Ist Main Road, BSK IIIrd Stage
IIIrd Phase, IIIrd Block,
Bangalore - 560 085 (India)
Visit us at: www.anmolpublications.com

Muslim Kingdoms of South

First Published, 2007

ISBN 81-261-2957-3

PRINTED IN INDIA

Printed at Mehra Offset Press, Delhi.

Contents

Preface

India is a great country, which boasts of a rich history, richer than many a nation in the world. It's history is vast and illustrious by all counts. The term 'India' finds its origin in the 'Indus Valley Civilisation' that flourished on the banks of the river Indus. The history of India is one of the most interesting and enlightening ones in the midst of a plethora of world histories. For the purpose of ease, it can broadly be divided into three distinct periods, namely; Ancient Period, Medieval Period and the Modern Period.

The first period, *i.e.*, the Ancient Period begins several centuries before Christs' birth and extends to around 1000 A.D. The period boasts of great kings like Chandragupta Maurya, Ashoka, Chandragupta Vikramaditya and Harsha. The second period, i.e., the Medieval Period starts with the expeditions of Sultan Mahmud of Ghazni to India. Earlier, in 712, Muhammad bin Qasim had conqured Sindh, which became a province of Omayyad Caliphate. Thereafter, a chain of rulers from different dynasties, such as Slave dynasty, Khilji dynasty, Tughlaq dynasty, Sayyed dynasty, Lodi dynasty and Mughal dynasty, reigned over the country. All these monarchs ruled over a vast empire, spanned over, the sub-continent and enjoyed this country's rich and opulant resources. The last of these dynasties, the Mughals, whose period ranges from 1526 to 1857, left the most indelible marks of their grandeur and splendid life-style after them. Hindu-Muslim Culture, Urdu, Red Fort, Taj Mahal and Delhi's Jama Masjid are the symbols, to name a few.

The third Period, i.e., the Modern Period starts from the Portuguese attacks in the 15th century. The formation of East India Company in 1600, through a charter signed by Queen Elizabeth I, which granted permission to trade with India gave a new turn to contemporary history. Though, the company had to face tough resistance from the Dutch and French. However, the British company succeeded in destabilising them and soon the company's business operations expanded into political ambitions. After being remained under the British rule for almost one hundred years, Indians made a brave effort to turn them upside down. In 1857, the first-ever large-scale revolt took place which shook the British at least for some time. Within a month of the capture of Delhi, the revolt spread like a wild-fire to different parts of the country. The most important element in the occurrence of the Revolt was Hindu-Muslim unity. People exhibited patriotic sentiments, without a touch of communal feelings. All revolutionaries, unanimously recognised Bahadur Shah Zafar as India's emperor. Begun as a mutiny of soldiers, it, soon, turned into a big revolt. Unfortunately, the great revolt, known as the first freedom struggle, failed due to certain reasons. But, it sowed a seed, which later flourished into a strong tree. During a second phase of slavery, spanning over ninety year, a popular freedom movement came up under Mahatma Gandhi and Congress. At last goddess of freedom smiled, the British yoke was lifted and India's independence was declared on 15 August 1947.

The devoted works of a generation of scholars have thrown a flood of light upon the subject. But the results of their research have been chiefly intended for the specialists or are limited to some specific aspects of the vast subject—Indian History. Today, when India is on the path of rapid progress in diverse fields of life, it becomes all the more important for all of us to explain to the world through a comprehensive and a realistic account of its past grandeur and the status, it enjoyed. It will be an injustice to belittle or ignore any aspect, whatsoever, while producing a grand work on a grand subject. This modest, exclusive, comprehensive and multi-volume series of books, namely, *Encyclopaedia of Indian History, Culture and Civilisation*, fulfills that very aim. It consists of thirty books—each being an independent entity, with a separate title.

This book is titled: ***Muslim Kingdoms of South.***

The targeted readership of this voluminous and splendid work comprises one and all belonging to elitists' group or scholars and as well as the rank and file—researchers and students. It hopefully, would quench everyone's thirst upto a saturation point. Nevertheless, all positive remarks and responsive suggestions are bound to help us enhance its usefulness to great academic standerds.

—Editors

1

Major States

Bahmani Kingdom

The foreign Muslim nobles in the Deccan revolted against Sultan Muhammad Tughlaq, occupied Daulatabad and chose Hasan as their Sultan. Hasan assumed the title of Abul-Muzaffar Ala-ud-din Bahman Shah and, thus, laid down the foundation of the independent Bahmani kingdom in 1347 AD. Ferishta wrote that Hasan in his early life, was a servant of a Brahmana named Gangu and therefore, assumed the title of Bahman Shah as a mark of respect to his previous master. But Bahman Shah himself claimed to be a descendant of the famous Persian hero Bahman, son of Isfandiyar. The Bahmani kingdom remained a powerful state of the South and possessed a large part of it for nearly two hundred years.

Bahman Shah proved a capable and ambitious ruler. He made Gulbarga his capital. He extended the territory of his kingdom and, thus, succeeded in making extended from the Wainganga river in the north to the river Krishna in the south, and from Daulatabad in the west to Bhongir in the east. Bahman Shah was an efficient administrator. He divided his kingdom into four provinces (tarafs) whose capitals were Gulbarga, Daulatabad, Barar, and Bidar. He died in 1358 AD.

Bahman Shah was succeeded by his son, Muhammad Shah-I. Muhammad Shah fought against the neighbouring Hindu states of Warangal and Vijayanagara which were established in the southeast and the southwest of his state respectively during the reign of his father. The ruler of Warangal, Kapaya Nayaka and Bukka, the ruler of Vijayanagara, probably made an understanding between each other and claimed the fort of Kaulas and Krishna-Tungabhadra-doab respectively. Muhammad refuted their claim and fought against both of them. He was more successful against Kapaya Nayaka and snatched away the fort of Golkunda from him which was accepted the boundary line between the two. He reached an understanding with Bukka as well by which it was agreed that none would kill the prisoners of war and unarmed subjects of each other. Muhammad died in 1375 AD and was succeeded by his son Ala-ud-din Mujahid. He ruled only for three years and constantly fought against the kingdom of Vijayanagara. While returning from one of his campaigns he was murdered by his cousin Daud. But Daud was murdered by Mujahid's partisans within a month of his accession to the throne and then his brother Muhammad- II was raised to the throne. During this period of internal strife in Bahmani kingdom, Vijayanagara occupied a part of its western coast. Yet, Muhammad-II did not fight against Vijayanagara.

He was a scholarly king, patronised scholars and pursued a peaceful policy. He died in 1397 AD and was succeeded by Ghiyas-ud-din and Shams-ud-din respectively who ruled only for short durations. Shams-ud-din was deposed by Taj-ud-din Firoz Shah who became king in 1397 AD. Taj-ud-din fought against Vijayanagara thrice. He was successful twice but was defeated the third time which reduced his respect. Taj-ud-din was an enlightened ruler. He constructed the new city of Firozabad and improved the ports of Chaul and Dabhol. He was deposed by his brother, Ahmad Shah in 1422 AD who then became the king.

Ahmad Shah (1422-1436 AD) conquered Warangal, plundered part of the Vijayanagara kingdom and successfully attacked Malwa. But he failed against Gujarat. He transferred his capital to Bidar in 1425 AD and remained there till the close of his reign. The quarrels between the foreign and Indian Muslim nobles which became one of the primary reasons of the weakness of the Bahmani kingdom began during his reign. Ala-ud-din-II, his son, succeeded him after his death. He brought to submission the Hindu kingdom of Konkan, married the daughter of the Hindu king of Sangameshwar, failed the attack of Khandesh, and fought against Vijayanagara. He was succeeded by his son Humayun after his death in 1457 AD.

Humayun was a tyrant and was known as zalim. He died in 1461 AD and was succeeded by his minor son, Nizam Shah. Her mother, Maqdoom-e-Jahan formed a regency council consisting of herself, Mahmud Gavan and Khwaja Jahan Turk to look after the administration. The rulers of Malwa and Orissa attacked the Bahmani kingdom during his reign but failed to gain anything. The boy-king died in 1463 AD and was succeeded by his brother, Muhammad-III. The queen mother had become suspicious towards Khwaja Jahan Turk who was now murdered. Mahmud Gavan was then appointed the Wakil-us-Sultanat (wazir) of the kingdom.

Mahmud Gavan was a Persian who came to the Bahmani kingdom as a trader. He proved to be the ablest wazir of the Bahmani kingdom. He subjugated the Hindu ruler of Konkan, captured the fort of Khalna from the king of Sangameshwar, plundered part of the Vijayanagara kingdom and snatched away a part of Goa from it. He also conquered the forts of Rajamundry and Kondavir and successfully plundered the state of Orissa. Besides a successful commander Mahmud Gavan was a capable administrator as well. He strengthened the Central government and raised the number of provinces from four to eight. He tried to abolish the Jagirdari-system and, instead of assigning jagirs to his officers paid them in cash. He paid proper attention towards the training and discipline of the soldiers and, thus, strengthened the Bahmani kingdom militarily. With a view to increase the economic resources of the state, he introduced the system of measurement of land and collected revenue directly from the peasants.

The peasants were provided the facility of paying revenue either in cash or kind. The success of Mahmud Gavan provoked jealousy among the Indian Muslim nobles who succeeded in getting death orders for him from the king while he was drunk. He was then executed on April 5, 1481 AD. Mahmud Gavan was a successful man. He served well the Bahmani rulers for three generations. He established a good college at Bidar. Mahmud Gavan himself was a scholar. He wrote himself two texts—Rauzat-ul-Insha and Diwan-e-Asra. However, he had one shortcoming. His religious policy remained reactionary. The conflict between the foreign Muslim nobles and the Indian Muslim nobles became further sharp after his death which, ultimately, led to the disintegration of the Bahmani kingdom. Muhammad Shah-III died in 1482 AD.

Muhammad Shah-III was succeeded by his son, Mahmud Shah. As he was a minor, the real power of the state passed into the hands of Malik Naib, Hasan Nizam-ul-mulk. The foreign Muslim nobles (pardesis) were dissatisfied due to the execution of Mahmud Gavan and therefore, refused to obey the new king. The foreign Muslim nobles consisted of the Turks, the Mughals, the Persians and the Arabs while the Indian Muslim nobles had Abyssinians on their side. The two groups fought against each other primarily not because of racial differences but to capture the power of the state. Besides, they were divided on religious ground as well. While the foreign Muslims were mostly Shias the Indian Muslims were Sunnis.

The foreign Muslims had come to the Bahmani kingdom in large number, gained strength and formed a distinct party. The Indian Muslim and the Abyssinians grew envious of their growing power in the state and combined themselves against them. Therefore, the court of the Bahmani kingdom was divided into two powerful rival groups which were determined to destroy each other. The weakness of later Bahmani rulers gave encouragement to these groups. Nizam Shah who was a minor failed to check their conflict. Mahmud Gavan who was a foreign Muslim tried to keep a balance between the two groups but finally fell a victim to the conspiracy of Naib Malik who was an Indian Muslim.

The execution of Mahmud Gavan brought the conflict of the rival groups in open and Sultan Mahmud Shah failed to check it. Malik Naib fled away for the safety of his life but the governor of Bidar killed him. The Indian Muslims, in turn, attacked the palace and tried to capture the Sultan but they failed and were killed in large numbers. The Sultan, Mahmud Shah felt so disappointed because of these quarrels that he left the administration in the hands of one Turk noble, Qasim Barid. The provincial governors, however, refused to accept the power of Qasim Barid. First, Malik Ahmad Nizam-ul-mulk, son of the murdered Naib Malik, refused to obey the orders of the state and established his independent rule in 1490 AD at Ahmadnagar. His example was followed by Adil Khan at Bijapur and Imad-ul-mulk at Berar. Thus, the Bahmani kingdom was divided and its provincial governors became independent rulers though none assumed the title of Sultan during the reign of Sultan Mahmud.

Their only bond was jihad (holy war) every year against the idolaters of Vijayanagara. Sultan Mahmud died in 1518 AD. He was succeeded by four weak rulers successively who remained puppets in the in 1538 AD. The Bahmani dynasty and its kingdom came to an end with his death. The Bahmani kingdom was then split into five independent kingdoms, namely, the Adil Shahi of Bijapur, the Qutb Shahi of Golkunda, the Nizam Shahi of Ahmadnagar, the Barid Shahi of Bidar and the Imad Shahi of Berar.

These five Muslim states of the South fought against each other but their primary enemy remained the Hindu kingdom of Vijayanagara. Ahmadnagar conquered Berar in 1574 AD and Bijapur annexed Bidar in 1618-19 AD. The Mughal emperor Akbar occupied part of Ahmadnagar during his reign and the rest of it was conquered by Shah Jahan. The states of Bijapur and Golkunda were finally annexed by the Mughal ruler Aurangzeb.

Administration of Bahmani Kingdom : The rulers of the Bahmani kingdom accepted Abbasaid-Khalifas as their overlord though, in fact, they were independent rulers and behaved accordingly. The first ruler of the kingdom, Bahman Shah could not get much time to look after the administration as he mostly remained busy in fighting.

Muhammad Tughlaq had divided his territories in the Deccan into four provinces Bahman Shah kept that arrangement as it was except that he appointed his own officers everywhere. Muhammad Shah I divided the kingdom into four Atrafs (provinces) whose capitals were Daulatabad, Berar, Bidar and Gulbarga respectively. Provincial governors called Tarafdars with extensive administrative and military powers were appointed in each of these provinces.

Tarafdar collected revenue from his province, organised the provincial army and appointed all civil and military officers of his province. Sometimes Tarafdars were appointed ministers of the king as well. When the kingdom became further extensive and Mahmud Gavan worked as prime minister, the number of provinces was raised from four to eight. Mahmud Gavan attempted to restrict the powers of provincial governors and, for that purpose, fixed some land as the land of the Sultan in each province which was managed by the officers of the central government. Provinces or Atrafs were divided into Sarkars and Sarkars were divided into Parganas for the convenience of administration. The lowest Unit of the administration was the village.

The head of the state was the Sultan who enjoyed all executive, legislative and judicial powers within the state. There was no legal limit to his powers and some of them called themselves the representatives of God on earth. But, in practice, the powers of the Sultan were limited by the powers and advice of powerful ministers and nobles. The Sultan was assisted by ministers in the administration. The prime minister was called Vakil-us-Sultanat, the finance minister Amir-e-Jumla and the foreign minister Wazir-e-Asraf. There were two other ministers called the Wazir-e-kul and the Peshwa but their responsibilities were not fixed up. Sometimes the provincial Tarafdars were also appointed as ministers. The chief judicial officer, after the Sultan, was called the Sadr-e-Jahar. Besides being the judicial officer, he looked after religious affairs and charitable works performed by the state.

The Bahmani kingdom constantly fought against neighbouring Hindu states and therefore, had to keep a large standing army. The head of the army, after the Sultan, was called the Amir-ul-umara. The Sultan kept his personal bodyguards called the Khas-e-Khel. The Bahmani kingdom maintained an artillery as well besides the cavalry, the infantry and war elephants. Shihabuddin Ahmad I introduced Mansabdari system in the army wherein the military officers were assigned jagirs according to their mansabs or ranks to meet the expenses of the armies raised by them. The civilian officers were also assigned mansabs with a view to fix up their salaries. However, the Jagirdars were required to submit the statement of their income government. The officers incharge of Kiledars were also directly responsible to the central government.

Sultans, mansabdars and the nobles enjoyed all sorts of luxuries which was a proof that the Bahmani kingdom was prosperous. However, no evidence is available regarding condition of ordinary people. Probably, as in other parts of India, the common people led a simple life.

The Bahmani kingdom helped in the growth of Muslim culture in south India. Followers of Islam from north India and foreign countries established themselves in the Bahmani kingdom. Different rulers patronised Muslim scholars and religious preachers. Even after the disintegration of the Bahmani kingdom, the rulers of those states which arose on the ruins of it patronised Muslim saints, scholars, artists, etc. and constructed madrasas and several other buildings, and, thus, participated in spreading the Muslim culture in south India.

The conflict with Hindu rulers of south India also forced the rulers of the Bahmani kingdom to provide political and cultural leadership to Islam in the South. Thus, the Bahmani kingdom contributed towards the politics and culture of south India for a long time.

Khandesh

The independent state of Khandesh was established by its governor, Malik Raja after the death of Firoz Tughlaq. It was situated in the valley of the river Tapti. Khandesh could never become a powerful state. It had to fight constantly for its existence against its powerful neighbouring state, the Bahmani kingdom and therefore, remained dependent on the support of Malwa and Gujarat. Most of the rulers of Khandesh accepted the suzerainty of the rulers of Gujarat with whom they had, matrimonial relations as well. Finally, the Mughal emperor Akbar annexed it to his empire in 1601 AD.

Malwa

Malwa was annexed to the Delhi Sultanate first by Ala-ud-din Khalji It remained a part of it till the reign of later Tughlaqs. Dilawar Khan who was appointed governor of Malwa by Firoz Tughlaq in 1390 AD made himself an independent ruler in 1401 AD though he did not assume the title of Sultan. He died in 1405 AD. His son and successor Alp Khan assumed the title of Husang Shah. Husang Shah was once defeated and captured by Muzaffar Shah, ruler of Gujarat, but was left free and sent to suppress the revolt of Malwa Husang Shah utilised that opportunity and once again made himself independent ruler of Malwa. He built up Mandu and made it his capital. Husang Shah fought many battles against Ahmad Shah, the ruler of Gujarat who had succeeded Muzaffar Shah.

But no concrete result came out of those battles. He also failed to capture Gwalior. However, he captured Kalpi and successfully plundered the Hindu states of Orissa. Husang Shah was an ambitious ruler and engaged himself constantly in wars of conquest. But he failed to extend the territory of his kingdom because there existed equally powerful states in his neighbourhood. He died in 1435 AD. He was succeeded by his son Ghazni Khan under the title of Muhammad Shah. He, however, proved himself incompetent and his wazir, Mahmud Khan, succeeded in dethroning him after a year.

Mahmud Khan assumed the title of Mahmud Shah and laid down the rule of Khalji dynasty in Malwa. He ruled between 1436-1469 AD and proved himself the ablest ruler of Malwa. He fought against the rulers of Gujarat, Delhi, Bahmani and Mewar. He extended the territory of his kingdom and got approval of his title of Sultan from the Khalifa of Egypt. He was a just and successful ruler though he was a bigot and pursued an intolerant religious policy towards the Hindus. He died in 1469 AD.

Mahmud Shah was succeeded by his son Ghiyas-ud-din who mostly pursued a policy of peace with his neighbours and enjoyed the pleasures of life. However, he invaded Mewar twice but failed. He allowed the ruler of Gujarat to capture Champaner. He was a bigot and even surpassed his father in certain respects. Probably, his son Nasir-ud-din got him poisoned and sat on the throne in 1500 AD. Nasir-ud-din Shah was a tyrant. He died in 1511 AD and was succeeded by his younger son, Azam Humayun who assumed the title of Mahmud Shah-II.

During the reign of Mahmud Shah-II, his Hindu and Muslim nobles contested for power against each other which helped Medini Rai to build his power even against the Sultan. The Sultan sought the help of Muzaffar-II, the ruler of Gujarat against Medini Rai but was foiled in his attempt because, Medini Rai, in turn, got the support of Rana Sanga, the ruler of Mewar. Mahmud developed enmity with Bahadur Shah, the ruler of Gujarat and was defeated by him in 1531 AD. He was, afterwards, killed and Malwa was occupied by the state of Gujarat. The Mughal emperor Akbar annexed both Malwa and Gujarat to his empire afterwards.

State of Malabar

Malabar and the Portuguese: The whole of the western coast of India, from Goa to Quilon, was outside the Tughluq Empire, and consisted of a number of small principalities, mostly Hindu. Ibn Batuta gives a short account of some of these States which he visited on his way to China in AD 1343-44.

Ibn Batuta boarded a sailing vessel at Gandhar near the mouth of the Narmada, and after, passing through a few harbours reached Sandapur, modern Goa. It was an island, surrounded by a creek, in the midst of which were thirty-six villages and two cities, namely, the old one, built by the old Hindu rulers, and a new city built by the Muslims, when they first conquered it passing through a small island, probably Anjidiv, Ibn Batuta reached Hinawar (probably modern Honavar) inhabited by Muslims who were "powerful at sea" and "earned their living by maritime trade". The ruler was a Muslim, Jamal-ud-din Muhammad, but he acknowledged the suzerainty of a Hindu, probably the Hoysala king.

Though Ibn Batuta speaks in a general way of the coast of Malabar—the pepper country—as extending from Goa to Quilon, it appears from his detailed description that Malabar proper was reached three days after he left Hinawar.

Ibn Batuta found twelve Hindu States in Malabar. Some of them were very powerful, possessing an army of fifty thousand men, while others were very weak, and could not muster more than three thousand. Yet they lived in peace and amity. That the rulers were all Nairs follows from the statement that "the rulers in this land bequeath their sovereignty to the sons of their sisters and exclude their own children".

Although the rulers were Hindu, there was a strong Muslim community in each State. Though they usually lived apart, they received very fair and liberal treatment and enjoyed perfect freedom of worship which the Muslim rulers denied to the Hindus. In Fakanar (a place in South Canara) the thirty warships of the Raja were in charge of a Muslim commander. The ruler of Jurfattan which has been identified with Cannanore, possessed many ships which went to Oman, Fars, and Yemen.

After a brief halt at Calicut, to which reference will be made later, Ibn Batuta proceeded by way of river to Quilon. On his way he passed through a Jewish settlement at Kunjakari living under a Jewish chief, but paying tax to the Hindu ruler of Quilon. This Hindu Raja held the Muslims in high regard, and they had a prosperous settlement under their own chief and judge, both of whom hailed from Persia.

State of Calicut

The most powerful chief in Malabar, during the 14th and 15th centuries, was the ruler of Calicut, called Zamorin. Reference has been made above to the rule of the Perumals in Kerala and the last king of this dynasty, Cheraman Perumal. Various stories are current about his pilgrimage, after abdication and conversion to either Christianity or Islam. These traditions have little historical value, and were evidently circulated to explain the growth of Muslim and Christian settlements in Malabar about this time.

The date of Cheraman Perumal is not definitely known, but most probably he flourished between AD 750 and 825. The end of the rule of the Perumals gave rise to a number of small principalities in Malabar, the most important of which was Calicut. Many traditions are current, tracing the line of the rulers of Calicut, called Zamorin, in an unbroken line of succession from Manavikraman, the son of Cheraman Perumal and a Nair girl belonging to the family of the Eradis of Nediyiruppu. It is said that as this son could not succeed his father under the matriarchal system prevalent among the Nairs, Cheraman Perumal, at the time of his abdication, gave him, "as a special mark of regard and affection his sword and the small strip of territory on the coast which later on became the port of Calicut".

Whatever we might think of this story or of the traditional account of the kingdom in subsequent times, there is no doubt that it was the most powerful kingdom and the chief centre of trade in Malabar as early as the beginning of the fourteenth century AD.

The riches derived from trade enabled the Zamorin to extend his authority along the Malabar coast from Cannanore to Cochin. The Hindu ruler of Cochin traced his descent from the Surya-Kshatriya clan to whom Cheraman Perumal is said to have given the country round Cochin when he divided his empire. In course of time the kingdom was split up among five branches of the dynasty, who formed a sort of federation, the oldest male member among all the branches taken together having the right to succeed to the nominal headship. This naturally gave rise to internal dissensions, full advantage of which was taken by the Zamorin of Calicut. By offering his help to one of the rival parties, he could easily establish his political influence in Cochin, and in this way he conquered a large part of the region round Cochin and reduced the Raja to a state of vassalage.

According to the historical chronicles of Kerala, "the Cochin Raja paid an annual tribute to his suzerain (Zamorin), obtained his overlord's recognition before his accession, sent contingents to the Zamorin's army, and refrained from striking coins and roofing his palace with tiles. He had to send all his pepper to Calicut, and the Christians were deprived of the right of navigation which was transferred to the Moors". This is partly corroborated by the Portuguese accounts according to which the kingdom of Cochin, like Cannanore, was subject to the Zamorin, who often drove the king of Cochin out of his kingdom and restored him at his pleasure. The king of Cochin, we are further told, gave him every year a certain number of elephants and could not strike coins nor roof his palace with tiles.

Ibn Batuta, who visited the city of Calicut no less than six times, and stayed there for nearly three months on his first visit, has left an account of its commercial importance. It was "one of the chief harbours of the country of Malabar, where people from China, Sumatra (Jawa), Ceylon (Saylan), the Maldive islands (Mahal), Yemen and Fars come, and here gather merchants from all quarters of the globe. And the harbour of Calicut is one of the largest in the world".

The trade and commerce were in the hands of Muslims, mostly traders from Arabian ports. Ibrahim, a merchant from Bahrein, was the head of the merchants in this town and held the office of 'Shah Bandar' or 'receiver-general of duties'. He was the chief officer in the customs house with whom foreign merchants and captains negotiated. The judge of Calicut was also a Muslim. Another Muslim, the shipmaster Misqal, "possessed great riches and many ships for trading purposes in India, China, Yemen and Fars".

Thus, although the ruler was Hindu, the Muslims strongly dominated not only the commerce but also the politics of the kingdom of Calicut. The king gave absolute freedom of Muslims, though he forbade the slaughter of cows and beef. The religious toleration, the good administration which guaranteed security and impartiality of treatment to all, the friendly attitude of Zamorin to all foreign trader some of the causes that made Calicut the chief centre of trade in Malabar.

But these very virtues of the Zamorin proved his undoing on the advent of the Portuguese.

Gujarat

Raja Karan (Rai Karan) was defeated by the forces of Ala-ud-din Khalji and Gujarat was annexed to the Delhi Sultanate in 1297 AD. Gujarat then remained a province of the Delhi Sultanate till 1401 AD when Zafar Khan, the governor of Gujarat, declared himself as an independent Sultan. He assumed the title of Muzaffar Shah in 1407 AD. Muzaffar defeated Sultan Hushang of Malwa and occupied his capital, Dhar, though restored his kingdom to him afterwards. Muzaffar died in 1411 AD.

Muzaffar was succeeded by his grandson Ahmad Shah. Ahmad Shah ruled for thirty-two years. He fought against the neighbouring rulers of Rajasthan, Malwa and south India. He was a successful ruler. He built up a new city, Ahmadabad and made it his capital. He died in 1433 AD. He was succeeded by his eldest son Muhammad Shah-II who died in 1451 AD. Muhammad Shah-II was succeeded in turn by Qutb-ud-din Ahmad Shah and Daud Khan. The last two rulers proved themselves incompetent. While Qutb-ud-din ruled between 1451-1458 AD, the reign of Daud Khan was limited only to some days. In 1458 AD, the nobles dethroned Daud Khan and chose Fateh Khan, son of Muhammad-II, to be the ruler. Fateh Khan assumed the title of Abul Fateh Mahmud and is famous in history as Mahmud Begarha.

Mahmud Begarha ruled between 1458-1511 AD and has been regarded as the greatest Sultan of his dynasty. He fought many battles. He suppressed those nobles who desired to place his brother, Hasan Khan on the throne and defeated those Hindu Chiefs who challenged his authority. He supported the Bahmani kingdom against Malwa and his maternal grandfather Jam Nanda against his rebellious Hindu subjects. However, his best success was capture of the forts of Girnar and Champaner. This success brought him the nickname Begarha.

Mahmud fought against the Portuguese and was supported by the Egyptian fleet but he could not check their influence on the sea, and finally, compromised with them. Mahmud raised Gujarat to the status of one of the powerful states of northern India. Besides, Gujarat prospered during his reign and progress was achieved in the field of literature and fine arts. Mahmud, however, was a bigoted Sunni and pursued an intolerant religious policy towards his Hindu subjects. Mahmud Begarha was succeeded by his son Khalil Khan who assumed the title of Muzaffar Shah-II. Muzaffar Shah supported Mahmud Khalji, the ruler of Malwa against his wazir Medini Rai and succeeded in restoring his authority in Mandu though Chanderi remained with Medini Rai. He fought hard against the ruler of Mewar, Rana Sanga who was supporting Medini Rai and other Rajput rulers against Muslim rulers.

But he did not succeed against the Rana. He died in 1526 AD. Muzaffar was succeeded by Sikandar and Mahmud-II respectively. Both of them proved incompetent and could rule only for some months. Then, in July 1526 AD, Bahadur Shah ascended the throne and his period of reign marked the zenith of the power of the state of Gujarat. He conquered Malwa in 1531 AD and plundered Chittor, the capital of Mewar. However, the Mughal ruler Humayun proved his greatest enemy. Humayun once succeeded in capturing the entire Gujarat. Bahadur Shah was murdered by the Portuguese in 1537 AD. After him, no capable man ruled over Gujarat and it was finally conquered by the Mughal ruler Akbar in 1572 AD.

Rival Kingdom

Political History : The foundation of the Vijayanagara kingdom on the southwest coast of India was laid down by two brothers, Harihara and Bukka, two of the five sons of Sangama. They were ministers in the state of Kampili. When

Sultan Muhammad Tughlaq conquered Kampili he imprisoned these two brothers, took them to Delhi and forced them to embrace Islam. Afterwards, when there occurred a revolt in Kampili, Muhammad Tughlaq sent them there to suppress that revolt. They failed in their attempt because of the resistance of the people of Kampili who were inspired by the spirit of independence. The success of Kapaya Nayaka and Ballala-II in liberating the Andhra, and Dravida Pradesh inspired the two brothers to lead the liberation movement of the Hindus in the southwest.

One saint, Vidyaranya encouraged them to accept Hinduism once again and pleaded to his guru, Vidyatirtha, the chief priest of Advaita-matha at Sringeri for it. Vidyatirtha converted them to Hinduism and they decided to liberate their people from Muslim domination. In 1336 AD, Harihara founded the independent kingdom of Hampi-Hastinavati and was crowned as its first king. On his coronation day, he founded the capital city of Vijayanagara (Vidyanagara). This very small state grew up as the mighty kingdom of Vijayanagara afterwards.

Harihara I ruled between 1336-1356 AD. His first capital was Anegondi but he shifted it to Vijayanagara after seven years. Harihara was a capable ruler but he had to struggle hard against his neighbours. Qutlugh Khan, the governor of Devagiri did not like the establishment of a Hindu state by his side. Even Vir Ballala-III, Kapaya Nayak and his friend Prolaya Verna who were leading the independence movement of the Hindus in the South were not friendly to him. Yet, Harihara succeeded in extending the territory of his kingdom.

While Ballala-III was attempting to conquer Madura, Harihara captured part of his eastern territory. Afterwards when Ballala was murdered in 1342 AD, Harihara annexed his entire kingdom. He then conquered the state of Kadamba and defeated the Sultan of Madura. Harihara also established a sound system of administration, encouraged agriculture and strengthened the fortification of the forts of Badami, Udayagiri and Goofy. His civil administration lasted until the very last days of the Vijayanagara empire.

Harihara was succeeded by his brother Bukka-I. Bukka centralised the administration, brought provincial governors under his effective control and conquered Tamil Nadu. He came to an understanding with the ruler of Warangal and then pressed the Bahmani ruler, Muhammad Shah-I to hand over Krishna-Tungabhadra-Doab to him. From that time started the prolonged struggle for power in the South between the Bahmani and Vijayanagara empires. During the reign of Bukka, the river Krishna was accepted as the boundary line of the two states. However, the most important conquest of Bukka was that of" Madura because of which his empire extended up to Rameshvaram in the extreme south.

Thus, Bukka extended further the territory of that kingdom which he had inherited from Harihara. The same way, Bukka also proved himself as a capable ruler. He claimed to be the protector of Hinduism and assumed the title of Vedmarga-pratishthapaka or the establisher of the path of the Vedas. (Neither Harihara nor Bukka assumed the title of the king.) Yet, he pursued a liberal religious policy and all religions, viz., Jainism, Buddhism, Islam and Christianity were provided equal freedom by the state which remained the settled policy of the Vijayanagara empire till its extinction. Fresh commentaries were written on the Vedas and the allied religious texts during his reign. He encouraged Telugu literature and was a patron of Nachana Soma, greatest Telugu poet of the age. Bukka died in 1377 AD.

Bukka-I was succeeded by his son Harihara-II (1377-1404 AD) who assumed the title of Maharajadhiraja (king of kings). He conquered Kanara, Mysore, Trichnapali, Kanchi, etc. and forced the king of Sri Lanka (Ceylon) to pay him tribute. Bahmani Sultan Mujahid Shah attacked Vijayanagara in 1377 AD but failed to get any success and was murdered while returning from his campaign. Taking advantage of the dissensions in the Bahmani kingdom. Harihara attacked Konkan and northern Karnataka and captured the ports of Chaul and Dabhol as well as Goa which made him the master of the entire west coast of the Deccan. Bahmani Sultans, Muhammad Shah II and Firoz Shah respectively attempted to capture Krishna-Tungabhadra-Doab from him but failed.

Thus, Harihara II extended further the territory of his empire. He was a successful commander and proved himself equally successful administrator. When he died in 1404 AD there ensued a war of succession among his sons. First, Virupaksha I crowned himself but was overthrown just after a year by his brother Bukka II. Bukka II, in turn, was overthrown by Devaraya I who ascended the throne in 1406 AD. Firoz Shah, the Bahmani Sultan attacked Vijayanagara immediately after his accession to the throne but failed to achieve any success. Devaraya I strengthened his cavalry and recruited Turkish-archers in it.

The last years of Devaraya's reign passed on peacefully and Vijayanagara became the centre of learning in the South. He died in 1422 AD and was succeeded by his son Ramachandra who ruled only for some months and, in turn, was succeeded by his brother Vijaya I. Vijaya I ruled between 1422-1430 AD but he left the administration primarily in the hands of his son Devaraya, who ascended the throne after his death. Devaraya II fought against the Bahmani kingdom twice but that wielded no concrete result. However, he succeeded in defeating the rulers of Orissa and Andhra Pradesh. He also recruited Turkish-archers in his army.

The Italian traveller, Nicolo Conti and Abdur Razzaq, the Persian ambassador visited Vijayanagara during his reign. Both described Vijayanagara as the most prosperous and powerful state of south India. Devaraya II was succeeded by his brother Vijaya II who left the throne after a year in favour of his nephew, Malikarjuna who ruled between 1446-1465 AD. The states of Orissa and Bahmani attacked Vijayanagara during his reign and Orissa captured the forts of Kondavidu and Udayagiri from it. Malikarjuna was, probably, murdered by his cousin, Virupaksha if who captured the throne in 1465 AD. But the provincial governors refused to obey him which weakened the Vijayanagara empire.

It resulted in the loss of a part of its territory to Orissa and the capture of Goa, Konkan and northern Karnataka by the Bahmani kingdom. However, the empire was saved because of the efforts of Saluva Narasingha, the chief of Chandragiri. The incapability of Virupaksha-II led to the downfall of his dynasty. He was murdered by one of his sons in 1485 AD who, however, renounced his claim to the throne in favour of his younger brother, Praudha Devaraya. But Saluva Narasingha soon dethroned him, captured the throne in 1485 AD and laid down the foundation of the rule of his own dynasty i.e., the Saluva dynasty.

Saluva Narasingha remained the first and the last ruler of his dynasty. He failed to capture Krishna-Tungabhadra-Doab from the Bahmani kingdom. However, he saved the Vijayanagara empire from further disintegration by successfully keeping the provincial governors under his control. He died in 1490 AD. Before his death, he appointed Naras Nayaka as the guardian of his two minor sons and the regent of the kingdom.

Naras Nayaka placed one of his sons, Timma on the throne though enjoyed all the powers of the state himself. Naras Nayaka died in 1503 AD and his son, Vira Narasingha who became regent in his place got Timma murdered in 1505 AD. Now Vira Narasingha became the ruler and founded the rule of a new dynasty, the Taluva dynasty.

Vira Narasingha ruled only up to 1509 AD. Yet, he strengthened his army, made his subjects warlike, concluded a treaty with the Portuguese governor, Almeida for purchasing all the horses imported by him, pursued a liberal policy in administration and foiled invasions of the Bahmani kingdom. Vira Narasingha was succeeded by his brother, Krishnadevaraya who ruled till 1529 AD. Krishnadevaraya proved himself as the greatest ruler of Vijayanagara. The empire reached at the zenith of its power and prosperity during his reign. By that time, the Bahmani kingdom was divided into five independent kingdoms. Yet, all these five states were the determined enemies of the Vijayanagara empire.

Therefore, his main contest was against those Muslim states which were determined to destroy Vijayanagara. Sultan Mahmud Shah declared jihad and attacked Vijayanagara in the very beginning of his reign. Krishnadevaraya, however, not only defeated him but hotly pursued him. Yousuf Adil Khan, the ruler of Bijapur was killed in the battle and Krishnadevaraya captured Krishna-Tungabhadra Doab, and the forts of Raichur and Bidar. However, he returned Bidar state to Mahmud Shah by which he desired to bring about a division among the five Muslim states. Next, he captured Warangal and snatched away the forts, of Udyagiri and Kondavidu from Orissa. Golkunda and Bijapur also attacked Vijayanagara in turn. Both were defeated.

The army of Bijapur was pursued and its capital Gulbarga was captured by Krishnadevaraya. However, he returned after placing on the throne the eldest son of Muhammad Shah II. Thus Krishnadevaraya defeated all his enemies and recaptured all territory and forts of the Vijayanagara empire which were lost by its previous rulers. He remained undefeated in the battle. Besides, he was a capable administrator and patron of fine arts and literature. He founded the city of Negallapur, built up many Gopurams and Mandapas and beautified his capital city, Vijayanagara. Felugu literature made tremendous progress during his reign. The Vijayanagara empire reached to its zenith in peace, order., power, prosperity and learning during his reign.

The Mughal emperor, Babur described Krishnadevaraya as the most powerful ruler of India in his autobiography Baburnama.

Krishnadevaraya was-succeeded by his brother Achyuta Raya (1530-42 AD). He proved himself a weak ruler. The central authority weakened during his reign. He was succeeded by his nephew, Sadasivo Raya in 1542 AD. He too was an incapable ruler and the real authority of the state passed into the hands of his minister, Rama Raya. Rama Raya was an able administrator but failed as a diplomat. He tried to create dissensions among five Muslim states which once formed the Bahmani kingdom. He helped one against another, in turn. But, ultimately, this policy failed and all these states united themselves against Vijayanagara in the name of Islam.

The combined army of Bijapur, Ahmadnagar, Golkunda and Bidar attacked Vijayanagara and the famous battle of Talikota took place on 23 January 1565 AD. The army of Vijayanagara was completely defeated and the invaders completely destroyed the capital city of Vijayanagara.

The battle of Talikota crippled the Vijayanagara empire but could not entirely destroy it. The brother of Rama Raya, Tirumala transferred the capital to Penugonda and maintained the existence of the empire. The mutual jealousy of the victors prevented them to unite among themselves once against Vijayanagara. That also helped the efforts of Tirumala. In 1570 AD, Tirumala dethroned Sadasiva Raya and captured the throne for himself. He, thus, laid down the foundation of a new dynasty, the Aravidu dynasty. Tirumala was succeeded by his son, Ranga-II who was a successful ruler. He in turn, was succeeded by his brother, Venkata-II. The empire began to disintegrate during his rule. The last important ruler of this dynasty was Ranga-III. He could not keel) the provincial governors under his control. Independent kingdoms were established at Mysore, Bednur, Madura, Tanjore etc. and the Vijayanagara empire reached its end.

An Estimate : The Vijayanagara empire was one of the successful results of political contest of the Hindus against Muslim aggression in south India. The founder rulers Harihara and Bukka were inspired by the contemporary Hindu saint, Madhava Vidyanaranya to establish it primarily in defence of Hindu religion. They largely succeeded in their aim. Of course, the rulers of Vijayanagara also fought against the Hindu rulers of Orissa, Warangal and others for their political gains, yet, their main enemies remained the Muslim rulers of Bahmani kingdom or rulers of those five states in which Bahmani kingdom was divided afterwards.

The causes of the conflict between the Vijayanagara and the Bahmani kingdom were economic, political and cultural. Both, primarily, contested for capturing the Krishna Tungabhadra-Doab. The Doab was on the boundary of both the kingdoms and both desired to capture it with a view to extend their territories.

The Doab was not only very fertile but also rich in minerals, e.g., iron, and also had diamond mines which allured both the kingdoms to fight against each other for economic gains. Besides, on the one hand, while the Muslim rulers of the South were determined to destroy the strong hold of Hindu political power and culture represented by Vijayanagara empire, on the other hand, the Hindu rulers of Vijayanagara fought back to save their political existence and Hindu culture in the South and they succeeded in their efforts for a long time.

The rulers of Vijayanagara followed the traditions of Hindu polity in administration. The king was the head of the state and he was regarded as the God's representative on the earth. He was the lawmaker, the highest administrator, the supreme commander of the army and the highest judicial authority in the state. Yet, the kings of Vijayanagara were not tyrants but enlightened despots. The king was assisted by a council of ministers in administration and its advice was binding on the king at times. The king was guided by the rules of Dharma and the rulers of Vijayanagara looked after the welfare of their subjects as defined by Dharma. Besides, the ministers, there were many other high officials in the state. Different departments looked after different activities and thousands of civil servants worked in those departments.

The empire was divided into six provinces for the convenience of administration. The head of a province was called Prantpati or Nayaka. Mostly the relatives of the king were appointed to these high offices of the state and they enjoyed wide powers in relation to their respective provinces. The provinces were divided into smaller units. A province was divided into Mandals and Mandals were further subdivided into smaller units called Nadu, Sthal, Kottam etc. However, the smallest unit was the village. Certain historians have described that one distinguished feature of the administration of the Vijayanagara empire was the existence of a particular, type of feudalism.

The king used to assign land called Amarama to his feudal chiefs who, in return, paid fixed yearly amount to the king and also kept a fixed number of soldiers to assist him in wars. They were called Amara Nayakas were fairly independent in their internal administration, owed more responsibility in administering their territories as compared to provincial governors and mostly became hereditary owners of their lands or Jagirs. In the middle of the 16th century, their number was nearly two hundred. The village constituted the smallest unit of administration where the village-assembly (Panchayat) looked after the administration of the village but enjoyed little autonomous powers.

There were some officers for the village. These officers of the village enjoyed hereditary rights. The officer called the Sentayava looked after the income and expenditure of the village, the Chaukidar of the village was called the Talra and the Begra looked after unemployed ones, labourers and their wages, etc. Besides, there were twelve administrative officers jointly called the Ayagaras who were appointed by the government to look after certain specific duties in the areas assigned to them. They were not paid wages but were exempted from taxes in return of their services to the state.

The primary sources of the income of the state were the land-revenue, irrigation-tax, grazing-tax and import-export duties on merchandise goods. The land-revenue was 1/5th or a little more of the produce. The Vijayanagara empire kept a large standing army which constituted of war elephants, cavalry and infantry. The kings recruited Turkish-archers in their army. They also kept an artillery but it was in a crude form. There was a separate department to look after the military administration.

The head of military department was called the Dandanayaka or the Senapati. All sorts of coins, viz., of gold, silver and copper were issued by the rulers of Vijayanagara. Figures of different gods and goddesses were marked on coins. The justice of Vijayanagara kings was severe. Death-sentence, mutilation and confiscation of the property were the deterrent punishments for criminals. The rulers of Vijayanagara were devotees of Vaishnavism. However, they were tolerant towards all other religions. The Muslims, the Christians, the Yahudis and people of other faiths were provided equal protection by the state.

Thus, the kings of Vijayanagara established a liberal, tolerant and efficient civil administration. But, their military organisation remained weak and its primary weakness was a weak artillery. Besides, the kings gave extensive powers to provincial governors and Amara-Nayakas. That proved a weakness of their civil administration because when the central authority became weak, they assumed independence and, thus, participated in the disintegration of the empire.

Society was well organised in the Vijayanagara empire. Women were respected in the society. They were educated and were absorbed in government services. They were trained not only in fine arts like music, (lance, painting, etc. but also in fighting, wrestling and weapons of war. Women, therefore, were employed as bodyguards as well. Many scholarly women were patronised by the court. However, certain social evils concerning women as child marriages, polygamy, dowry system, practice of sati, Devadasi system etc., were prevalent in the society.

However, efforts were made by the state for improving the condition of women. Two clear proofs are available for, that. Because of child-marriages, the dowry system had become rampant in the society. The Brahamanas, therefore, requested the state to declare taking and giving of dowry illegal and the state accepted, it. It is proved by an inscription of 1424-25 AD. The same way, though the state charged marriage-tax from both the parties, it exempted people in case of remarriage of widow and, thus, encouraged widow-marriages.

The state did not encourage the practice of Sati though did not prohibit it. Brahmanas were respected in the society. Except the Brahmanas who avoided meat from their diet, there was no restriction of any sort on other castes in matters of food except the flesh of oxen or cow. Animal sacrifices were common. Mostly buffaloes and sheep were sacrificed on occasions of important festivals.

The people wore both cotton and silk clothes. Man wore Dhoti, shirt, cap or Pagri and a Dupatta on his shoulder. Woman used Dhoti and Choli while rich woman used Petticoat as well. Shoes were used only by rich people. Both men and women used ornaments. The state did not arrange for the education of the people but temples and Matths did it and the state provided ample financial assistance to them. The Agraharas provided education only of the Vedas.

The Vijayanagara empire was the most prosperous state of its time. Several foreign travellers who visited Vijayanagara during the fifteenth and sixteenth century gave glowing description of the wealth and prosperity of the state and its people. The Italian traveller Nicolo Conti, the Portuguese traveller Domingos Paes and the Persian ambassador Abdur Razzaq praised the riches of the Vijayanagara empire.

They described that not only the king and the nobles were rich but even the common people enjoyed prosperity. The common people could afford to wear ornaments in their ears, necks, arms, fingers, etc. Besides the gold, pearls, diamonds and other precious stones were used to prepare ornaments. There was no dearth of any commodity; the prices of all articles were low and everything remained stored up in case of need. All travellers also praised the beauty and splendour of the city of Vijayanagara. Nicolo Conti wrote:

> "In this city there are estimated to be ninety thousand men fit to bear arms. The king is more powerful than all the other kings of India."

Barbosa described:

> "(The city is) of great extent, highly populous and the seat of an active commerce in country dealing in diamonds, rubies from Pegu, silk of China and Alexandria and Cinnabar, camphor, musk, pepper and sandal from Malabar."

The rulers of Vijayanagara were largely responsible for this prosperity of their state. They had encouraged agriculture, trade and commerce and provided every facility to their subjects for their development. There had been, therefore, tremendous progress in every field and the fruits were enjoyed both by the state and its subjects.

The kings were very much tolerant towards people of all faith and therefore, got cooperation from all. Barbosa praised King Krishnadevaraya very much. He wrote: "The king is extremely liberal in religious affairs. The Christians, the Yahudis, the Muslims, etc. can come and go, live wherever they like and pursue their religion freely in his kingdom." Iranian traveller Abdur Razzaq praised the city of Vijayanagara thus: "I have never seen a city like Vijayanagara nor ever heard of a city in the world like it. 'The city has been encircled by seven walls, one inside the other, for protection." 'The Portuguese traveller Domingos Paes also wrote:

> "it is the most beautiful city of the world where wheat, rice, barley, pulses and every other article is available in abundance."

He again wrote:

> "The king has enormous wealth, soldiers and elephants because everything is available here in abundance .... You will find citizens of every country here because the people of this city carry on trade, in precious stones particularly in diamonds, with every Country of the world."

Besides brisk internal trade, the empire maintained trade relations with distant foreign countries as Malaya, Burma, China, Arabia, Iran, Egypt, Africa, Abyssinia and Portugal. The main articles of export were cloth, rice, iron, sugar, saitpetre, spices and perfumes while the articles which were primarily imported in the country were horses, pearls, copper, mercury, silk and velvet.

The trade was carried on both by land and sea and the Indians manufactured ships of their own. According to Abdur Razzaq, the kingdom of Vijayanagara had three hundred ports. The Vijayanagara empire kept a small navy as well. The main industries of Vijayanagara were cloth, perfumes and utensils of various metals. The industrialists and businessmen were organised into trade-guilds to look after the interests of trade and industry. Mostly gold and copper coins were used though there were some silver coins also.

Thus, the empire enjoyed widely prosperous economy. However, the system suffered from one serious defect. Mostly the burden of taxation was suffered by the common people which resulted in economic disparity among the people.

Literature and fine arts progressed within the Vijayanagara empire. The rulers encouraged Sanskrit, Tamil, Telugu and Kannada literatures and languages. During its early period, Sayana wrote commentaries of the Vedas. His brother Madhava Vijayaranya was also a scholar of repute. King Bukka I encouraged Telugu literature. He provided protection to a great Telugu-poet, Nachan Soma. King Devaraya II provided court-patronage to thirty four poets. King Krishnadevaraya made free Telugu from the influence of Sanskrit language and, thus, opened way for independent writings called Prabhanda. His court was graced by eight famous poets of Telugu including Pedanna.

Besides Telugu, he patronised scholars of Tamil and Kannada as well. Therefore, the rule of king Krishnadevaraya marked the zenith of the growth of various literatures. He himself was a scholar and patronised many scholars at his court. During the entire period remarkable texts on religion, philosophy, grammar, drama, music, dance etc. were produced. Fine arts like music, dance, painting and architecture also made good progress. The temple of Vitthalaswami and the Hazara temple built by Krishnadevaraya have been regarded as the finest specimens of Hindu architecture.

Thus, the Vijayanagara empire occupied an important place in the history of its own times. It occupies a remarkable place in Indian history because of its polity, economy administration and cultural progress. Its one remarkable success had been that it provided shelter and the opportunity to grow Hindu religion and culture in the South against Muslim onslaughts. Dr. A.L. Srivastava writes:

> "The Vijayanagara empire served a high historical purpose by acting as a champion of Hindu religion and culture against the aggressions of the Muslims in southern India."

Western Trade

In order to view the history of the Portuguese in India in its true perspective, it is necessary to make a few preliminary observations about the maritime trade of India. Economic factors have often profoundly influenced the course of history, and sometimes even revolutionised it. The foreign trade and maritime activities of India, during the period under review, suddenly changed the course of history, not only of India but also of the whole civilised world. Reference has been made in the preceding volumes to the maritime trade carried on by the Indians since remote antiquity, both in the eastern and in the western seas.

The rise of the Arabs as a great maritime power in the ninth century AD was the first direct challenge to the supremacy of the Indians in the Western Sea. An authentic account of the rivalry between the two maritime powers is not available. But the position in the fifteenth century AD may be summed up as follows:

1. Indian owned ships, from Gujarat, Malabar, and various ports on the eastern coast, brought spices and other costly goods from Malacca, "then practically the sole interrupt for China and the Spice Islands". On the west, Indian ships carried on trade with Hormuz in the Persian Gulf and various ports on the coast of East Africa, and pilgrim traffic to the Red Sea. The main centre of this trade was Gujarat, but Malabar and Konkan had also a large share, in it in the fourteenth century A. D., as is proved by the detailed statement of Ibn Batuta. A few junks from China still reached India, but most of them stopped at Malacca. The junks of China were strongly built, the timber being fastened by iron nails. The ships owned by Indians and Arabs (including Egyptians) were built mainly, if not exclusively, in India, but they were very frail as their heavy planks were made fast with coconut cordage and wooden pins.

2. The Arabs exercised a strict monopoly in the trade from Malabar to the Red Sea. The eastern goods brought by Indian ships to Malabar ports, together with the Indian pepper and cinnamon from Ceylon, were carried in Arab ships to Jidda and Ormuz. They also shared with Indian ships the carrying trade between Gujarat on the one hand and Red Sea, Persian Gulf, and East Africa on the other. From Ormuz Indian wares found their way in smaller boats, more suited to the navigation, to Basra, where the trade routes divided; some caravans started for Trebizond, and others for Aleppo and Damascus. On the shores of the Mediterranean the goods were purchased by Venetians and Genoese for distribution over Europe. Jidda played the same role in the Red Sea as Ormuz in the Persian Gulf. To the north of Jidda navigation was hampered by reefs and shoals, and so goods were transferred to smaller boats that went to Suez. From Suez the merchandize crossed the desert to Cairo on camels, and thence went down the Nile to Alexandria.

The most important consequence of this state of things was that the Arabs were almost the sole purveyors of the eastern spices which were much prized in Europe. They controlled the entire trade between India and Europe except the small volume that passed over land route, either from the northwest of India or from the head of the Persian Gulf. But the Arabs were also mere intermediaries. The goods carried by them to the Mediterranean ports were taken over by the Italian merchants, mainly from Genoa and Venice, who distributed them throughout Europe.

The cost of transmitting wares from India to Europe was very heavy, due to the large number of transhipments and high duties imposed by the various authorities through whose jurisdictions they had to pass. It has been calculated that when the wares from Calicut (in Malabar) reached Cairo, the ruler of the place, by various devices, exacted nearly one-third of their price as his own dues. In spite of heavy expenses the mercantile houses of Genoa and Venice reaped enormous profits, as the Indian goods fetched a very high price in European markets.

It could hardly be expected that the monopoly of Venice and Genoa in the profitable eastern trade would be looked upon with equanimity by the adventurous maritime nations like the Spanish and the Portuguese. The wonderful geographical discoveries by these two nations in course of the fifteenth century AD induced the Pope, Alexander VI, to regulate the enterprise into the unknown world by dividing it between them. He issued no less than four bulls for this purpose in AD 1493-94, by which the countries to the east of Europe were assigned to Portugal.

By this time the Portuguese had not only explored the entire western coast of Africa but even proceeded beyond the Cape of Good Hope. The lure of capturing the eastern trade naturally turned their attention towards an all-sea-route to India. For this would enable them to import goods from that country at a much cheaper cost and, by one stroke, transfer to them the huge wealth hitherto flowing to Genoa and Venice. Thus it was that Vasco da Gama was commissioned to find out a direct sea-route to India from Portugal via Cape of Good Hope. On July 8, 1497, Vasco da Gama left Lisbon with three vessels, of a tonnage varying from 60 to 150, on this perilous undertaking.

Coming of Portuguese

On May 17, 1498, the inhabitants of the small village of Capucad, eight miles to the north of Calicut, saw the strange spectacle of three sailing vessels at anchor manned by white-skinned peoples unknown to them. The rural folk were amused, perhaps a little bewildered, but little did they dream that these were harbingers of untold sufferings to them and to their country.

These were the vessels which, under the leadership of Vasco da Gama, by mere accident, touched the land at a point lying within the kingdom of the Zamorin of Calicut, to whom reference has been made above. It was almost providential that da Gama had not anchored off Gujarat, for this principality was then ruled by the Muslims, who were the sworn enemies of the Portuguese, their most deadly rivals in over-sea trade.

The Zamorin, as usual, welcomed the strangers and provided all facilities to them in Calicut which was then an important centre of spice-trade. This alarmed the powerful Muslim traders of Calicut who, not unreasonably, concluded that once the Portuguese got a footing in Calicut, they would extend their activities to all other ports and thus bring irretrievable ruin upon the Muslim traders.

They therefore sought by every means in their power to prejudice the mind of the Zamorin against the newcomers. One objection which they urged before Zamorin's officers proved to be prophetic. The Portuguese, they argued, had not certainly under-taken this long and tedious journey from their distant home "for mere purposes of trade, of which, being a wealthy nation, they had no need, but only to spy out the country with the view of returning and conquering it by force of arms and plundering it".

The machinations of the Muslim traders, aided by large bribes to the officials, brought about an estrangement between the Portuguese and the Zamorin, and the high-handed actions of the former almost precipitated a crisis. In a fit of anger the Zamorin ordered that the goods in the Portuguese factory should be seized, and Vasco da Gama, together with his companions who were already prisoners, should be killed. But the chief Brahmana (priest?) and other officers induced the king to rescind the order, and brought about a reconciliation between him and the Portuguese. So when Vasco da Gama left the Indian shore on August 29, 1498, he had collected valuable information regarding trade and the route, and established friendly relations with the ruler and Hindu population of Calicut. The successful venture of Vasco da Gama induced the king of Portugal to send a larger fleet of 13 vessels under Pedro Alvarez Cabral on March 9, 1500.

Cabral had a series of adventures on the way and reached Calicut with only six vessels on September 13, 1500. The Zamorin cordially welcomed him, and a treaty of peace and friendship was concluded between the two. Thereupon the Portuguese established a factory at Calicut, but the Muslim traders placed every possible obstacle on their way of successful trade in spices. Cabral complained to the Zamorin and, in order to hasten his decision, attacked and seized a Muslim vessel that was loading in the harbour.

These irritated the Muslim traders who attacked the Portuguese factory, killed Ayres Correa, the factor in charge, with fiftythree of his men, and destroyed the whole building. In revenge, Cabral destroyed ten Muslim vessels and bombarded the town of Calicut for two days. He then set sail and reached Cochin, another Hindu State, whose relation with the Zamorin has been noted above.

Cabral signed a treaty of friendship with the Raja of Cochin, promising to conquer Zamorin's kingdom for him, and established a factory. Here, too, the Muslim traders were actively hostile, but the Hindu Raja helped the Portuguese in every way, even to the extent of placing a guard over the factory building and allowing the Portuguese to sleep within the walls of his palace. When the fleet sent by the Zamorin to chastise the Portuguese was sighted near Cochin harbour in January, 1501, the Raja of Cochin warned them of the danger and offered assistance. The fleet of the Zamorin sailed away, chased by Cabral. While still at Cochin, Cabral received friendly messages of cooperation from the Rajas of Camianore and Quilon. On his return journey Cabral visited Cannanore and received on board an ambassador from the Raja to the king of Portugal with presents and the offer of free trade in his kingdom. Thus the two great feudatories of the Zamorin sought to recover their independence with the help of the Portuguese.

On the basis of the report submitted by Cabral, the Portuguese king now entertained the ambitious project, not only to divert all Indian trade to Portugal by curbing the Arab ventures, but also to plant the Christian religion in India. With these ends in view he despatched in 1502 a fleet of twenty ships under Vasco da Gama.

As the first discoverer of the direct sea-route between Europe and India, Vasco da Gama occupies a unique place in the history of the modern world. But in his treatment of the Indians he may be described almost as a monster in the disguise of human form, a worthy compeer of Sultan Mahmud and Tamerlane, though on a much smaller scale.

When his fleet reached Anjidiv, south of Goa, he committed a horrible cruelty described as follows by a European historian: "A rich Muslim pilgrim vessel on its way to India from the Red Sea was intercepted by da Gama's fleet, plundered and sunk; there were many women and children on board; but to these no mercy was shown; and we actually read that da Gama watched the horrors of the scene through a porthole, merciless and unmoved".

After halting at Cannanore for a few days, and renewing friendship with its king, da Gama proceeded to Calicut. The reputation of the Portuguese as a fighting power had reached so high that all the Indian and Arab ships had left the harbour, and the Zamorin, fearful of vengeance, sent a Brahmana as an envoy with the most conciliatory proposal. He sent twelve Muslims, who were guilty of outrages against the Portuguese during their last visit to the city, and a large amount recovered as fines for plundering the Portuguese factory.

But da Gama was not satisfied, and made the expulsion of all the Muslims out of the country a preliminary condition to peace. This being refused, da Gama bombarded the city for an entire day, killing many people and causing great damages to the city.

While still off Calicut, da Gama seized "a fleet of two large ships and twenty-two smaller vessels" which, laden with rice, had sailed from Coromandel. After having plundered the ships, da Gama "ordered his men to cut off the hands and ears and noses of all the crews. This done, their feet were tied together, and in order to prevent them from untying the cords with their teeth, he ordered his men to strike them on their mouths with staves and knock their teeth down their throats. They were then put on board, to the number of about 800, heaped one on the top of the other, and covered with mats and dry leaves; the sails were then set for the shore and the vessel set on fire". The refined cruelty reserved for the Brahmana envoy sent by the Zamorin has perhaps no parallel in the history of the civilised world. His hands and ears were cut off, and he was sent back with the severed limbs carefully packed and a letter telling the king to make curry out of them and eat it.

It has been truly observed that "da Gama had no bowels of compassion". But his lieutenants were worthy of the Captain. The friendly Raja of Cannanore having complained to da Gama against some Muslim ships leaving his harbour without paying the harbour duties and the price of goods, Vincente Sodre was sent to help him. Sodre at once decided to sink all the ships, but the Raja prevented this cruel deed.

The Muslim owner of the ships, an inhabitant of Cairo, settled all pecuniary claims to the satisfaction of the Raja, but as he was reported to have uttered some insulting words, Vincente Sodre "had him tied to the mast and flogged with a rope's-end until he fainted. Having filled his mouth with dirt, and tied over it a piece of bacon, he sent him back to his ship with his hands tied behind him". The Indians thus had a foretaste of the barbarous and inhuman cruelties which characterised the Portuguese almost throughout the period of their dominance in Indian waters.

Factory established in Cochin : Vasco da Gama established a factory at Cochin and erected a defensive palisade at Cannanore. He then returned to Portugal, leaving Vincente Sodre with six vessels and a caravel to patrol the coast. The Portuguese could not save Cochin from the revenge of the Zamorin who overran the country, forcing its Raja and his Portuguese friends to take refuge in an island. But in 1503 three Portuguese squadrons arrived in Cochin, one of them commanded by the famous Affonso d'Albuquerque. The troops of the Zamorin were driven away from Cochin, and peace was concluded between the rulers of Calicut and Cochin. It was on this occasion that the Portuguese built at Cochin their first fortress in India.

Francisco d'Alemeida, the First Viceroy : In 1505, the Portuguese king adopted a new policy. Instead of sending annual expedition, and leaving a small garrison to protect the factories, he decided to appoint a Viceroy who would reside in India for three years. Francisco d'Alemeida, the first Viceroy, arrived in September, 1505, and made Cochin his headquarters. He strengthened and rebuilt the fort there, and also erected forts at Anjidiv (south of Goa) and Cannanore. The former was shortly abandoned and the Portuguese troops were concentrated in Cochin and Cannanore. There were several clashes with Muslim trading vessels in which the Portuguese were uniformly successful.

The Zamorin of Calicut, alarmed at the growing power of the Portuguese in Indian waters, made a serious effort to drive them away. "In March 1506, an engagement took place between a large fleet of Muhammadan traders, armed and equipped by the Zamorin, and a Portuguese fleet of four vessels, resulting in the capture of the largest Muslim ships and a veritable massacre of their crews, with no casualties among the Portuguese".

The intention of the Portuguese to settle in India permanently, so clearly revealed by the establishment of a residential Viceroy and a standing fleet, as well as the construction of forts, alarmed the Muslim rulers of Bijapur, Gujarat and other smaller States. The establishment of Portuguese supremacy in Arabian Sea had also seriously affected the interest of Arabia and Egypt by depriving them of the duties levied on Indian goods. So when the Muslim rulers of India appealed to the Sultan of Egypt for aid, he readily agreed, and sent a fleet under Amir Hussain who, in January 1508, severely defeated a Portuguese fleet, sent against it, off Chaul, in Konkan coast, less than twenty miles to the south of Bombay. The son of the Portuguese Viceroy, who commanded the fleet, lost his life. But next year, in February, 1509, the Viceroy Almeida avenged the death of his son by inflicting a crushing defeat on the Muslim fleet off Diu on the Gujarat coast.

Albuquerque Governership : In November, 1509, Affonso d'Albuquerque succeeded Viceroy Almeida, under the lower title of Governor of India. Earlier in the year the Portuguese had made an unsuccessful attack on Calicut. One of the first acts of Albuquerque was to carry out the specific instruction of the king of Portugal to destroy Calicut, for, said he, nothing he would undertake with greater pleasure than the destruction of Calicut. The naval expedition arrived off Calicut on January 3,1510. The Zamorin was absent, as was already ascertained by the spies of the Raja of Cochin, and the town, which contained but few troops, was sacked by the Portuguese. But then the people drove away the Portuguese who sailed back. Albuquerque himself received two wounds and a number of high officers were killed.

The first achievement of Albuquerque was the conquest of Goa which belonged to the 'Adil Shahi rulers of Bijapur. On March 4, 1510, he occupied the defenceless city which offered little resistance, though he was forced to abandon it in the face of an attack by Yousuf 'Adil Khan. But Albuquerque stormed the city in November, 1510, strengthened its fortifications, and decided to make it his head-quarters. In order to increase its commercial importance Albuquerque took steps to force all ships to put into Goa. He also provided all encouragement and facilities to traders, so that even Muslim traders in spices settled there. In order to have a substantial number of friendly people, he authorised a large number of Portuguese to marry Indian wives, and encouraged them by allotting lands, houses and cattle. The Muslim Sultan had increased the taxes, but Albuquerque reduced it to the rate prevalent under Hindu rule. He further conciliated the Hindus by appointing them to government offices in larger numbers. He established a mint for the coinage of gold, silver, and copper money.

The fall of Goa and the defeat of the Sultan of Bijapur made a profound impression on the Indian rulers. The Captain of the Egyptian fleet, who had been waiting at Cambay for reinforcements, now sailed back to Suez. The Muslim Sultan of Gujarat released the Portuguese prisoners and sent an ambassador to Albuquerque to conclude a treaty of peace by offering.Diu to the Portuguese for erecting a fort. The Zamorin also made friendly overtures, offering a site within his kingdom for the construction of a Portuguese factory. This was established in 1511, but finally abandoned in 1525.

The greatest achievement of Albuquerque was the conquest of Malacca in 1511. It was a masterstroke of policy, designed to ruin the profits enjoyed by the Muslim rulers of Arabia and Egypt and the trade of Venice with them. The capture of Malacca was hailed with joy in Portugal, and the Pope celebrated it by a series of splendid ceremonies. Taking advantage of the absence of Albuquerque, the Sultan of Bijapur had sent a force under Pulad Khan, who seized not only the mainland territories of Goa but even the island itself. Pulad Khan then fortified himself in Benasterim, only six miles from the city of Goa, which commanded the principal passage from the mainland to the island of Goa. A new commander, Rassel Khan, with a large force and artillery, replaced Pulad Khan and besieged the city. As soon as Albuquerque returned to Cochin he made arrangements for the relief of Goa. He himself reached the place in October 1512 and after a gallant attack forced the Bijapur commander to surrender Benasterim and evacuate the island (1512). This victory enhanced his reputation and the Sultans of Bijapur and Gujarat again sent envoys to conclude peace.

Albuquerque then proceeded to Aden and Jidda in 1513, and, apart from diplomatic success, obtained possession of Ormuz, an important centre of trade. He died in December, 1515, after an eventful career in course of which the power and reputation of Portugal were firmly established in the eastern countries.

Four governors succeeded Alfonso d'Albuquerque, the last of whom, Vasco da Gama, now sixty-four years old, reached India in September, and died in December, 1524. During the next five years there were three governors, the last of whom, Nino da Cunha, reached India in November, 1529. One of his first acts was to transfer the headquarters of the government from Cochin to Goa. This scheme had been originally proposed and highly favoured by Alfonso d'Albuquerque, but was strongly opposed by a large section of the Portuguese officials in India. They sent a strong remonstrance to the king of Portugal against it, and even suggested the rendition of Goa to the Sultan of Bijapur in order to gain his friendship and cooperation. Albuquerque sent a long reply, answering all the arguments of his hostile critics. On receipt of this letter King Dom Manoel of Portugal decided to retain Goa, and fifteen years after the death of Albuquerque it became the Portuguese capital in India.

2

Mysore

Mysore under Haider Ali

Nawab Bahadur Haider Ali Khan: Nawab Bahadur signifies incomparable Knight; the Bahadurs in India being what the knights were in Europe. A great sovereign or general among the Mughals, after a battle, gives the dignity of Bahadur to a man of distinction, one of the principal officers who has behaved with honour.

If there has formerly existed any ceremony for the creation of a Bahadur, it is now out of use: all that is done at present is, that the general publicly praises his actions, and in his discourse always calls him Bahadur; which title is afterwards given him by all the world indiscriminately. A Bahadur has great privileges; he may go everywhere completely armed, causing a gilt mace to be carried before him and may appear thus even in the King of the Canarins and Corgues, Dayva of Mysore, Sovereign of the Empires of Cherquile and Calicut, which contain the kingdoms of Cananore, Cochin, Travancore; Nawab of Bangalore, Ballapur, Bassapatnam, or Bisnagar, *etc.*

Lord of the Mountains and Vallies, standing militia of one lac and eighty thousand (180,000) men, under various denominations. The year 1786 appears to have been occupied by the Sultan in internal regulations; inspection of his forts, and examination of his treasures and stores.

Return to Seringapattam

Soon after his return to Seringapattam, he ordered an inventory to be made of his property of every kind. The treasure, jewels, and other valuable articles, were estimated at eighty millions sterling. He had also 700 elephants, 6,000 camels, 11,000 horses, 400,000 bullocks and cows, 100,000 buffaloes, 600,000 sheep, 300,000 firelocks, 300,000 matchlocks, 200,000 swords, 22,000 pieces of cannon, of different calibres, and an immense quantity of gunpowder and other military stores. His regular army consisted of 19,000 cavalry, 10,000 artillery, and 70,000 infantry. He had besides 5,000 rocket men and 40,000 irregular infantry, and also a militia of 180,000 men. Tipu Sultan, at this period, formed a new code of regulations for his army. He reduced his cavalry, and augmented the infantry. He adopted Persian and Tartar terms for the words of command, which were formerly given in English or French, and gave new names to the different divisions of the army.

Rise of Haider Ali

Haider Ali Khan, son of Nadim Saeb, general of ten thousand horse in the army of the empire, was born in 1717 at Divanelli, a small fortress or castle between Kolar and Oscota in the country of Bangalore. This land was given in fief to his father, who was particularly attached to Nizam El Moulouc, Grand Vizier and Suba of Deccan.

Haider Ali claimed the honour of being by descent a Quereshi, and consequently of the same tribe as the Arabian Prophet Muhammad. When his ancestors emigrated from Mecca to India, is not known but to his family alone, and it is stated, that they were much respected in the district of Kohir, which is situated about the middle of the Peninsula, between Hyderabad and Goolburga; and that several of them held the honourable office of Judge.

After the death of Nizam El Moulouc, Nadim Saeb retired to Divanelli with his two sons, Ismael Saeb and Haider. Ismael Saeb was much older than his brother. He entered into the service of the king of Mysore; and in a short time became his first general. The king of Mysore, as a reward for a victory he had obtained over the Marathas, gave him the country and fortress of Bangalore; which put him into a situation of having a body of troops of his own, that composed part of the army of the king of Mysore, when Naserjung made a descent upon the coast of Coromandel in 1750. Haider, then about thirty four years old, had never quitted his father's house. His father gave him the command of the quota of troops he was bound to furnish to the army of the Suba, for his lordship of Divanelli. It consisted only of fifty horsemen and two hundred soldiers armed with matchlocks. Ibrahim Saeb, the maternal uncle of Haider, served him instead of a Mentor.

Haider being at the battle where Naserjung was slain, the bravery of the French, who, to the number of eight hundred, seconded by four thousand Sepoys, had the courage to attack the army of the Mughals, then more than three hundred thousand strong, made such an impression on his mind, that he was persuaded the French were capable of undertaking the most difficult enterprises. Having followed Muzzafarjung, successor to Naserjung, to Pondicherry, the observations he made in that city, upon the manners, discipline, fortifications, buildings, arts, and industry of the French, gave him the highest esteem for that celebrated and warlike nation, and more especially for M. Dupleix who was then governor.

Muzaffarjung withdrew his Army: In 1751, Muzaffarjung having withdrawn his army to Golconda, Haider, whose father was dead, went to join his brother in Mysore. On the account the young man gave of the advantageous arms of the Europeans, and their address in managing great guns, Meer Ismael Saeb dispatched a Guebre to Bombay, to purchase cannon, and muskets with bayonets. This Persian, who died in 1767, purchased two thousand muskets, and six pieces of cannon, of the governor of Bombay. He likewise enrolled thirty European sailors, of different nations, that he collected on the coast of Malabar, to serve as cannoneers. Meer Ismael Saeb, brother to Haider, was thus the first Indian who formed a corps of Sepoys armed with firelocks and bayonets, and who had a train of artillery served by Europeans. This procured him new advantages over the enemies of the king of Mysore, and increased the esteem and friendship of that prince for him.

Nand Raja, brother to the king of Mysore, and Dayva, having formed an army to make a descent upon the coast of Coromandel, and join that of the English, Haider, at the recommendation of his brother, obtained the command of the cavalry of this army. The English, aided by the Mysorians, forced the French troops, combined with those of Chanda Saeb, to surrender themselves prisoners of war, and to give up the Pagod of Schirnigam, in which they had taken refuge. It was on this occasion that Chanda Saeb was made prisoner. Nand Raja afterwards quarrelling with the English, M. Dupleix formed an alliance with him; and it was agreed to lay siege to Trichnopoli, a strong place on the river Kaveri, with an army composed of French forces, together with those of Mysore, and those of Chanda Saeb, Nawab of Arcot. The English, who were the allies of Muhammad Ali Khan, competitor of Chanda Saeb, had then a garrison in Trichnopoli.

French Set out from Pondicherry: When the French set out from Pondicherry, in 1752, to join Nanda Raja, they were harassed in their march by a body of Maratha cavalry, commanded by a chief allied with the English. On this occasion the commandant of the French troops wrote to the regent of Mysore to send him a reinforcement.

Haider was sent to his assistance, at the head of eighteen hundred horse. It was then that Haider began to be known to the French, and to acquire some reputation among the Europeans, whence he had his pretended name of Andernec.

Before that time, the French, the English, and other European nations, had very little connection with, or knowledge of, the interior parts of the country; and there were not perhaps two Frenchmen at Pondicherry that could converse in the language of the Mughals, which is a kind of Persian, and is commonly called Moors.

The officers and soldiers had no other interpreters than their Dabashis, or Malabar domestics, who knew only their own language and a sort of corrupt Portuguese. The Malabar language, though very regular, is perhaps the poorest language in being: so that the word *Dore* signifies Mr. or Sir; and to express the word governor, or general, or *the superior Sir,* they say *Peri-dore,* which is *the great Sir,* or *Master;* and in the same manner, to denote any chief whatsoever, the Malabar language has only the word *Naik;* and they use *Tanjaor Naik* to signify the king or Raja of Tanjaor; and *Narim Naik,* and *Chabri Naik,* to denote the Serjeant Narim, or the corporal Chabri: and the name *Haider Naik* implying the chief Haider, the French have formed it into Andernec.

It is this name of Naik that has caused it to be imagined that Haider had been a corporal of Sepoys. He was then called Haider Saeb, which is the same as Mr. Haider. His name was enlarged in proportion as his power increased, as the custom is among the Mughals; and he is now called Haider Ali Khan Bahadur or Bahadur Shah.

When the French army had joined that of Mysore, Haider, whose camp then formed the left wing of the Mysorian army, came and encamped himself to the right of the French, in spite of all the arguments of the French commandant, and the regent of Mysore; and, however disagreeable it was to the French to see themselves as it were cooped up, he would not remove from the station he had assumed. He informed the commandant that he wished to be near the French, that he might learn from them the art of war. In fact, he was very attentive and exact in observing everything that passed in the French camp; and caused several of their evolutions to be repeated, as well as was in his power, in his own camp.

This repetition caused some diversion to the French officers and soldiers, whom he was attentive to please by his politeness and good manners. But it was not with any satisfaction they observed that Haider had drawn the most active and intelligent French soldiers into his service. He had still in his service, in 1770, the Sieur Stenet, son of a *Cent-Suisse* of Versailles, who was a volunteer at the siege of Trichnopoli in 1753: he took him at that time into his service, and sent him to his brother in Mysore, as he did every other Frenchman that chose to engage in his service. These enrolments were made with some dexterity; and, as there was need of his services, the French commandant winked at the irregularity of the proceeding.

General Lawrence, who was then only major, attempting to throw some succours and a convoy into Trichnopoli, received a considerable check; of which, in his Memoirs, he gives all the honour to Haider and his cavalry. English jealousy perhaps induced him to dimmish the merit of the French; but it is certain that Haider distinguished himself highly on this occasion.

Nand Raja Quit the French: In 1755, Nand Raja having quitted the French to return to Mysore, Haider made a particular treaty with M. Dupleix, by which he engaged to remain with his troops, forming a body of six thousand men, till the capture of Trichnopoli; and he did not return to Mysore till Mr. Godehen, successor to M. Dupleix, had made a truce with the English, and given orders to raise the siege of Trichnopoli. In 1756, Haider being informed of the death of his brother, as he was on his way to rejoin him, hastened to receive the succession that had devolved to him by the law; his brother having no male children. This death put him in possession of a handsome fortress, a fertile territory, and a body of troops, which, joined to his own, amounted to above fifteen thousand men, including two hundred Europeans, and three thousand of excellent cavalry. The king of Mysore having the same confidence in him as his brother Ismael, appointed him generalissimo of his army.

The kings of Mysore being Brahmans, had united the royal dignity and the priesthood; and, to be more venerable in the eyes of their people, they affected to appear in public only twice a year; namely, on those days when they presided at the solemn ceremonies of their religion. And in order to appear solely occupied with the sacred mysteries, which they celebrated with pomp and magnificence, they abandoned the government to a Dayva, or regent, who, till the time of Nand Raja, had always been one of the king's nearest relations. But a Brahman, named Canero, favourite of this prince, persuaded him to assume the government himself, and forsake his brother Nand Raja. This last, who, had neither the capacity nor the application, nor even the firmness, necessary to support himself in this dignity, made no resistance; and preferred banishment to the frontier to the hazard of making the least remonstrance.

Canero having taken entire possession of the mind of the king, was declared his minister, and charged with the administration of affairs. Haider kept his command of the army.

Haider's Love for Power

The power, the reputation, and the love of the soldiery that were possessed by Haider, ought to have secured him from the envy and jealousy of this ambitious minister; but Canero, sacrificing every thing to those passions ventured even to make a private treaty with the Marathas enemies of the state. In consequence of this treaty, the Marathas army entered Mysore in the rainy season, at the moment when Haider least expected them and, deceived by Canero, has dispersed his troops.

The approach of the Marathas, and their superiority in number, obliged him to advance towards Seringapattam, capital of the kingdom, that offered him a sure asylum in the island on which the city is situated, and which cannot be entered, when the Kaveri is swelled by the rains, but by the bridge of Seringapattam.

Canero, who in another situation, would have done his utmost to have prevented Haider from entering the royal city, pressed him to pitch his camp on the island. Haider fell into the snare of the perfidious Brahman. He passed the bridge and went through the town with his army, which he encamped at the opposite extremity of the island. The Maratha army soon appeared, and invested that part of the river, where it is fordable in the usual state of the waters.

Haider, having no suspicion of the treachery of Canero, depended on the well-furnished magazines of the city for the subsistence of his troops. But he was in the highest astonishment, the day after the arrival of the Marathas, when he beheld the gates of the city shut; and was informed that Canero had determined that the whole army should perish, either by hunger or the cannon of the city, unless they delivered up Haider to the king, who had strong reason for securing his person. This account convinced Haider that Canero had sworn his destruction. He sent several officers to treat with him; but the day was consumed without effect. When the night was closed in, he sent for the chiefs of the different corps into his tent. He thanked them for their fidelity to him, and assured them that he would not be the cause of the loss of so many brave men. He advised them to arrange their affair, at the break of day as well as they could, with Canero; and informed them that he should determine for himself in the course of that very night.

At the same time he gave six month's pay and gratification to the whole army, which was distributed to the soldiers before any treaty was made with Canero. He then embraced the principal officers, telling them he depended on their friendship when a favourable opportunity might arrive; and afterwards dismissed them. About midnight, assembling thirty of his men on whose fidelity and bravery he could rely, he committed a quantity of gold to the charge of each; and, putting himself at their head, attempted to pass the river by swimming. He succeeded; and happily eluding the Maratha army, kept a direct course, without stopping, till he arrived at Bangalore, which was thirty leagues distant from Seringapattam.

When he came near this fortress, he sent one of his friends to his uncle Ibrahim Ali Khan to whom he had entrusted the government, to inform him, that though he had formerly possessed lands, fortresses, treasures, and an army, he had now no more remaining than thirty friends, who were determined to share his fortune; that he therefore begged him to say, with sincerity, whether he could still rely on his friendship; and that his answer would determine whether he should come to Bangalore, or seek an asylum elsewhere.

His uncle having received this message, mounted his horse, and returned with the messenger of Haider. "Courage I" said he, on meeting his nephew, nothing is lost that you have trusted in my hands; and God will assist you to recover the rest. Haider embraced him, and they entered Bangalore.

Seeing himself thus in possession of a strong place, he began to hope for the re-establishment of his affairs; and his wishes were soon partly realised, by the unforeseen arrival of almost all his cavalry, which the brave Meer Mughdum Ali Khan, his brother in-law, brought after him.

At the time that Canero was in treaty with the chiefs of Haider's army, Mughdum seizing the instant of a sudden and unexpected decrease of the Kaveri crossed the river at the head of three thousand horse; and overthrowing every force the Marathas brought to oppose him, he opened a passage and arrived at Bangalore by favour of the woods and mountains he was perfectly acquainted with, having lost a very inconsiderable number of men.

Haider made use of every resource. He raised troops with the utmost celerity; and being necessarily on the defensive, he began a war of stratagem with the Marathas, seconded by his brother-in-law, and assisted by the nature of the country.

In the year 1760, at the time he was busied in defending his own proper home, Pondicherry being in great danger, he detached seven thousand men, at the request of M. Lally, to assist the French, under the command of his brother-in-law Mughdum.

Mughdum, in his way to Pondicherry, placed a garrison in the fortress of Thiagar, which the Sieur Mariol put into his hands, by order of M. Lally; and the garrison of that place, consisting of three hundred French and twelve hundred sepoys, having joined the army of Haider, Mughdum after repelling a party of the English, who pretended to dispute the passage of a river, encamped on the glacis of Pondicherry, where he remained two months; and threw several Convoys into the place, without being able to prevail on M. Lally to encamp without the town. He returned to Haider, bringing with him all the French cavalry under the Sieurs Alain and Hughel, and such workmen as were at Pondicherry: a precious acquisition, which has highly contributed to the success of Haider, by furnishing him with skilful armourers, carpenters, and other workmen from the arsenal of Pondicherry, collected with much expense and trouble by the French.

Mughdum, on his return, passing by Thiagar, withdrew his garrison; and the French replaced some sepoys in the same; Mughdum saying, with a generous spirit of integrity, that as the place was to have been the reward for delivering Pondicherry, justice required him to restore it, since he had failed in the attempt.

This action, however, may perhaps have been more political than generous. But the fact is, that Thiagar was not surrendered to the English till after the capture of Pondicherry.

Haider made Truce with Marathas: During the absence of Mughdum Haider made a truce with the Marathas, a nation very averse to long wars. This Nawab esteeming the French in the highest degree, saw with great satisfaction a fine corps of cavalry of that nation in his army; and he was still more rejoiced to behold them accompanied by a body of workmen, for want of whose assistance he was in no small distress. His brother-in-law, who had conciliated the affection of all who knew, him, was doubtless entitled to the most honourable reception. Haider, on the contrary, received him with coolness, and even with indignation; making it a crime that he had not accomplished the object of his mission, by raising the siege of Pondicherry; and, without waiting for his reply, he degraded him to the rank of simple cavalier, as being unworthy of any command.

This treatment, which astonished all the world, was highly mortifying to the officers and soldiers who had borne a part in the expedition. Many of them, particularly the French, spoke to Haider in favour of his brother-in-law; but he appearing always in anger, but at the same time willing to do justice, consented to assemble all the chiefs of his army, and allowed the friends of Mughdum to give a detail of his conduct during the expedition to Pondicherry. The whole assembly unanimously extolling the merit of Mughdum. Haider ordered his grand sawari to be immediately prepared; and being on his march to the house of his brother-in-law, followed by the whole assembly, he met him in the bazaar, where he was walking on foot like a common soldier.

As soon as Haider saw him, he descended from his elephant, approached Mughdum and embraced him cordially several times, and addressed him nearly in these words: "I find by the account of your "friends, that I was wrong in blaming your conduct, and was going to "your house to make an apology for my error. I am happy that I "have met you, that the satisfaction I make may be the more public." Then causing him to mount the king's own elephant, he conducted him to his own house, riding before him on horseback, with all his attendants in procession, and followed by the people and soldiery; who, happy at the reconciliation of Haider and Mughdum, sang his praises, in which his brother-in-law was not forgotten.

The conduct of Haider in this transaction was founded in justice; but, according to all appearance, it was not less the effect of policy. He was then looking forward at a great fortune, and was desirous of convincing his officers, that, as he had not spared his brother-in-law, who was his dearest friend, he should not fail in punishing any neglect of duty in them.

Haider Turned French to His Advantage: Haider lost no time in turning the arrival of the French to his advantage. He spread the news by his emissaries, magnifying their number; and, avowing his intention to march to Seringapattam, he invited all the great men of Mysore to join him for the purpose of delivering the king from the power of the treacherous Canero, and to restore the government in conformity to the laws of the kingdom.

Nand Raja, who had always held a secret correspondence with Haider, quitted his exile and joined him; and it as said that he furnished him with large sums of money to raise troops and increase his army.

Canero, knowing the activity of Haider, was not remiss in his preparations. He collected an army vastly more numerous than that of Haider; and, by virtue of caresses and rewards gained to his party those Europeans who managed the artillery of Haider before his flight. His artillery was besides, far superior in number and quality, so that he did not fear to go out of the town and waited for Haider at Senapattam, an open village several leagues distant from Seringapattam.

The two armies were encamped at the distance of three leagues asunder. The dependence of Haider on his own troops, and hopes he had been encouraged to form from his French succours, did not prevent his employing stratagem against his enemy. Success attended his attempts.

There was a lady at Seringapattam, commonly called the old Dayva, because her husband, brother of the king and of Nand Raja, had been regent or Dayva of the kingdom.

This lady had possessed great power during the regency of her husband, who left her extremely rich. Nand Raja, her brother-in-law, on his accession to the regency, had not that respect and consideration she thought were due to her: from that moment she declared herself his enemy, and contributed much to his loss of the regency.

This princess had always protected Haider and his brother; and, as her conduct was not very exemplary, the scandalous chronicle affirmed, that Haider and his brother shared her private favours. Though distant from Seringapattam, Haider had always kept up an intimate correspondence with this lady, who was not a friend to Canero, though apparently, from policy, much attached to him. On the assurance that Haider gave her, that Nand Raja should never be regent, she promised to serve him to the utmost of her power, and even supplied him with large sums of money.

Haider, to make every advantage of the friendship of this lady, on whom he had an entire reliance transmitted to her fictitious letters, addressed to the principal heads of the army of Canero, in which he appeared to prescribe in consequence of an agreement long established, operations to be made by them upon certain signals appointed by Haider. The intension of these manoeuvre was apparently that of surrounding Canero at the commencement of the battle, and preventing his escape.

The lady having received these letters, repaired to the camp of Canero the night preceding the battle: she gave him the letters, and by an artful conversation on the business, increased the consternation of the minister: the consequence was, that he immediately retired to Seringapattam, leaving the command of the army to an old general named Peer Khan, whom he believed to be in his interests, but who was really the friend of Haider.

Haider, informed of every thing as it happened, marched with his army at the break of day to approach that of Canero, thrown into great agitation by his departure. The news of this precipitate march augmented the confusion, and the general was by no means desirous of removing it. A number of deserters from Canero's army arrived in the camp of Haider, with the news of his flight. As soon as that Nawab heard their report, he caused his army to halt, and sent a messenger to the general of the other army to propose a conference, publicly assuring him, that his exertions were directed against the traitor Canero, and not the king and kingdom of Mysore. Peer Khan, after taking the advice of the principal chiefs of his army, consented to a conference with Haider and Nand Raja, in the presence of the two armies; when it was resolved, to the great satisfaction of the soldiers, that they should unite, and form but one army; and that a deputation should be sent immediately to the king of Mysore, praying him to drive the traitor Canero out of the kingdom, as a declared enemy of the king and the state.

When the two armies were united, Haider, to the surprise of every one, commanded before him the Europeans who had formerly been attached to his service and that of his brother: he made them ground their arms and giving everyone a stroke after the manner of the Indians when they dishonour or degrade any one, he drove them out of his camp. He was induced to this severity, as he said, because these soldiers having been loaded with favours by his brother and himself, were the only men of all his troops who had presumed to carry arms against him. The French cavalry from Pondicherry were present at this execution, and pretended to approve it.

The deputation from the army being arrived at Seringapattam, the answer of the king dictated, no doub by

Canero, was that they were traitors, and that the king would punish them. On this answer, it was resolved to lay siege to Seringapattam; which was immediately done, to prevent Canero from calling in the assistance of the Marathas.

The inhabitants of the city had no sooner heard the report of a few cannon, than they assembled, and remonstrated in strong terms against Canero, excited, most probably, by the dowager Dayva; who at length prevailed on the king to deliver Canero to the army, and to declare Haider regent instead of Nand Raja, who expected the appointment, and supposed Haider would be contented with the post of generalissimo.

Upon his accepting the regency, Haider made every submission to appease Nand Raja. He gave him a considerable territory, and made a promise, both in writing and by oath, that he would never make any attempt on his liberty, property, or life, but would always regard him as his brother.

Haider afterwards caused the Brahman doctors to be assembled to judge Canero. He was condemned to death for having invited a foreign enemy into the kingdom, and levying war against the king's most faithful subjects. By virtue of his power as regent, Haider spared his life, and commuted his punishment into that of being shut up in an iron cage in the middle of the most public place of Bangalore; where it is still to be seen, with the bones of this unhappy favourite, who lived two years in the cage, exposed to the insults of a populace that adored Haider.

As a beginning of his performance of the duty of a regent, Haider caused an exact account to be made out of the royal revenues, together with the treasure and jewels. He found that the greatest part of the jewels, instead of being in the treasury were in pawn with the court banker, who had advanced money when Salabatjung, Suba of Deccan, accompanied by M. Bussi, came as far as the gates of Seringapattam, and forced the king of Mysore to pay contributions.

Haider being informed that this man had acquired the whole of his immense fortune in the service of the state, was displeased that he had demanded pledges on lending money to the government. He ordered the jewels to be taken out of his hands, and his due paid him; but at the same time nominated a commission to inspect his accounts. The commissioners having found him guilty of fraud and extortion in his dealings with the state, condemned him to perpetual imprisonment, and confiscation of all his property. The luxury of this banker was enormous.

It is said that his children had cradles of gold suspended from the ceiling by chains of the same metal. Haider caused the judgement to be put in execution, but gave him a pension to subsist on; and placed his sons in the service, where they have been preferred.

Establishment Order and Regularity: Order and regularity were soon established in the finances, and Haider then proceeded to compel a number of petty tyrants, known by the name of Palleagars, to evacuate their fortresses. He was under the necessity of using force with some of them, but the greater part treated with him in a friendly manner. He compelled likewise many Rajas, vassals and tributaries to the kingdom of Mysore, to acknowledge their dependence, and pay the tribute with punctuality and exactness. He likewise obliged many neighbouring kings, such as the kings of Canara, the Marathas, and the Patan Nawabs of Canour, Curpa, Sanour, and many others, to restore the lands they had usurped from the kingdom of Mysore. But he did not accomplish all this without declaring war, and obtaining many victories over them.

The Patans were dreaded through all Hindustan, for their valour and their perfidy. Haider acquired great reputation by the signal victory he gained over the three Nawabs, near Sanour; for which he was indebted to the bravery and spirited evolutions of the French cavalry under M. Hughel.

This victory of Sanour induced Busalatjung, Nawab of Adonis, and brother of Nizam Ali Khan, Suba of Deccan, to send an embassy to him.

Those princes were at war with the Marathas, who had lately received a considerable check on the banks of the Krishna, in a battle they had lost against the united armies of the Grand Vizier of the empire and of Abdali, king of the Patans, in which sixty thousand Marathas were left on the spot.

Busalatjung had laid siege to Scirra, a strong place situated between his dominions and the kingdom of Mysore and gives the title to a Subaship; of which the whole district has been either seized by the Marathas, or united to the Subaship of Deccan. This prince imagined, that taking advantage of the defeat of the Marathas he should easily get possession of Scirra, and, by that means, become of equal rank with his brother, by acquiring the title of Suba. But his army not being equal to the undertaking, he experienced a resistance that would have reduced him to the shameful necessity of raising the siege, if he had not been advised to form an alliance with Haider; who was glad to assist him.

He did not, however, consent to join his army till he had previously made an advantageous treaty. In this treaty it was agreed, that Haider should appear before Scirra with his large army, and a numerous artillery: that Busalatjung and himself should carry on the siege conjointly, till the place was taken; that as soon as it should surrender, each army should take possession on its respective side of attack; that all the artillery, ammunition, and in general everything that could be carried away, should be the share of Busalatjung, who should either take it in kind, or receive the value from Haider; and, that this last should take possession of the place.

Haider being arrived before the place with a well-disciplined army and a grand train of artillery served by Europeans, made his attack in a manner very different from that made use of by Busalatjung. By successful undermining, he blew up two bastions and the curtain, which forced the besieged to surrender at discretion, and increased the terror his arms had spread over the extensive empire of India.

In the execution of the treaty between these two princes, Busalatjung, who was always afterwards called the Merchant by Haider, preferred the receiving money for his share of the capture; and it was now that Haider was declared Suba of Scirra, by the Emperor sending him an embassy with all the highest honours annexed to the title, and marks of the dignity of Suba, such as the rich round palankeen, and Mahee Muratib, the fish's head, set with precious stones. It was thus that Haider, born a private gentleman, found himself raised to the rank of the greatest princes of India.

At the time of his receiving the title and honours of Suba of Scirra, he engaged to make war on the Marathas; who had then seen the end of their empire, if the sons of Nizam-ul-Moulouc had possessed as much courage and intelligence as Haider; and if, more especially, the king of the Patans had not abandoned his allies, and returned into his own country, satisfied with the immense plunder he had obtained, Haider, continuing the war with success against Marathas, took Marksira and Maggheri, strong places in the district of Scirra, at well as the kingdom of Bisnagar or Bassapattam. But the Marathas having collected their forces against him, he, by the pusillanimity of his allies, had nearly lost his life, having received a stroke on the head with a sabre, in a battle in which neither side gained the victory. A few days afterwards he concluded a truce for three years; and preserved his conquests by paying a sum of money to the general of that nation.

This war was scarcely finished, when a new opportunity presented itself for extending the power and reputation of Haider. The son of the Queen of Canara had escaped from Rana Bidnoor, capital of that kingdom, and came to the Suba at Bisnagar, to implore his assistance, that his mother might be compelled to put him in possession of the kingdom of his ancestors—the regency of which she had held since the death of her husband, the late king, and father of the young prince, and still retained it, though her son had arrived at the age prescribed by law for him to take charge of the government himself. As the kingdom of Canara was comprised in the subaship of Scirra, the prince could carry his complaint with propriety to no other tribunal than that of Haider. The young prince was, therefore, favourably received, and his mother was cited, by an ambassador of Haider, to appear before the Suba at a time fixed.

This woman, who possessed a degree of courage unusual in her sex, and who, from the anarchy that had long reigned in the Mughal's empire, was habituated to despise the orders of the emperor and his officers, replied to the ambassador of Haider, that she was queen, and knew no superior. On this answer which Haider, expected, war was determined on against the queen; but the nature of the country promised to throw many difficulties in the way of the expedition.

Rana Bidnoor, capital of the kingdom of Canara, is one of the largest and best peopled cities of India. It contains at least sixty thousand souls; among whom are about thirty thousand Christians, who have great privileges. This considerable population is, however, by no means proportionate to the extent of the city, whose circuit exceeds three leagues.

It will not be found that this is an exaggeration, when it is considered, that there are streets in it, nearly in a right line, of two leagues in length. Besides, the greatest part of the ground on which the town stands is inhabited by great men and nobility, whose houses are each in the midst of a large garden, enclosing vast basins or reservoirs of water, as well for the purposes of pleasure as utility. A prodigious number of trees, planted in these gardens, shade all the streets; which are watered on each side by a rivulet of clear and limpid water, and have no other pavement than a fine gravel.

This beautiful city is situated near a small mountain, at whose summit is a considerable fortress, since much more strongly fortified by Haider. The mountain is in a plain about five or six leagues in diameter, environed by mountains and forests that extend for more than twenty leagues every way, and are not to be passed but by narrow passages, defended by forts at a small distance from each other.

These circumstances render the access to the city extremely difficult for an army, that may be checked at every step by an inconsiderable force, and cannot encamp but in the length of a stony passage, where it is liable to be attacked by the people of the country, who know all the secret passages, and can continually lay in ambush to annoy their enemy. The woods cannot be cut down, much less burned, without infinite labour; and they are filled with tigers, bears, elephants, and every species of venomous reptiles.

A mass of such almost insuperable obstacles as presented themselves to Haider ought to have deterred him from his enterprise, if he had not been accompanied by the young prince who was beloved by the people and the men in power while the queen, his mother, was detested by them, as well for her haughtiness and pride, as for having contracted a second marriage with a Brahman contrary to the law of the place, which prohibits the widows of their kings from marrying a second time.

Leaving of Bisnagar by Haider: Haider, determined to make the attempt, left Bisnagar, carrying with him the Prince of Canara, at the head of 6,000 men of his best cavalry, and some Caleros, men habituated to traverse the mountains and forest. He was followed by a number of oxen, loaded with rice; and, with no other baggage, he advanced by forced marches towards the capital of Canara. His movement was so rapid, that he passed on without finding any obstacle, and arrived on the plain of Bidnoor before the queen had received any news of his march. His cavalry, accustomed to every kind of ground, terrified the Canarins, who had never beheld a legion of that kind. The good discipline observed by his troops, and the sight of the legitimate prince, caused Haider to be received everywhere as a tutelar divinity.

On his appearance in the plain, his cavalry easily dispersed a part of the queen's army that attempted to oppose his passage; and that princess, who had scarcely time to make her escape, was pursued, taken, and conducted into the presence of the conqueror.

Haider used his victory with the greatest moderation. He received the queen in the most gracious manner, and reconciled her with her son; who granted her a considerable pension, allowing her to live with her husband. To satisfy the people, who ardently desired it, the young prince was proclaimed king; he made homage to the empire for his kingdom, and signed the treaty, as well as his mother, and the principal great men of the country.

While these transactions were performing in the kingdom of Canara, the army of Haider advanced into the country, and his infantry took possession, without resistance, of all the posts that were necessary to secure his return, and the success of anything he might think proper to undertake.

Before he engaged in the war that was to place the Prince of Canara on the throne of his ancestors, Haider made a treaty with him, by which the prince yielded to the Suba the port of Mangalore, with a tract of country to form a communication from thence to the frontiers of the kingdom of Mysore. In execution of this treaty, Haider, after causing the new king to be crowned, marched with a party of his troops to take possession of Mangalore, leaving a part of his army encamped at the gates of Rana Bidnoor.

The Queen of Canara, enraged to find herself deprived of the sovereignty, had pretended to be reconciled with her son, and to acknowledge him as king, with no other intention than to wait for an opportunity of destroying Haider. With this hope, and completely to gratify her vengeance, she resolved on the death of this generous Suba. She therefore endeavoured to gain the confidence of her son, whose feeble and pusillanimous spirit she well knew. She reproached him, with a dissembled tenderness, that, to hasten the beginning of his reign, he had inconsiderately delivered up his kingdom to the barbarians, the enemies of his religion, who would leave him only the empty name of king, after depriving him of the most valuable part of his dominions, and most probably would finish him by entirely robbing him of the whole.

At length, by force of insinuation and under the appearance of a highly disinterested person, who had resigned a kingdom to him, she succeeded in her endeavours to make him regret the treaty with Haider; and, continuing to act on his fears of the future intentions of the Suba, she acquired such an empire over his mind, that he was brought to consent to the assassination of Haider, which she had projected in a manner that, in its own nature, was almost certain of success.

During his stay at Rana Bidnoor, Haider had dwelt in the palace of the kings of Canara, and was, of course, to reside there on his return. From this palace to a famous pagoda there was a subterranean communication, known to very few except the queen. The queen had resolved to undermine the palace, and to blow up Haider the night of his return, when he should be at table with his principal officers, hoping that, at the instant of the catastrophe, the people and soldiers of Canara, animated by her son, might easily put the troops of Haider to the sword in their first confusion and disorder.

This project might have been easily put in practice by means of her husband, the superior of the Brahmans, who belonged to the pagoda. The day of Haider's return was come, and the moment approached in which this Suba and his retinue were to perish by treachery; when the plot first came to the knowledge of a Brahman, chief of a pagoda some leagues distant from the city. Whether he was actuated, as the Brahmans affirm, by a detestation and horror for the crime or whether his hatred for the queen and her husband, who were united contrary to their law, was his leading motive—he conveyed himself in secret to Rana Bidnoor, and presenting himself before Haider, as if to compliment him on his happy return he advised him openly, in the presence of the king and queen of the conspiracy, and the danger he was in. This astonishing recital made the whole assembly tremble, but made no impression upon Haider, looking round, discovered the guilty persons without difficulty. He ordered them to be seized. The witnesses were heard, and the truth being established on the spot, the queen, her husband, and all their accomplices, were put to death, except the King of Canara, who was carried prisoner to Maggheri, near Scirra, and his kingdom was confiscated.

The discovery of this conspiracy was worth a fine kingdom to Haider, rich in all sorts of productions, and having a valuable extent of sea-coast, with a good number of sea-ports. The immense quantities of rice, pepper, cinnamon, cardamoms, coral, sandal wood, and ivory, that abound in this kingdom, have caused it to be called the granary and warehouse of all India. In the mountains there are mines of gold, diamonds, rubies, and other precious stones; and even in the very fortress of Rana Bidnoor, there is a rich gold mine. When Haider took possession of the place, he found an immense treasure in gold, coined and in ingots, in trinkets and precious stones, that was indeed stupendous, if credit may be given to the accounts of the French, who accompanied him in that expedition. They say that the prince caused pearls and precious stones to be measured in their sight with a corn measure; and that, having made two heaps of gold in ingots and trinkets, they surpassed the height of a man on horseback.

On this happy occasion Haider gratified all his troops with half a year's pay, not excepting those, that were in garrison in different parts of his dominions. He changed the name of Rana Bidnoor into that of Haider Naga, or Royal city of Haider and the name of Mangalore into that of Corial or Port Royal. He assumed at the same time the title of king of Canara and of the Corgues, a small kingdom situated at the southern extremity of Canara, and separated from that kingdom, as well as from the Malabar, district, and the kingdom of Mysore, by mountains that entirely enclose it. It has long been in subjection to the kings of Canara.

Visit to Several Parts: Haider, after taking possession of the capital, visited the several parts of his new dominions, and was everywhere acknowledged sovereign with scarce any opposition. But being desirous of reuniting certain cantons of this kingdom, in possession of the Portuguese, he did not find the viceroy of Goa disposed to make this restitution; and, as he was far superior in force to the Portuguese, he did not hesitate to attack them. With little difficulty he got possession of the country of Carvar and its fortress of Opir, situated in the country of Sunda, formerly dismembered from the kingdom of Canara.

As he was preparing to lay siege to the fort of Rama, a fortress on the point of a cape of the same name, and the only barrier that could stop his progress to Goa, the French, who were under his command, refused to give him the least assistance, preferring rather to retire into the fort of Rama than to combat with the Portuguese: M. Hughel, siding with the French, abandoned him likewise.

Haider, knowing it to be impossible to take this fort with his own troops, did not hesitate in making peace with the Portuguese, who yielded him the country of Carvar. This inconstancy of the French, and other similar events, gave Haider to understand that he should not well support a war with any European power, and that he could not depend upon the Europeans in his service, excepting when they themselves were attacked.

When Haider came a second time to Mangalore, at his return from the war with the Portuguese, he received a solemn deputation from a nation originally from Arabia, but now dispersed over the whole coast of Malabar, and known by the name of Mapelets. At the head of this deputation was Ali, Raja or Prince of Cananore. This Ali, son of one of the most rich and powerful Mapelets, had the good fortune in his youth to be beloved by the daughter of the Raja of Cananore, a Nayre prince. The father, in spite of the diversity of religion, and the prejudice of his nation, which forbids all alliance with a different cast, and much more with strangers of another religion, consented to the marriage of his daughter with Ali, and dying, left him his principality, or the small kingdom of Cananore.

The Mapelets seem to be Arabs of Marcate and Sahar, who have settled in India for the sake of commerce. This nation, forming no alliance with strangers, has preserved its peculiar manners, and a particular physiognomy, much resembling that of the Arabs of Marcate, who have generally the face long, the chin square and turned up, and the beard thin. They are lean, and of a short figure, not in the least resembling the other Arabs, who are large and handsome men, with black thick beards.

The inhabitants of the coast of Malabar having suffered the Mapelets to take possession of all the commerce of their country, as well by sea as by land, this nation has become rich and numerous, and that with still less difficulty, by reason that the princes and nobles of the country, having frequent occasion for money, have often had recourse to the Mapelets, who lent them large sums of money at exorbitant interest; sometimes upon pawns, and sometimes in advance upon the harvests of pepper, cardamoms, and rice. These repeated usuaries have increased the riches of the Mapelets, and impoverished the princes or Nawabs of the Malabar coast, known by the name of Nayres. The Mapelets grew proud in consequence of their wealth, and attracted the envy and jealousy of the Nayres.

These last, especially the more powerful of them, were not very exact in fulfilling their engagements with the Mapelets; who, on their part, were still more arrogant, when they saw Ali, a prince of their nation, elevated to the rank of prince of the country.

Master of Canara Kingdom

In this state of things, Haider became master of the kingdom of Canara; and, consequently, a neighbour of the Malabar coast, of which the principality of Cananore is the frontier on the Canara side. Ali Raja, and the Mapelets, concluded that they should insure the possession of their states by putting themselves under the protection of Haider, who was of the same religion, and whose power and reputation were capable either to protect or subjugate them.

The deputation of the Mapelets was honourably received by Haider. He loaded their deputies with magnificent presents, and assured them of his protection and good-will. The Mapelets are navigators. Ali Raja had many vessels then well-equipped and ready to set sail. Haider, who had resolved to have a fleet, in order to defend his coast from the incursions of the Marathas and other pirates, created Ali Raja his high admiral, and made his brother, Sheik Ali, intendant of the marine, of the ports, and of the maritime commerce of his dominions. He entrusted him likewise with considerable sums for the purposes of purchasing or of building vessels.

Haider with justice regarded his kingdom of Canara as the most precious gift Providence had bestowed on him and the best inheritance he could leave to his children. He designed Haider Nagar to be the capital of all his dominions. He caused all his family to repair thither, except his first Begum, the sister of Mughdum and mother of Tipu Sultan, his eldest son, who desired to reside at Bangalore. The intentions of Haider were, to establish in this kingdom a government calculated to make himself beloved by his people; and he succeeded beyond his hopes. The government of his other states was shared among his relations.

He left the government of Bangalore and its dependencies to Ibrahim Ali Khan, his uncle, who had so long enjoyed it. To Mughdum Ali Khan he gave the government of the kingdom of Mysore; to Mirza, that of Scirra, and all its district; and to a son of his uncle, named Amin Saeb, the government of the kingdom of Bisnagar.

Conquest of Maldives

Ali Raja having formed a fleet, at the commencement of the fair season made the conquest of the Maldive island, under the pretence of some injustice done to his nation; and after taking their king prisoner, he had the cruelty to put his eyes out. This conquest was made in the name, and on the account of Haider, whose colours were borne by the fleet. Ali Raja had embarked on board a number of Sepoys, or disciplined soldiers; so that Haider's colours had no sooner appeared at sea, but they enforced respect.

Ali Raja having brought back his victorious fleet to Mangalore, came to Nagar to do homage to Haider, and presented to him the unfortunate king of the Maldives. Haider, whose character is far from cruel, was so irritated at the barbarity of Ali Raja, that he instantly deprived him of the command of the fleet; which he afterwards gave to an Englishman named Stanet. Shocked at the inhumanity of Ali Raja, he entreated the king of the Maldives to forgive the outrage his admiral had been guilty of; and after expressing how much he was afflicted at the event, and using every argument in his power to console him, he gave him one of his palaces for a retreat, with a revenue sufficient to procure all the pleasures his situation permitted him to enjoy.

The courtiers and poets of this conqueror's court, little acquainted with geography, having learned that their master was become king of twelve thousand islands, added to his titles that of king of the Islands of the Sea. The conquest of the kingdom of Canara, that had withstood the efforts of the Emperor Aurangzeb, and that of the Maldive islands' unknown to the greatest part of the Mughals, added so much to the reputation of Haider, that almost all the princes of Hindustan dispatched ambassadors to congratulate him on his numerous conquests. The poets, likewise, did not fail, in their poems, to set him above Alexander and Timur.

It was now more than a year that Haider had not quitted the neighbourhood of Nagar, and that occupied with the cares of government, and his pleasures, he appeared to be delighted with a state of repose till then unknown to him. At this juncture it was that the protection he had granted to the Mapelets recalled him to the head of his troops, and gave him an opportunity of making new conquests.

The Mapelets, proud of the protection of Haider, gave up that respect and complaisance they had till then preserved for the Rajas and the other Nayres; they even threatened to do themselves justice by force of arms, if the Nayres did not perform the engagements made with them. The Nayres, whose expenses had compelled them to multiply the sums borrowed of the Mapelets were so beset by that nation of usurers that they were unable even to pay the interest of the sums due, and saw nothing but ruin in the menaces of the latter.

Irritated as well by the arrogance as by the extortions of a race of people they were in the habit of despising, they resolved, at any rate, to dissolve the connection between them: for this purpose several assemblies were held at Calicut, where the Zamorin, or chief of the Nayres resides, at which it was unanimously resolved, that on an appointed day a general massacre of all the Mapelets should be everywhere made.

This conspiracy was in part put in practice, and more than six thousand Mapelets were murdered; though the greater part escaped. Their vessels, spread over, all the coast, favoured their escape; and in many places, being forewarned, they assembled in sufficient numbers to resist their enemies.

The greater number took refuge at Cananore, where they found themselves in security, by reason of its vicinity to the dominions of Haider, as well as from the two fortresses of Cananore, one of which belonged to the Hollanders, and the other to Ali Raja. The Mapelets, in their distress, hastened to send deputies to Haider, to inform him of the catastrophe,and implore his protection.

This nation, being fanatic Mohammedans, their deputies represented to Haider in their harangue, that God, and the prophet whose relation he was, had made him powerful for no other reason, than that he might protect the true believers; and that the crime of the infidels, which ought to be punished by their destruction, would give him an opportunity of forming new conquests.

Haider, who was already instructed in the power and force of the empire of the Nayres, and was acquainted with the difficulties that might oppose him in the conquest of the country, did not hesitate to promise justice and protection to the Mapelets. He quickly assembled twelve thousand of his best troops, of which four thousand were cavalry, and the rest infantry, and began his march to the coast of Malabar, directing his route by Mangalore and Cananore. All the artillery he took with him consisted of four pieces of cannon; and he ordered his fleet to accompany him along the coast, to furnish him with assistance, as it might be required.

On his arrival at Cananore, he found more than twelve thousand Mapelets under arm; ill armed, it must be confessed, but superior in courage to the Nayres, and animated by the desire of vengeance and the hope of recovering their losses at the expense of their enemies.

Haider encamped on the banks of the river at Cananore, and dispatched an embassy to Calicut, composed of the most distinguished Brahmans of his court. They had orders to represent to the Samorin, and all the Nayre princes, the injustice of the cruelties they had been guilty of to the Mapelets; and to inform them, that he was come with his army to see justice done them: but that, before he employed force, he judged it expedient to offer his mediation; promising, that if they would punish the principal offenders, and give a just and reasonable satisfaction to the Mapelets, his army should not advance into their country; and that he would even undertake the troublesome office of rendering justice to every one.

The Nayre princes had agreed to support each other; and upon the report that Haider was coming against them to the assistance of the Mapelets, they assembled an army of more than one lac men. The deputies of Haider having finished their harangue, the Nayre princes replied, that they were astonished at the conduct of Haider, with whom they had never had any connection or dependence; and that if his troops did anything more than drink the water of the river of Cananore,—if they even presumed to set their feet in the river, they should be attacked and punished for their temerity.

On this answer the ambassadors of Haider returned to their master; and the Nayres, having collected all their forces, appeared with the firm resolution to prevent Haider from passing the river. The arrival of Haider and his army on the Malabar coast induced all the European nations who have establishments there to send deputies to him.

Upon the great reputation of Haider, it was not doubted but he would make a conquest of the whole country. The deputies of every nation were in haste to treat with him for the security of their factories and their commerce. As they expected to find this great conqueror at the head of a numerous army, they were astonished to see so small a number of troops; many of them could not help expressing their surprise to the European officers of the army; magnifying at the same time, the forces of the Nayre princes, which they affirmed to exceed one hundred and twenty thousand men.

The officers answered, that since the Nawab, who had it in his power to assemble a much greater army, had brought no more than twelve thousand men with him, it was to be presumed, that he was certain that the number he had brought was sufficient to defeat his enemies. This proper answer, which, to instructed and enlightened men, would have had its due force, made very little impression on the deputies, who had no notion of the military art, and still less of tactics; they made haste to return to their counting-houses, well convinced that the little army of Haider would be destroyed by that of the Nayres, who had lined the opposite bank of the river with a numerous artillery, and were continually firing and making rhodomontades.

Haider, perfectly acquainted with the genius of all the people of India, held himself assured of the victory, and founded his expectation on his cavalry; which was a body of troops absolutely unknown to the Nayres, no foreign army having penetrated as far as the Malabar coast, where no horses had been ever seen, except a few belonging to the European chief of the factory, and purchased by them more for pleasure than untidily: for this country, intersected by rivulets, and covered with woods, besides being subject to continual rains for seven months in the year, is absolutely improper for the breeding and keeping of horses.

To succeed in his attempt, in spite of this numerous army and the artillery, Haider caused his fleet to enter the river. His vessels sailed up as far as possible; and, drawing up his infantry in order of battle in a single line in face of the enemy, with his twelve pieces of cannon, he waited for the ebb of the water. When the river was at the lowest he entered it full gallop, at the head of his cavalry, which he had till then kept out of sight of the Nayres: they were led on by fifty of the French hussars, lately arrived from Pondicherry. As the rapidity of the current was diminished by his vessels, he traversed the river without difficulty at a place where it was a league in breadth, sometimes swimming, and sometimes wading: he soon came to the other river, where the Nayres were busied in attempting to oppose the infantry, who pretended to be on the point of passing over.

They were frightened at the sudden appearance of the cavalry, and fled with the utmost precipitation and disorder, without making any other defence but that of discharging a few cannon, which they were too much intimidated to point properly. Haider, foreseeing this event, had given orders to pursue the fugitives full speed, cutting down all they could overtake, without losing time, either by taking prisoners, or securing plunder.

This order being executed with the utmost strictness, nothing was to be seen in the roads, for the distance of four leagues round, but scattered limbs and mutilated bodies. The country of the Nayres was thrown into a general consternation, which was much increased by the cruelty of the Mapelets, who followed the cavalry, massacred all who had escaped, without sparing women or children: so that the army advancing under the conduct of this enraged multitude, instead of meeting with resistance, found the villages, fortresses, temples, and in general every habitable place, forsaken and deserted.

It was not till they were near the environs of Tellicherry and Mahe, French and English establishments, that they began to find people who had taken refuge near those places.

Notwithstanding this general defection, the army was in want of nothing: they everywhere found cows, oxen, poultry, rice, and all sorts of provisions that could be wished for in a fertile country; the fugitives having abandoned everything, without daring to load themselves with the least article that could impede their flight.

Haider caused his army to halt near these settlements, and sent an offer of peace to the Samorin, and other princes, on reasonable terms. The Samorin, who was old, remained quiet in his palace, and sent word that he waited for the conqueror, and trusted to his discretion.

This halt of the army, the sending of several Brahmans, and more especially the tranquillity of the Samorin, encouraged the inhabitants, who returned for the most part to their houses; they were still more encouraged at finding that the Mapelets committed no outrages, except on the persons or property of Nayres; but the Nayres continued to conceal themselves in the woods and mountains, from whence they carried on a kind of concealed war with the Mapelets.

March to Calicut

Haider marched for Calicut, and found no other resistance in his route but from a large pagoda, built on a mountain, and fortified. In this place the nephew and presumptive heir of the Samorin had taken refuge, and found means to make his escape from thence, though it was invested: after his departure, the Brahmans opened the gates to Haider. The conqueror continued his journey to Calicut, and took up his residence at the English factory, where his fleet arrived before him. He inquired for the Samorin on his arrival, and was informed that he was in his palace, without any guard, waiting the commands of the conqueror; from whom he hoped for mild treatment, as he had always formally opposed the resolution to massacre the Mapelets, and had foretold the consequences to his nephews.

On this intelligence, Haider returned into his palanquin, and gave orders to advise the Samorin of his approaching visit. He met this prince, who came forth and threw himself at his feet; Haider hastened to raise him, and the Samorin offered his presents, consisting of two small basins of gold, one filled with precious stones, and the other with pieces of gold, and two small cannons of gold, with carriages of the same metal. The two princes having entered the palace, Haider testified his respect for the Samorin, and promised to restore his dominions (on condition of his paying a small annual tribute) as soon as his subjects had laid down their arms, and the affair of the Mapelets was amicably settled.

These two princes parted, apparently much satisfied with each other; but the world was highly astonished, the next day, to behold the palace of the Samorin on fire; and though Haider himself assisted in procuring help, it was impossible to save anything, the edifice being entirely wood; and the Samorin, with all his family, and, as it is presumed, much treasure, perished in the flames.

This prince had himself caused the palace to be set on fire, being resolved to terminate his life in that manner, on account of some letters he had received form his nephews and the kings of Travancore and of Cochin. These letters contained the bitterest reproaches and execrations, treating him as the betrayer of his country, and apostate to his religion, which he had abandoned to the Mohammedans.

The Brahman who had conveyed these letters to him, avowed to him at the same time, that he was degraded and excluded from his caste; and that all the Brahmans and Nayres had sworn never to have any communication with him. The tragical end of the Samorin affected Haider extremely; and he was so irritated against the nephews of that prince, that he publicly swore he would never restore their dominions.

Collection of Huge Army by the Princes of Calicut: The princes of Calicut, assisted by the kings of Travancore and Cochin, had collected a considerable army on the river of Paniani, twelve leagues from Calicut, where they appeared disposed to make better opposition than they did near the river of Cananore.

They had even collected together some European cannoneers and Portuguese artisans; but upon the approach of Haider, they had not the courage to face him, and saved themselves by precipitately withdrawing their whole army.

Haider passed the river, and attacked Paniani, which made little resistance, though the best and almost the only fortress in the country. He continued to pursue his enemies till he arrived at the environs of Cochin, where, by the mediation of the Hollanders, he made peace with the king of that place, on his engaging to pay tribute.

The example of the King of Cochin was followed by the submission of all the Nayre princes; who sued for peace, and obtained it on condition of doing homage, paying tribute to Haider, and rendering ample justice each to the Mapelets in his respective districts. On these terms they were all put into free possession of their dominions; the nephews of the Samorin only being excluded from theirs.

After putting garrisons in Calicut and Paniani, Haider bestowed the government of this state on the Raja of Coimbatore, a Brahman, prince of a country dependant on Mysore, and separated from the Nayres only by the mountains. He hoped that this prince, entitled to respect from the Nayres, as being a Brahman, would be capable of maintaining peace and order, on account of his intimate knowledge of their manners and customs. The rainy season, which is very long and tempestuous on the coast of Malabar, began to appear, and obliged Haider to quit the country; but in order to be at hand to watch his new conquest, he retired only to Coimbatore, the residence of the raja, whose palace he occupied.

This country is beyond the mountains called *Gates*, and is not subject to the rains that overflow the coast of Malabar, from the middle of April to the end of September.

Passing by Madigheri, a large town and fortress on the frontier of the Malabar, at the distance of six leagues from Coimbatore, Haider left Raza Saeb, son of Chanda Saeb, in quarters with three thousand infantry.

Haider imagined that the Nayres, awed by his power and contented with his moderation, would peaceably support the yoke he had placed upon them; but he was not yet sufficiently acquainted with the characters of that haughty people, who, once offended, never pardon their enemies, however great their wrongs.

The month of May was not yet elapsed, when a general revolt of the Nayre manifested itself over all the coast of Malabar. It commenced by the massacre of a small garrison of about two hundred men, that were surprised by the inhabitants of a large town, called Pondicherry, situated at the foot of the fortress. They carried their cruelty so far as to cut off five French soldiers, deserters from Mahe, who, intending to enter in the army of Haider, arrived in the town the day after the massacre: and, as a still greater instance of the inhuman rage by which they were actuated, they ripped up two women who accompanied these unfortunate soldiers.

According to every appearance, this revolt was the effect of the secret intrigues of the King of Travancore, and the nephews of the Samorin. It would doubtless have been less general, if the Raja of Coimbatore, Ali Raja, and his brother Sheik Raja, who were entrusted with the charge of seeing the Mapelets re-imbursed, had been more temperate in their rapines and exactions.

As the immense quantities of water that fall in the Malabar country convert the smallest rivulets into large rivers; and as this country offers an almost insurmountable obstacle, by the torrents caused by the overflowing of the waters, that are met with almost at every step, during the rainy season; the Nayres, habituated to their climate, and going absolutely naked in the stormy months, believed, with reason, that they should have time to take Calicut and Paniani, and destroy the Mapelets, before Haider could enter their country; but they were yet to learn that their conqueror was not to be stopped by obstacles much greater than those they depended upon. They had taken their measures so effectually, that Raza Saeb, commandant at Madigheri, and Haider, were still ignorant of their revolt.

Calicut and Paniani were already invested by the army of the Nayres, when the news came to Haider, by means of a Portuguese sailor, who, on the promises of a handsome reward from the governor of Paniani, ventured to ascend the river of the same name alone, in a canoe made of bamboo, and covered with skin. This sailor, travelling only in the night, notwithstanding the danger of wild beasts and noxious reptiles, and with no other guide than a pocket composed, arrived at Madigheri. He apprized Raza Saeb of the revolt, and the danger to which Haider's troops at Calicut and Paniani were exposed.

This general, without loss of time, caused the Portuguese to be conducted to Haider at Coimbatore and himself immediately marched with his forces towards Paniani, in spite of the rains, and the inundation under which almost all the country was laid by the overflowing of the rivers.

This precipitate march made some impression on the revolters, as soon as they were apprized of it, but hearing that he had brought no cavalry, they detached a party of their army, which harassed Raza Saeb at the crossing of each river, and at length succeeded (perhaps by the fault of his guides) to draw him into a place between the meeting of two rivers that joined near Pondiaghari, where he found himself shut up, without being able to pass on either side, by reason of the depth and rapidity of the water; and cut off from returning by the defiles he had passed, which were every where rendered difficult to pass, by felling of trees, and the Nayres, who were in ambuscade in various parts.

Haider no sooner heard of the revolt than he recalled a party of his cavalry that had been luckily cantoned near Coimbatore. While he was thus collecting the strongest part of his army from Mysore and other parts of his dominions, he commanded a select party of his infantry to be in readiness to march on the shortest notice: however, in expectation that Raza Saeb might disperse the mutineers, he waited for news, before he exposed to so insalubrious a season troops designed for very different operations. Raza Saeb having contrived to send advice of his situation, Haider immediately marched with three thousand horse, and ten thousand Sepoys or Topasses. He ordered his cavalry, both officers and men, to ride without saddles; and commanded his infantry to quit their habits, and march naked, excepting a pair of light drawers and shoes. Each soldier was provided with a waxed cloth to wrap up his knapsack; and the three hundred Europeans lately arrived from Pondicherry and Colombo, were offered parasols, as they did not choose to quit their habits. Their refusal was the cause that they were almost the only persons in the army that were attacked by the dysentery.

All the artillery of this small army consisted in twelve light pieces of cannon, that were carried by elephants.

It is scarcely possible to form an idea of the species of war to which Haider led his troops this campaign. Imagine an army of fifteen thousand men marching from the break of day through a mountainous country, in roads or passages scarcely admitting more than three men abreast exposed from morning till night to a constant shower, equal to those that fall in the greatest storms, attended with frequent thunder and lightning, excepting for three hours after noon, in which the sun shone out with almost insupportable lustre and heat; frequently obliged to cross rivers up to the chin in water, and sometimes swimming; and passing the night in towns or villages deserted by their inhabitants, where, however, they found plenty of the necessaries of life. Their path was every where marked by ruin and destruction, for their orders were to burn and pillage, and they exerted themselves so much in this horrible work, that they left behind them nothing but heaps of ruins, where houses had formerly stood.

Unexpected March

This unexpected march obliged the Nayres to collect all their troops, and gave some relief to the troops of Raza Saeb, though not sufficient to prevent his losing many of his men for want of necessaries, and in consequence of the hardship they were subjected to.

The Nayre princes, though half defeated by the fear of the consequences of their revolt, nevertheless expected Haider with confidence in a retrenched camp near Pondiaghari, which on its left wing had a village fortified with a ditch and parapet planted with pallisades, well furnished with artillery, and maintained by the most resolute, who had determined rather to perish than yield. Haider, for the attack of this retrenched camp, disposed of hit army so that four thousand of his best Sepoys, forming the right wing, were charged to attack the village; this corps was commanded by a Portuguese lieutenant-colonel, lately arrived from Goa, with different officers of his nation.

The left wing, composed of Topasses, was commanded by an English officer; and Haider himself commanded the main body, having behind him a reserve of Europeans almost all French, with whom were joined those who are called the *Bara Aadmees,* or *Great Men,* a corps composed of all the young nobility and courtiers, without excepting even the generals, who have not appointed posts or command on the day of battle. They were all on foot, and armed with sabres and bucklers, having voluntarily put themselves under the command of the officer of Europeans, whom they promised to follow wherever he might lead them.

The cavalry, that could not be of service till after the entrenchment was forced, was formed behind the corps-de-reserve. According to the orders, the Portuguese officer attacked the retrenched village with his four thousand Sepoys, by conducting them bravely to the edge of the ditch; but, without advancing a step farther, he contented himself with causing his troops to fire as if at their exercise. These unfortunate Sepoys, totally exposed, were destroyed with impunity by their enemies, who fired from pent-holes, or from behind the hedges. This firing, which lasted upwards of two hours, highly enraged Haider, who receiving every moment news of the state of the attack, learned with the utmost mortification the unavailing loss of his best troops.

The French officer, commandant of the Europeans, who lately arrived, and had not yet had an opportunity of distinguishing himself, offered to advance with the corps-de-reserve, and put himself at the head of the Sepoys. Haider answered, that he might do as he thought proper; and he immediately joined his troop, which was impatient for the combat, and burned with a desire to revenge the French who were inhumanly massacred at Pondiaghari. Headed by this active and courageous officer, and joined by the Bara Aadmees, they ran with violent eagerness to the attack.

The intervals between the battalions of Sepoys afforded them a passage: they jumped into the ditch, and hastily ascending the retrenchments tore up the pallisades, and were in the face of the enemy in an instant. They gave no quarter; and the enemy, astonished to the last degree at their impetuosity and rage, suffered themselves to be butchered even without resistance.

The flames of the village on fire, and the direction of the cannon now pointed on the distracted Nayres, evinced to Haider that the village was carried, The whole army, in consequence, moved to attack the retrenchment; but the enemy, perceiving that Haider's troops had stormed their outpost, and catching the affright of the fugitives, fled from their camp with disorder and precipitation.

Haider had supposed his enemies would have exhibited more firmness on this occasion. This brave and fortunate attack, which was much exalted by the young nobility that shared the glory, gave him infinite pleasure. He created the French commandant Bahadur upon the spot; and in the evening presented him with a patent, appointing him general of ten thousand horse, which is the highest military post among the

Mughals; at the same time declaring him general in chief of his artillery. He likewise gave a gratification of thirty rupees to every soldier, and twice that sum to each of the wounded; of which there was a great number, though no more than one died. As the Nayres had no bayonets, the wounds were only cuts with the sabre, little dangerous where ready assistance is to be had.

The Europeans inspired the Malabars with a new terror by this exploit; and Haider, to increase it, spread a report that he expected many thousand men from Europe; he added, that they were a cruel people, and devourers of human flesh; and that his intention was, to deliver all the coast to their outrages. The rage and fury by which his small handful of French were urged on to revenge their murdered countrymen, gave much force to the belief the wretched inhabitants were disposed to afford to his reports.

Wherever he turned, he found no opponent, nor even any human creature; every, inhabited place was forsaken: and the poor inhabitants, who fled to the woods and mountains in the most inclement season, had the anguish to behold their houses in flames, their fruit-trees cut down, their cattle destroyed and their temples burned.

The perfidy of the Nayres had been too great for them to trust the offers of pardon made by Haider, by means of Brahmans he despatched into the woods and mountains to recall these unhappy people; who were hanged without mercy, and their wives and children reduced to slavery, whenever they were found in the woods by the troops of Haider; severity and mildness being both equally ineffectual in making them return to their homes. Ali Raja and the Mapelets, who saw themselves thus involved in the ruin of the Nayres, persuaded Haider to return to Coimbatore, in hopes that his absence might remove the timidity of the people: and it is highly probable that the dysentery that raged in his army was a much more effectual reason that induced him to leave the country.

The officers and Europeans, who had retained their clothing, and had more particularly abused the liberty of doing as they pleased, were the most exposed to this dangerous malady.

Nayres was Deprived of all Kind of Privileges: Before he quitted the country, Haider, by a solemn edict, declared the Nayres deprived of all their privileges; and ordained that their caste, which was the first after the Brahmans, should thereafter be the lowest of all the castes; subjecting them to salute the Parias and others of the lowest castes, by ranging themselves before them, as the other Malabars had been obliged to do before the Nayres; permitting all the other castes to bear arms, and forbidding them to the Nayres, who till then had enjoyed the sole right of carrying them; at the same time allowing and commanding all persons to kill such Nayres as were found bearing arms.

By this rigorous edict Haider expected to make all the other castes enemies of the Nayres; and that they would rejoice in the occasion of revenging themselves for the tyrannic oppression this nobility had till then exerted over them.

This ordinance being found to make the submission of the Nayers absolutely impossible, because they would have thought death preferable to such a degradation, he made a new edict, by which he re-established in all their rights and privileges such Nayres as should embrace the Mohammedan religion. Many of these nobles took the turban on this occasion; but the greater part remained dispersed and chose rather to take refuge in the kingdom of Travancore than submit to this last ordinance. Though the approach of the fine season, and the terror he had spread, might have left little apprehension of another revolt, yet he left several bodies of troops in the country, distributed in posts so situated as to assist each other in case of necessity, and quartered the rest of his infantry in the neighbourhood of Madigheri, taking only his cavalry with him to Coimbatore, which he was obliged to spread over the country, on account of the scarcity of forage.

Haider Arrived to Coimbatore: On his arrival at Coimbatore, Haider found there a body of four thousand Maratha cavalry lately arrived. More than a year had elapsed since he had ordered this corps to be raised, and since the chiefs had received the necessary sums of a Brahman, named Chamrao, formerly attached to Mons. Bussi, but since entered into the service of Haider, whose confidence he had acquired. This Brahman had not been sufficiently sparing of the money; and when the Marathas had received it, they were in no haste to complete their engagements. Instead of three months, they were scarcely ready to march in eight. Their horses, instead of being of the height and quality agreed on, were mostly small.

In short, instead of a regular body of cavalry, it was nothing more than a collection of peasants and vagabonds, incapable of forming a line, or indeed of doing any thing, but rob and pillage. Secure in possession of the Brahman's money, they paid little regard to his complaints; and, in order to avoid losing the whole, he was obliged to take the troops, such as they were. When they were on their journey, they advanced very slowly, and made continual stops; so that instead of one month, they employed four in making their journey; and even that degree of expedition was not obtained, but in consequence of repeated sums advanced by the distressed Chamrao.

The Marathas would not have acted in this manner, if they had been acquainted with the character of Haider; who, for the sake of economy, was in the habit of requiring an exact account of the sums expended for the maintenance of his troops, and was not easily deceived. In fact, having passed them in review the day after his arrival, he found them in so bad a state that he could not avoid expressing his surprise to the Brahman. Chamrao had long since written to Haider, complaining of the mutiny and disobedience, not only of the private men, but of their officers.

Haider complained to the chiefs, that his orders were so ill executed: he signified to them, that, on account of their disorderly appearance and bad equipment, he would receive the troops, as his custom was with all his cavalry, and reform all those that were not agreeable to the agreements made with Chamrao, his agent; that he likewise expected they would account for all the money employed in raising the troop; and besides, to show them his displeasure to find that, regardless of every thing that could be urged by the person entrusted with his orders, they had employed in their journey four times the space necessary to perform it in, he had given orders to his treasurer to deduct from their account the time they had voluntarily lost by passing through unusual roads.

These Marathas, who, according to their own account, had large sums to receive, murmured loudly at finding themselves obliged to renounce a considerable part of their claim. Not at all habituated, in their own country, to be commanded despotically, they resolved with one accord to return to their camp; with menaces to do themselves justice, if refused it by fair means.

They who knew Haider, and how circumspect he is, could not conceive how he could so indiscreetly put himself in the power of these Marathas; having kept with him at Coimbatore no moje than five hundred Sepoys, and thirty Europeans, who were their commandant's guard.

Fortunately, the Marathas troops were not ignorant that Haider was able, in a very short time, to collect military of every denomination; in the meantime they demanded payment within the hour, or in default they threatened to mount their horses, and return into their own country, destroying and pillaging all that might offer in their way.

Haider reproached himself secretly for the vivacity that had led him to use menaces with those people, at an instant in which he was not prepared to give law to them. Though he had little to fear personally, it would have been more prudent in him to have retired at this juncture into the fortress of

Coimbatore; but that courage, which never abandoned him, led him to surmount the difficulty and danger that now presented itself.

In this embarrassment Mahfuz Khan, ancient Nawab of Arcot, and brother of Mohammed Ali, advised him to send for the French commandant, and give him the charge of reducing this mutinous cavalry to reason. Haider approved of the thought, and sent for the officer; he explained the affair to him, and informed him that by the advice of the Nawab of Arcot he requested he would undertake to bring those vagabonds to hear reason; whom he could easily reduce by force of arms, but that he wished to use milder methods.

The French officer consented to shew himself worthy of the confidence Haider honoured him with, though he saw all the difficulty attending the execution of the business: however, he undertook it with ardour, being desirous of continually rendering himself more useful and necessary.

To begin his negociation, he sent word to the Maratha chief, that he was desirous of paying him a visit, in order to cultivate an acquaintance with him and the other great men of his nation: at the same instant he sent an express for Madigheri, with orders for all the Europeans to march for Coimbatore; and, together with his letter, he dispatched an order from Haider to the commander-in-chief of the cantonment, to send off all the Topasses, which amounted to a body of above four thousand men.

The Maratha chief having accepted with joy the visit the French officer proposed, received him with the greatest politeness, as did the other chiefs who were assembled on the occasion. In order to obtain their confidence, the commandant, after making the usual compliments (that is to say, speaking highly of the valour and merit of the Maratha nation) proceeded to inform them, that he wished to visit them, because the French and himself were nearly in the same situation as the

Maratha cavalry; and it might be found advantageous to unite their pretensions, and made a common cause.

The fact in reality was, that the French troops arrived in Haider's dominions at the very juncture in which the revolt of the Nayers demanded his attention, and had remained a considerable time at Seringapattam. It is true, that he had received considerable sums by order of Haider; but, though he had already been engaged in actual service, no agreement had yet been made for the emoluments and pay of himself and his troops.

This overture having insured the confidence of the Marathas, they began to exclaim against Haider, and accused him of breach of faith, by speaking almost all at once; their chief at last found an opportunity of speaking alone: he spoke highly of the conduct and behaviour of his troops, and placed their pretensions in the most favourable point of view; and the French officer, seeming to give credit to their words, was careful not to shew any intimation that he was charged with any commission from Haider: he gave them reason to suppose the contrary; and even acquainted them (as in confidence) that he expected his troop the next day, who, impatient to know their fate, would come expressly to decide it: that therefore he judged it expedient for them to wait till the Europeans were arrived; and in the meantime, he would go to Haider, as if from himself, and offer his mediation: the Marathas unanimously approved this project, and accepted his offer with gladness.

Things thus adjusted for the present, there was no question concerning the expediting of business: the Marathas promised the French officer, that they would return his visit the following day at the same hour, to learn the effect of his intended conference with Haider: and they parted good friends. All the country resounded with the valour of the French; and the Marathas, had the highest opinion of them, on account of the defeat of Nasirjung, and the exploits of M. Bussi, were highly flattered with this kind of alliance with them.

The following day the few Europeans that were at Madigheri, to the number of four hundred men, began to appear, but irregularly, in small numbers, consisting of three or four at most in a party. By this artifice, they appeared to be coming in all day, without its being possible for the Marathas to judge of their number; and those who arrived did not fail to acquaint the inquirers, that the main body would soon arrive: accordingly, at the close of the night, a column of infantry passed by the Maratha camp, with drums beating and colours flying, composed of Topasses, who had been sent from Madigheri, and were headed by the Europeans who, by another route, had gone out of Coimbatore to join them.

This artifice caused the Marathas to believe the Europeans were much more numerous than they really were; and their notion was strengthened by the hats of the Topasses, and their drums and fifes, which resemble the others; and as they played the same marches, and it was almost dark when they appeared, it was not easy to perceive the difference.

The principal Maratha chiefs waited on the French commandant; who receiving them with most attentive politeness and regard, acquainted them, that he had found Haider disposed to act in the most amicable manner with them, and had accepted his mediation; but that he had promised to keep strictly to the agreement made with his agent, Chamrao: that he consented, either that himself alone, or with such other person of consequence as the Marathas might choose, would pass in review, one by one, the horsemen and their horses, for the purpose of reforming those that were not according to the agreement: and likewise, that after having taken an account of the length of the journey they had to perform, arbitrators should decide the time they ought to have employed. The French commandant added, that these propositions having appeared to him equitable, he had judged it proper to submit, and accept them; being well convinced of the candid and noble manner of thinking that distinguished the Maratha nation.

They, who did not find their account in this method of adjusting the affair, exclaimed much against the facility of the officer, and assured him that they would not consent to be thus passed in review; and more particularly because Chamrao, the envoy of Haider, had seen and approved the horses, which had not since been changed; and that with respect to his demand concerning the time employed in the journey, it was at the very request of Chamrao, they affirmed, that they had so sojourned on the road, in order that they might not arrive at Coimbatore during the absence of the Nawab, being informed that forages were very rare.

These Maratha officers having persisted in their determination, maintained firmly that the propositions made to them were unreasonable; and that they could not accept them, nor abate their pretensions, without the consent of all the chiefs, of whom they would convene an assembly. The night approaching, they returned very dissatisfied with their visit, and the resolution of Haider.

The French officer, not to render himself suspected by paying too great attention to the situation of their encampment, thought proper to commit that charge to one of his adjutants. This officer reported that the camp was in a meadow situated between two banks, one serving to retain the water of a great tank, and the other as a passage at the time of rain; that the meadow was bounded at one end by a hill impracticable to cavalry, because covered with fruit-trees, and intersected by hedges and walls of earth, that divide the property of different persons; that at the extremity of the bank, that served for a road, there were some houses, and a small pagoda; and lastly, that he was of opinion, that two hundred men, and some pieces of cannon, placed in this hamlet, would be able to prevent the Marathas from going out of their camp.

In consequence of this advice, cannon were conveyed in the night to this post, and 250 men, who entrenched themselves. A barbette battery of ten pieces of cannon was constructed, which was by no means an agreeable sight to the Marathas when day-light appeared. Their chiefs having sent to the officer who commanded the post, to demand with what intention those cannon were pointed at their camp, received answer, that they had been placed there by his commandant, with orders to fire on the first Maratha that should attempt to get on horseback; and that if they desired further information, they must apply to the commandant. On this they dispatched two of their officers, who complained of this act of hostility, but with much politeness, and an air that sufficiently exhibited their fear.

The commandant did not hesitate to answer, that having been so little satisfied the preceding evening with their reception of the propositions of Haider, which to him appeared just and reasonable; and fearing that, by a precipitate resolution of returning into their own country, they might betray his faith and honour, pledged to the sovereign on their account, he thought it incumbent on him to take these precautions. But, nevertheless, he wished to continue his mediation, and would certainly join them, if Haider refuse to do them justice. This discourse having encouraged them, they protested they were ready to treat; and that, trusting entirely to his promises, all the chiefs would wait on him at an hour to be appointed, for a conference with Haider's ministers.

On the assurance given them that no act of hostility should be committed, provided they remained quiet in their camp, they returned to their quarters. The commandant repaired to Haider to inform him of their good dispositions; he found him alone with Mahfuz Khan, who likewise offered himself as mediator and interpreter, for which he was qualified by speaking very good Portuguese.

In consideration of the advanced age and high rank of this personage, the French officer begged he would consent that the meeting might be held at his house. Advice was given to the Marathas, who repaired thither at the close of the evening.

Two Brahmans, secretaries to Haider, likewise attended, and everything was arranged in two days; Mahfuz Khan having removed all the difficulties with a degree of address and intelligence very uncommon, but acquired by fifty years' experience in this sort of negotiations.

It was agreed, that none should be dismissed, but such horses as were absolutely incapable of any kind of service; that they should all pass in exact review; that such as should be judged in a state to serve as good cavalry, should be paid at the rate of forty rupees a month, man and horse, according to the agreement made with Chamrao; and that the others should be reduced to five and twenty, and should serve as irregular cavalry. The time allowed for the journey was set at three months.

After this review it was found that one hundred and fifty horse only were entitled to forty rupees, and the rest were reduced to five-and-twenty. The principal chief, whose troop was well mounted, and who alone possessed eight hundred horse, had none dismissed; perhaps there was indulgence shown him, on account of the pains he had taken to accommodate the difference.

Affairs Adjusted Satisfactorily: The affair being thus satisfactorily adjusted, Haider made a present of twenty two horses to the French officer, to mount twenty Europeans, to serve him as a guard, and accompany him everywhere: at the same time he gave orders to the Baksi and the secretary at war, to settle the pay and emoluments of all the Europeans; Haider being in the custom never to settle pecuniary affairs himself, but committing the charge of them to ministers, who have no permission to conclude any business without the precise orders of their master.

To make their court, the Baksi and his colleague exclaimed against the exorbitant pretensions of Europeans, and proposed abatements that were flatly rejected; but as the corps of

Europeans was not numerous, the subject of these discussions was of small consequence to Haider: to end them therefore, and to make a parade of generosity that he thought suitable to his rank, he ordered the commandant and principal officers before him, and addressing himself to the former, "I hear, with concern," said he, "that you do not agree with the Baksi and Narimrao. Why did you not apply to me ? have you forgot that I have, both by writing and conversation, informed you, that you may dispose of everything I possess; and that the French are highly esteemed by me ?" Upon which he gave orders to Narimrao to prepare the Basti, and he signed them before he dismissed the officers; at the same time inviting them to an entertainment to be given at the palace the next day.

As it could not be expected that the coast of Malabar would ever enjoy a state of tranquillity while the Nayre princes were on the frontiers, and in the country of Travancore, Haider resolved to make the conquest of that kingdom; for which, however, he could urge no better reason than that the king of that country had assisted his enemies. Though this kingdom is of small extent, it is very populous; and its king, Ram Raja, has acquired a reputation for his valour and prudence, which gave reason to conclude that the undertaking would be attended with much difficulty.

Haider knew that his enemy had long exerted himself in disciplining his army; that he had a numerous corps of Sepoys well armed, and a train of artillery, served by good cannoneers, procured from the Danes, the English, and the Dutch. He likewise knew that the country was not to be penetrated, but by way of narrow passages through mountains, where Ram Raja had caused fortresses to be constructed, which he was firmly resolved to defend to the utmost.

Neither was he ignorant, that the English, jealous of his power, had assembled troops in Madura and Marava, countries dependant on Mohammed Ali Khan, and frontier to Travancore: but, habituated to overcome all obstacles, he was determined to pursue his intention. He trusted to the promises made by the English deputies, who had waited upon him on the coast of Malabar; to whom he had granted not only a confirmation of all their former privileges, but had, besides, given permission to establish a factory at Onoor; and he was likewise persuaded, that the English troops were assembled for no other purpose than to protect the dominions of Mohammed Ali from insult.

Mahfuz Khan had lately been induced to take the part of Nizam Ali Khan, who had sent him presents of great value. He knew that the Suba of Deccan was engaged in wars with his vessals, in which he was assisted by a party of English, commanded by General Smith. He therefore concluded that he had nothing to fear on his part.

In order to secure himself from any interruption in the war he had projected, Haider wrote to Mirza Ali Khan, governor of Scirra, and his brother-in-law, to renew the truce with the Marathas, which was on the point of expiring: a business not difficult to be performed, by means of a sum of money properly distributed among the chiefs. The intended war, and the necessity of placing strong garrisons in the conquered country, obliged Haider to make considerable levies for the augmentation of his army; and, being willing to derive every advantage from the time preceding that in which he intended to march against Ram Raja, he caused all his troops and his artillery to be exercised by the European officers, he himself assisting every day with his sons and generals at the different exercises and evolutions.

After consulting the commandant of Europeans, whose knowledge and intelligence he greatly valued and depended on, he established, by his advice, a corps of five thousand grenadiers, divided into battalions of five hundred men, composed of four companions of one hundred and twenty five men each. Two of those battalions were selected out of the Topasses, and the rest from the Sepoys; each being commanded by an European officer. There was, besides, in each company, an European adjutant or serjeant-major. The officers and private men of every company were chosen by Haider himself, who regarded tallness less than a martial air, and the activity and robust temperament of the individual.

The Grandiers

These grenadiers received ten rupees a month, instead of eight which is the pay of the other Sepoys. They were exempt from all works of labour, and even mounted no guard, except that of their commandant; and, that nothing might prevent their being ready to march at the first signal, every escouade, composed of seven men, including an inferior officer, were allowed a cook servant, and an ox to carry their tent and baggage. Every company was augmented by an escouade of seven men, destined solely to guard the baggage. These were as it were apprentices, being youths of about seventeen years old, intended to replace the grenadiers who fell, and to render the corps capable of affording great advantages by the rapidity of their motions.

From the time of their first establishment, they were exercised every morning in handling their arms, by their own officers; and every afternoon, from three till six, five battalions, by turns, were exercised in their evolutions by the French commandant; after which they were made to march from six to eight, marching out at the ordinary pace, and returning home with a quick step.

All the officers, with exception, were obliged to do this exercise as well as the common soldiers. This constraint at first occasioned much murmuring among them, but luckily it did not come to the hearing of Haider. However, whether through a sense of duty, or from example, they became accustomed to it, and their assiduity afforded great encouragement to the soldiers. It was thus that this sovereign formed a body of troops, to whose rapid movements the English afterwards attributed all his successes.

The English had no sooner heard of Haider's preparations, which fame had rendered still more considerable, than they conceived umbrage at them, as well as at the long stay he made at Coimbatore, the capital adjoining to Madura, of which we have already made mention.

In their uncertainty respecting his intentions, they resolved to dispatch his wakil from Madras, a Brahman, named Menagi Pundit, to carry him a letter from the governor and council of that settlement. This letter announced a solemn embassy, composed of Colonel Call, chief engineer, and Counsellor Boschier, brother to the governor.

Haider being persuaded that they intended to make propositions to him, relative to Travancore and the coast of Malabar, contrary to his views and intentions, thought it was necessary to elude the receiving to embassy. He immediately despatched an answer to the letter of the council, assuring them that he was very much flattered with their letter, and thanking them for the honour they intended him in sending so distinguished an embassy; but at the same time he added, that Coimbatore, being only a camp or military station, by no means proper for the reception of ambassadors with those honours they were entitled to expect, he could not decently receive the embassy till he should arrive at Seringapattam, a royal city, to which he proposed to return in a short time; and that he would be careful to advise the governor of Madras of his arrival there.

Haider was too well acquainted with English politics to suffer himself to be seduced by the pompous honour with which they hoped to dazzle his sight; and, far from being flattered by this embassy, he was determined no longer to defer his expedition against Travancore. The order was already given for the army to be in readiness to march, when an unforeseen event convinced him that he had more enemies than he suspected, who were anxiously intent upon his destruction.

Recruitment of Turner

There was an Irish officer in his army, named Turner, who had been admitted into his service, by virtue of a letter of recommendation from Governor Boschier. He was a man of strong understanding; and who, possessing all the talents required in a good soldier, especially in the art of tactics, had in a very short time gained the affection of Haider, who committed the most important operations to his care. This man, who was not in the slightest degree suspected, was commander of the first battalion of Topass grenadiers; and, in this quality, he was regarded as general of that military, which forms a body of about five thousand men.

It must be allowed that an officer recommended by an English governor ought to have been treated with less confidence and security; but this man had behaved so well, in the war on the coast of Malabar, that, far from having any mistrust of him, he had acquired the confidence of his generals. Taking advantage of the good opinion they had of him, he waited till the time of payment, which is made the fifth day of every lunar month after the moon has appeared; and when he had received his appointments, and the pay of his men, the made his escape by the road that leads towards Cochin.

His quarters were a short league distant from Coimbatore. The officers of his corps waited on him to receive their pay; but, under the captious pretence of his secretary being absent, he begged them to wait till the next day, which was without difficulty granted. To put his project in execution he mounted his horse, being accompanied by a young Swedish officer, to whom he had communicated his design, and disappeared, carrying every thing of value he possessed with him; taking the precaution first to acquaint his domestics that he was going to supper with the commandant-general at Coimbatore.

The intensity of the heat in the day, and the beauty of the nights, in India, induce people of distinction to sit up very late, more especially as they have the custom of sleeping in the day from three till six. Some officers, who were in this habitude, called upon him, and were astonished to find he was gone to supper at Coimbatore; but far from harbouring any suspicion, they concluded, on the contrary, that it was a gaming party, knowing him to be a great gamester; the night being fine, they resolved to take the advantage of it; and, thinking to surprise him agreeably, they mounted their horses, and repaired to the commandant's quarters at Coimbatore, where they arrived about midnight. Their astonishment was highly increased, when they found everybody in the most profound sleep.

They inquired to no purpose for Turner, as no one could give any account of him; and the suspicion that consequently arose in their minds induced them to apply to the commandant himself. On their account of the absence of their officer, the commandant sent to inquire of the posts that guarded the entrance of the passes, whether any one had passed them; and was informed that two European officers had departed three hours before. The first captain of Turner's corps, named Minerva, an Irishman, offered to pursue him instantly with a party of fifty Europeans: his offer was accepted, and he departed at two in the morning. At eight they had stretched over upwards of six leagues, and arrived at the frontier of the country of Cochin. They discovered the horses of the officers they were in quest of, and environed the house, in which they found them both asleep. They immediately secured their persons and conducted them bound to Coimbatore.

Escape of Turner and Recapture: Haider being informed of the escape of Turner and the Swedish officer, and their recapture, gave orders to judge them as in a similar case in Europe. In consequence, a court martial was assembled, at which the two criminals were tried, and convicted of carrying off the public money; sentence was accordingly pronounced, that they should be degraded and hung, and their bodies afterwards exposed on the high road.

The council, in compassion to the youth of the Swedish officer (who, according to all appearance, had been seduced by the other, and still more, because he carried away no property of any other, and was only culpable in having departed without leave) thought proper to intercede with the Nawab in his favour, who commuted the punishment of death into that of imprisonment. As to Turner, he was conducted to the place of punishment, and there discovered to the council, that the English, conjointly with Nizam Ali Khan, intended to attack Haider.

He confessed that he was a Sepoy employed by the government of Madras, and begged pardon of the sovereign for having so long abused his confidence; that he should not have made his escape, if he had not lately been nominated major of a regiment on the Bombay establishment: he intreated his judges, in consideration of the importance of his discoveries, that they would spare him the indignity of being hanged, and as he deserved to die, would give orders for him to be shot; this request was allowed him. Before he suffered, he distributed all his money to the soldiers appointed to put him to death; to the Sieur Minerva he gave his sword and watch. After his death he was suspended on a tree near the road-side conformably to the latter part of his sentence.

The discovery of the intentions of the English, caused the departure of the army for Travancore to be suspended. Haider without delay caused Mahfuz Khan to repair to Hyderabad, where he was charged to attempt, by the intrigues of his friends and his creatures about the Nawab, who were in great number (Basalatjung, brother of the Suba, being the first) to avert the storm that threatened him from that court.

In the meantime he continued to exercise his troops, and train them to all kinds of evolutions. This spectacle, entirely new to the Indians, and the long stay of the sovereign of so many states in Coimbatore, drew so great a concourse of people to that place, that their number amounted to more than 100,000, exclusive of the army, which exceeded 60,000: but it will scarcely be credited, that this country is so abundant with all the necessaries of life, that a sheep or a dozen of fowls never cost more than two shillings; and twelve measures of rice, one of which is sufficient to serve a man a day, were sold at the same price.

The immense population of this country is proved by the two markets which are held weekly; where, at each, is commonly sold twenty thousand pieces of silk, each fourteen cubits long. This country, through which lies the ordinary passage from Mysore and the coast of Coromandel to the coast of Malabar, produces a considerable revenue to Haider, who enjoys the tolls, to the exclusion of the Rajas of the country.

It is estimated, that thirty thousand oxen, loaded with tobacco, annually pass through Coimbatore: this assertion is rendered very probable, by the numerous magazines of that commodity at Pondiagheri. Besides tobacco, there are great quantities of silks of every kind, and pepper, cardamom, clove, ivory, *etc.*, brought from the coast of Malabar.

During the long stay of Haider at Coimbatore, many events happened, which, though of no great importance, are yet sufficiently interesting to be related. They may serve not only to give the reader a more perfect idea of the genius and character of Haider, but likewise to throw light on the manners of the people, of whom the Nawab became the sovereign. The first of these events is a process or suit at law, carried on against the missionary Jesuits of the dominions of Haider.

The news of the expulsion of the self-named Jesuits from Portugal and France having arrived in India, a missionary of that order, a Portuguese by nation, and residing in Mysore, quitted his cure in 1767, and retired to Goa; being determined, as he said, to shew himself a faithful subject of his king, by no longer continuing in a body of men declared to be enemies of his country. A year and a half after his departure, he wrote to a Portuguese lady, named-Madam Mequinez widow of a Portuguese officer, who had rendered signal services to Haider, and was afterwards slain in a battle against the Manillas; Haider in return, had given his widow the regiment of Topasses her husband had possessed, with the appointment of colonel, till an adopted son of her husband's was of age to command the regiment himself.

This lady accompanied her regiment everywhere: the colours were carried to her house; and she had a private sentinel at the door. She received the pay, and caused the deductions to be made in her presence from each company. When the regiment was collected, she inspected them herself, as well as all the detachments that were ordered out; but she permitted the second in command to exercise the troops, and lead them against the enemy.

This dame Mequinez having received the letter of the ex-Jesuit father, addressed herself to the Brahman Narimrao, secretary at war, and much esteemed by Haider. She complained that, during the life, and since the death of her husband, she had deposited in trust in the hands of the now ex-jesuit all her jewels, and the money she and her husband could spare: that this father having departed to Goa, she being in the army, wrote to him, and received for answer, that all the jewels and money she had deposited in his hand, were transferred under the same title into those of the provincial father resident at Xavier Paleam, to whom it was necessary for her to address herself for restitution: she added, that having carried this letter to the provincial father, he affirmed she had lost her senses: and that he had never heard either of her money or jewels: at the same time she placed in the hands of the secretary the letter received by her from Goa, together with a state of the jewels and money she reclaimed, amounting to a considerable sum.

The Brahman acquainted Haider with the particulars of this affair, and painted the Jesuits in the most odious colours by reciting what had passed in Fiance and Portugal concerning them. On this complaint, Haider immediately ordered a guard of four Sepoys and a corporal to every missionary found in his dominions, with orders not to lose sight of the reverend fathers; but at the same time to permit them to perform their functions, as well in their missions as in their churches, without impeding them in the least: but, on the contrary, they were commanded to treat them with every mark of respect.

Haider commanded this restraint to be laid upon them, because the complaint was made at the very time when the revolt of the Nayres demanded his presence on the coast of Malabar. On his return to Coimbatore, and the Brahman Narimrao having renewed the widow's complaint, he sent for the French commandant, of whose integrity and judgement he was well convinced: "You are, doubtless," said he, "acquainted with the suit urged by the widow Mequinez against the Jesuits; and, as I wish the affair to be terminated by an equitable decision, I have fixed upon you to take cognizance of the same, and shall give you every necessary power to be her judge." The officer answered, " That not being a man of the law, he could not pretend to undertake the distribution of justice, for fear of erring through ignorance. " Haider replied, "Certainly you, who are yourself a Christian, must be better acquainted with the law of the Haider, and all the 'Mohammedans, believe that Jesus Christ, like Moses and Mohammed, has given laws to Christians, which the judges are bound to follow in their decisions; and that Christian prince cannot evade them by contrary laws.

Christians than any judge in my dominions; and since my intention is that every one shall be judged by his own law, you cannot avoid accepting this commission; but I permit you, if it be necessary, to select, as assistants jointly with yourself, such officers of your nation, and religion as you think capable of seconding your own endeavours." There was nothing could be objected to his offer. The French officer, after thanking

Haider for the honour of his good opinion, consented to perform his orders to the utmost of his power: and the day following, Madam Mequinez and the reverend provincial father, being informed of the Haider Bahadur's determination, did not fail to wait on the French officer as their judge.

The lady arrived apparently in the utmost distress. She lamented, with signs of great affliction, that poverty, to which, she affirmed, the perfidy of the Jesuits had reduced her, and against whom she vented numberless invectives: her oration was so specious that almost all the Europeans, especially the French, who we're chiefly young men, were prejudiced in her favour, and were desirous that the Jesuits should be condemned to make restitution, and be burned, or at least hanged.

Italian Provincial Father

The provincial father was an Italian of about sixty year of age, of a commanding and venerable aspect, though at the same time affable and mild. He praised God for inspiring the sovereign with the choice of such a judge as his heart had long desired. After this short prayer he entreated the French commandant (making at the same time the most humble apology to the other gentlemen present) that he would be pleased to grant him a private audience, that he might be able to explain the affair in all its particulars; but which he could not do in public, because of certain persons who were involved in the business.

The French officer made a sign for every one to retire; and the reverend provincial father, being alone with him, expressed himself in these terms; You must be sensible, Sir, that, even in the most regular and holy societies, it is impossible to prevent Judas from sometimes appearing; and he who now has drawn this unexpected persecution on us, for the satisfactory termination of which we depend on you, may justly be called by that name. Before that man determined to retire to Goa, there were several scandalous stories came to my knowledge concerning him, that obliged me to reprimand him; for, in this country, when a man is once at the head of a mission, the superior has no other right than that of reprimanding him, for fear of a greater disorder. Being informed that my remonstrances produced no effect, I thought it my duty to watch over all his actions. I was advised when he quitted his cure, and that he had departed to Mangalore, in his way to Goa. I followed him without delay, and coming up with him before he embarked, I easily obtained an order from the commandant of Mangalore to prevent his quitting the place before I had published, in all the missions, that if any one had interests to discuss with that father, he should repair to Mangalore: many persons repaired thither, and among them the dame Mequinez, who reclaimed two thousand rupees, a pair of bracelets of rubies, and a collar of pearls, which were returned to her; as was acknowledged by an authentic act passed in the chancellory of the Portuguese factory at Mangalore, and witnessed by the signature of the French and Portuguese factors.

Since the exhibition of the widow Mequinez's complaint against us, I have applied to the chief and chancellor of the Portuguese factory for a copy of the act, which they have constantly refused of this trust having been abused. This custom is very ancient, and seems to have originated with the Portuguese. The monks, at all events, gain much money by the practice, because there are scarcely any women that die, who previously acquaint their husbands, or relations where they have placed sums in this manner.

Portuguese Factory at Mangalore : The Portuguese had a factory at Mangalore, on an eminence that commanded the river. In this factory they kept a small garrison of thirty Portuguese soldiers, commanded by a lieutenant, who was at the same time factor, and a kind of consul: this settlement had two pieces of cannon, and displayed Portuguese colours. The king of Canara submitted to this, and the Portuguese levied a small duty, as toll on the entering or going out of the river of Mangalore, which they pretended to defend against invaders. When the English took Mangalore in 1768, the Portuguese had neither the inclination nor the power to defend the entrance of the riser against the English army. Haider being desirous of constructing a citadel at Mangalore in 1774, M. Catini, his engineer, found that the site of the Portuguese factory was the most proper for building a citadel capable of defending the entrance of the river; and the Portuguese were obliged to resign their factory.

To procure this deed, which is absolutely necessary for the right decision of the cause, it will be proper, Sir, for you to make use of the authority of the Nawab. The bearer of his order must be a Frenchman who can be depended on, and who must compel the Portuguese factor to exhibit the registers of his chancellorship, in spite of all the resistance he may make, on account of the honour of his flag and garrison. I must entreat you likewise, sir, to conduct the business in which manner as that the Brahman Narimrao may not be apprised of the order given to force the 'chief of the Portuguese settlement to communicate his registers: for I have good reasons to suspect that this Brahman, whose avarice you are now stranger to, is interested in the plot, as well as the Portuguese chancellor and factor.

The Brahman would not fail, "in that case, to advise them of the intended order, and they would dispatch the registers to Goa. If you cannot clear up the affair by means of these registers, you may write to Mahe, to know who was the French gentleman who then resided at Mangalore. You may then apply to him, and perhaps his memory will furnish you with means to do justice to the injured.

The French officer, after having heard the recital of the provincial father, said, Be at your ease, my reverend father; I will do my utmost to search your affair to the bottom, without giving any suspicion of the communication you have made."

Provincial Fathers' Conference

Madan Mequinez, impatient to know the result of the provincial father's conference with the French commandant, hastened the next morning to wait up on him. There were then several French officers with him: he no sooner saw her, than he said, Madam, the provincial father made his confession to me yesterday; you must now absolutely make yours. The lady colonel, assured of the victory, consented with great readiness; and everybody having retired, he addressed her thus:

> "How could you thoughtlessly precipitate yourself into the abyss you are fallen in ? You enjoy a great revenue by the bounty of the Nawab; and you have presumed to impose on that prince, whom you know to be severely just: you are a Christian, and you have not scrapped to invent the most odious imposture, in hopes of enriching yourself by the plunder of the churches and altars, and with the intention of sharing your unjust demands with Brahman and a Monk, whose wickedness you are well acquainted with. But it is in vain that you hope any longer to conceal your conspiracy. I am informed of everything by the French gentleman who resided at Mangalore, and who will quickly arrive here, together with the chancellor of the Portuguese factory, who brings his registers, and is guarded by Sepoys. You have but a moment in your power to save yourself, by making a sincere declaration of the truth: for from this instant I will cause you to be arrested and guarded, without permission to speak to any one; and when your imposture shall be proved, you may expect that the Nawab will punish you as you deserve: but if, on the contrary, you make the confession I demand, I will find means of terminating the affair without noise."

The woman, who now saw herself unmasked, was almost dead at hearing a discourse so unexpected; and finished by falling on her knees. She confessed the truth, and threw the blame on the Monk of Goa, and the Brahman, who had prompted her with this infamous contrivance. The officer raised her, with the assurance, that by her confession she had placed herself out of all danger: he then went out, and fastened the door behind him; but soon returned with two officers of known discretion, to whom he had comunicated the particulars of what had passed: and the dame Mequinez, supposing them to be of the number of her judges, repeated before them everything she had before avowed to the commandant.

The provincial father being sent for, and informed of the confession of the widow, prostrated himself, on the earth, and then raising himself, returned thanks to God, that the truth was cleared up, and his brethren justified from the accusation so maliciously urged against them. He nevertheless entreated the commandant to conceal the detail of the affair from the Nawab; fearing, as he said, the consequence that might ensue to the widow: but more probably wishing to avoid the enmity of the Secretary Narimrao.

The officer having informed Haider that the affair was terminated, that prince was contented with saying, "I am persuaded that the whole is an iniquitous contrivance against the reverend fathers; for I am informed, that her conduct is such, as, if she does not take care, will finish by bringing no small mortification upon herself. However," added he, "since you and the reverend fathers forgive her, I shall say no more of it." He immediately gave orders to remove the guard he had placed over the Jesuits. The good fathers were not, however, disposed to pardon the lady spiritually: she was excommunicated, and condemned to public penance; to which, though it may seem astonishing, she submitted, with much apparent resignation.

The provincial father, in his letter, written to inform all the missions of the means by which his innocence was cleared up, spoke highly of the French officer; who, he said, was in the highest favour with the Nawab. This eulogium produced a letter from the archbishop of Cochin, who recommended to him a Malabar priest, of the number of the Christians of St. Thomas, whose diocesan the archbishop was. He was deputed, together with three other laymen of his country, to request of Haider the permission to keep fire-arms, under the pretence that, by not being armed, they ran the risk of being robbed by the Nayres, and the soldiers of the Nawab. The officer, who imagined he might safely give credit to the archbishop's letter, was much surprised when Haider said, he was no stranger to the antipathy that fomented their quarrel. "These people," said he, "have been disarmed, because they assassinated each other, being always at enmity on account of their priests, who are of different castes: I shall take care to place safeguards in the country, to prevent my people from molesting them, and I shall send troops sufficient to disperse the Nayres."

Christians of Saint Thomas

These Christians of Saint Thomas are of very ancient origin, being settled in India before the arrival of the Portuguese. It is demonstrated, that their St. Thomas was not the disciple of Jesus Christ. They are partly in subjection to the Pope, and partly under the patriarch of the Chaldeans, who resides at Merdin in Mesopotamia. This division causes them to detest each other; and, profiting by the troubles of their country, they were mutually engaged in a cruel war, when Haider caused them to be disarmed. The deputies who came to Coimbatore were stout men, with a ferocious air and manner: they had the figure of a small cross above their nose punctured in the skin, and a large scar on the right cheek, caused by the recoil of their muskets.

The archbishop, in his letter, offered to the commandant two young slaves, who, he said, he had himself educated, and were qualified to render services both of utility and pleasure, being instructed in writing and in music. As he did not obtain his desire, he sent an inconsiderable present; with an excuse, that the young slaves, at the moment of their departure, had cried and wept so immoderately, that his feelings would not suffer him to part with them. To this present were added a vast number of benedictions, and a promise that he would write to the Pope, then Clement XIII.

The same officer was employed by Haider in a law-suit between the French and English factors resident at Calicut. A merchant of that city had long been indebted to the French company; and having received a considerable quantity of wood from Haider, the French factor agreed with him, that he should pay his debt in that commodity, which was much wanted at Pondicherry, for the entire rebuilding that town, lately destroyed by the English. The quantity sold to the French factor being arrived at Calicut, the English factor prevailed on the Raja of Coimbatore to seize it, on pretence that the English company had a prior claim on the merchant: the Raja, who was guided by the English, adjudged, after hearing the parties, that the English factor should have the wood, which was accordingly carried by him to his factory: but on the appeal that the French commandant made to the Nawab himself, the Raja ordered the affair to remain in its then state, till the decision of the sovereign was known.

He wrote at the same time in favour of the English; and the French factor, persuaded of the goodness of his cause, begged the commandant of Europeans to intercede in his favour. This officer having impartially informed Haider of the difference between the factors, the Nawab made him this answer:

> "Neither you nor I are sufficiently informed to decide on this affair, especially as our attention is required to things of more consequence: but, that justice may be done, I have written to the Raja of Coimbatore, to put the decision into the hands of the chiefs of the Portuguese, Danish, and Dutch factors; and whatever their judgement may be, to put it in execution."

In persuance of this order, the delegated judges decided in favour of the French; but the English factor, to render the judgement illusory, caused all the wood to be sawed up, so that it was rendered unfit for any use except to be burned: a piece of business that he could not have performed without the connivance of the Raja, whose duty it was to have placed guard over the wood.

They French factor, not being able to receive it in that state, wrote to the Nawab, informing him of this disgraceful manoeuvre. On the account given by the French officer, Haider immediately wrote to the Raja to repair to court with the utmost dispatch. The governor had no sooner received this order, than, suspecting the business, he sent for the English factor and the wood-merchant, and sent the latter to the French factory to offer payment of the sum due to the company. The French chief, bound to promote the welfare of his employers, could not refuse accepting a payment that was much more advantageous than the wood; and accordingly gave the merchant a discharge.

The Raja, furnished with this piece, departed to wait upon Haider; who demanded, on seeing him, how the affair was terminated between the French and English ? The Raja, without being disconcerted, answered with an affected laugh: "The English have lost their cause; but, as they had spoiled the wood without waiting for the judgement, I have forced them to pay the value in money; and the French have given the merchant an acquittance, which he has put into my hands." Haider, who was not the dupe of his artifice, took this occasion to demand an account of the revenues and disbursements of the country he governed; and nominated commissioners to receive his accounts.

Though the Raja did not seem abashed at the discourse of his sovereign, yet he retired extremely chagrined that his stratagem had been turned against himself. On inspecting his accounts, the committee condemned the governor to pay three or four lakhs of rupees to the Nawab. To obtain either time or a mitigation of part of the sum, he complained for some days of the rigour of this judgement; which he affirmed would ruin him, as he protested he was not possessed of so large a sum. On his refusal, Haider placed guards about his palace, to provent water from being brought him, because, as a Brahman, he was obliged to wash himself many times in the day. This step forced him to open a secret repository of treasure in the very palace in which Haider then resided, but which is the ordinary residence of the Raja.

Care by French Surgeon

A French surgeon, who had cured him of a secret disorder for the sum of one thousand rupees, half paid in hand, and the other half due, by a written promise to pay when the cure was completed, not being able to obtain the latter five hundred, though the cure had long been made, thought the present instant favourable to his desire of being paid. Haider having heard his complaint, said, "Do as I did: let no water come into his house till you are paid." "But I have no soldiers," replied the surgeon. "But you have friends that have," answered the Nawab. Upon which advice the surgeon collected a number of French soldiers, by promising them a part of the sum: they took possession of the palace-gate; and the water-carriers not daring to approach, the surgeon received payment of his note, to the great diversion of Haider, who, notwithstanding what had passed, did not remove the Raja from his government.

Haider Ali, though in the midst of the most brilliant of courts, had become uneasy and thoughtful since the departure of Mahfuz Khan for Hyderabad. This lord, after making the utmost dispatch to arrive at the court of Nizam, had dispatched letters which removed to suspense of Haider, and confirmed the intelligence given by the Irish officer. He sent word that the English, by means of the Divan Rocun Dowla, had determined the Nizam to carry the war into Mysore; that all the friends of Haider had in vain attempted to dissuade him from the design; and that, having given himself up entirely to the suggestions of his Divan, he had bestowed the command of his army on General Smith, who had brought a considerable corps of Europeans and Sepoys from Madras.

Determined Expedition

Upon the receipt of this authentic advice, Haider determined to defer his expedition against Travancore till a more favourable opportunity, and to march to Seringapattam, the capital of Mysore, to be in readiness to meet in his enemies. Haider had been long absent from this kingdom, in which he first saw the light, and where his fortune first began to disclose itself. He was about to return, as one of the greatest sovereigns in India, to a kingdom he had left in the capacity of a subject; for the Dayyas, notwithstanding their great power, are only the first subjects of the king. It was the desire of Haider to make his entrance with all the pomp and state his rank demanded, and his Savari was therefore very numerous and brilliant. His daily march was a kind of triumph. The description we shall proceed to give will be so much the more agreeable to the reader, as it will convey an idea of the magnificence of the Asiatic processions.

Haider left Coimbatore with a fine army of about fifty thousand men; of which twenty thousand were cavalry, extremely well mounted, thirty thousand Sepoys, and four thousand Topasses, with their uniforms.

Every day of the march the cavalry lined the right side of the road by which the Nawab and his attendants were to pass. The prince was saluted by all the officers and the standards. When all the elephants on which the great men were mounted had defiled before one corps of the cavalry, that corps turned about to the left, and rode full speed to take their place at the other end of the line. Two regiments of hussars, and one of dragoons, which formed the whole of the European cavalry, took the post of honour, and were the first to salute the Nawab; after which they placed themselves at the head of the procession; they were preceded by five hundred couriers, well clothed, and mounted on dromedaries. Next marched two elephants bearing the great standards of the Savari, being gold embroidery on a blue ground; one representing the sun, and the other the moon and stars.

After the two elephants marched that which carries the great tumbles, called the grand tantum; they continually sound during the time the Savari is in motion, and may be heard at the distance of more than a league; there is even something grand and majestic in the noise; the orders of the general are communicated to all the army by means of these instruments. After this elephant came four others, carrying the music of the Savari, consisting of small tumbles, hautbois, flutes, and trumpets, the performers being thirty two in number. Five elephants, called elephants of war, succeeded the four: they carry towers, or a kind of octagon chair, of gold, on their backs, strongly fixed to the saddle of the elephant by straps and silver chains. In each of these chairs are six warriors, armed from head to foot in armour which is musket proof; their offensive arms being fusils, and a species of a very large conical bore, that discharge a whole handful of balls at once. One of these elephants is intended for the Nawab, but he never makes use of it in any battle.

The procession of elephants was succeeded by two regiments of Caffres or Abyssinian horse. The men were completely armed, one regiment having their arms polished, and the other bronzed, and both had large plumes of red and black ostrich feathers on their helmets, which hung down their backs: they bore lances, the steel work of which was highly polished; and the harness of their horses was red, with black silk fringes. The cavalry was followed by a number of men on foot, habited like Caleros; that is to say, almost naked, with large silk scarfs and close drawers, reaching to the middle of the thigh: they carried long lances, ornamented with ostrich feathers and small bells, that were made to sound by the motion of their march. The Caleros were succeeded by a body of men carrying small banners, or flags of red ground, with flames of silver.

The lance-bearers usually follow the prince to the chase: they are habituated to traverse the mountains and forests: the bearers of small standards are sent as safeguards to towns, villages, and castles: the appearance of these colours is sufficient to prevent the soldiery from entering any place; but the magistrates must attend at the gates or barriers, to furnish the army upon payment, with everything they may want.

After this crowd of people on foot came the nobility following the court, marching as they pleased, in order, though without distinction of rank; generals, bahadurs, and even princes, marched indiscriminately with simple volunteers. Nothing could be more brilliant than this troop; they were armed from head to foot, and mounted on the most beautiful horses; their arms were damasked and encrusted with gold and silver; many had their casques ornamented with white feathers, formed of pearls and precious stones; and great numbers had coats of mail, gilt and enamelled: the bridles of their horses were enriched with pearls and other valuable stones, and with plumes of feathers. The number of this troop varied every day, they being volunteers; but it was usually about six hundred. They all had auftabgeries, variously enriched.

Successor of Nobility

The nobility were succeeded by eight esquires or huntsmen of the Nawab, mounted on superb horses and followed by twelve grooms on foot, each leading of the Nawabs horses, richly harnessed: the first of these horses was a present from the general of the Marathas to Haider, and was extremely singular: he was of a mouse-grey colour, with a white mane as brilliant as silver, and so thick and long, that it reached to the ground; it was tied together with a rebound; his tail was answerable in beauty to his mane: but the most remarkable circumstance was, that he had a natural covering of a clear bay colour, which depended as low as his midthigh, and which commencing at the withers, finished at a small distance from the crupper; on this mantle flowers were artificially painted; so that, though the horse was absolutely naked, it was necessary to be very near him, in order to perceive that he was not covered with a cloth of some kind.

After the led horses followed a troop running footmen, with black staves headed with gold, who were succeeded by twelve ushers or Sauquedars on horseback, carrying gold and silver maces with small crowns at top. After these came the grand officers of the household, as the steward, the chief usher, the sword-bearer, *etc.*: they had each a large collar or chain of gold depending on their breast, as marks of their dignity. These officers preceded the grand almoner or Pirzada, who marched alone, mounted on an elephant covered with green. He was immediately before the Nawab himself, who rode on the white elephant of the queen of Canara, an animal formerly worshipped as an idol, but now in a state of slavery, having large silver rings on his feet, with chains of the same metal. This elephant, which is said to be equal in value to a thousand others, was far superior to them in height and magnitude; he was covered with yellow, a colour much affected by the emperor and the Subas.

The pavilion in which the Nawab sat was covered with stuff of the same colour, and had no other ornament than four small globes of silver; except that on each side, by silver chains, hung small hatchets or axes, such as the Samorin has carried before him. It is the custom of the Indians to assume the marks of honour of those they have vanquished. The elephant bore on his head a kind of buckler of gold, that represented a sun: he was led by two conductors, the one ranked as captain of horse in the Nawab's guard and the other was his usual keeper. In a small pavilion behind the Nawab was a valet to supply him with betel; and on each side an attendant stood upright on the foot-step, holding by the pavilion with one hand, and having in the other a large chowry to disperse the flies, made of white peacock's leathers, which he caused to move circularly, and produced a singular effect at a distance. About two hundred elephants followed that of the Nawab, two and two: they were rode by only three persons, the master, the conductor, and an attendant in the small pavilion.

The coverings and pavilions of these elephants were very different in colour and magnificence; some were bordered with gold and silver lace; many of the pavilions were wrought silver; and there were some even enriched with precious stones, as were those of the sons of Haider, and some others. The young princes were on the left of their father, and Raza Saeb on his right, but their elephants were not more than half the size of that of the Nawab.

After all the elephants in procession, came what are in India called the honours, borne by five elephants. The first carried a mosque of gold, and of exquisite workmanship, covered with white satin, that was taken off when the procession came near any town or city; the second carried, at the extremity of a red staff, the head of a fish, whose scales were formed of jewels and enamel, and a long horse's tail depended from the same; the third carried a large flambeau or white wax in a chandelier of gold; the fourth bore two small pots of gold, called chambou, at the end of a large red staff; and, lastly, the fifth elephant carried a kind of round chair without a canopy, coved on the outside with ivory inlaid, and ornamented with gold.

After the honours followed two regiments of Abyssinians by horseback like the two first; and the procession was closed by two hundred Caffres on foot, clothed in scarlet, with silver collars, and armed with lances varnished black, and interspersed with silver gilding: all the train was inclosed between a double rank of men on foot, clothed in white silk, having lances in their hands about fourteen feet long, varnished black, and adorned with plates of silver at the armed ends of which were small red streamers with silver flames: the lance-men marched at such a distance from each other as to inclose the whole by joining their lances.

Haider's Grand Welcome

This grand procession, on its march in the plain, had the most superb and striking effect. Haider was everywhere received with the most lively expressions of joy; the highest honours were rendered him, and the people crowded to see him, while their acclamations, of "Long live Haider !" were incessantly reiterated. Every village, town, and city, was ornamented; triumphal arcs, and other edifices, were erected in various places, according to the riches of the inhabitants; the houses, and even the walls, of towns and fortresses were painted, or at least new white washed; governors, commandants, and other great men, came out in state with their retinues, preceded by musicians, singers, and dancers, known by the name of Bayaderes, to meet the sovereign; flowers and sweet water were dispersed in his passage, and the canon were heard in all parts of the country.

It was in this triumphant march that he met his brother-in-law, Mughdum Ali Khan, at the distance of about a league from Seringapattam. This potentate was at the head of a numerous retinue mounted on elephants and marched before Haider to the island, where tents were magnificently dressed out near the city walls; all the army encamped on the island, and the situation of the camp brought to every one's recollection the great danger Haider had avoided in the time of Canero at the same place.

Haider came into Mysore without any fear of the events that might arise in the war he supposed himself to be engaged in with the Suba of Deccan: he perfectly knew the indolent and enervated character of that prince, and had no apprehensions from his army, which was defective in the essential articles of discipline, arms, and pay, and whose chiefs being proprietors of their own troops, were his friends and partisans. From this last circumstance he was assured that General Smith could make no movements without his receiving advice of them.

As he was abused by Mirza, his brother-in-law, who every day gave him reason to think the truce with the Marathas would be soon renewed, he went forward with cheerfulness, and in spirits; and arrived at Seringapattam with the conviction that he could easily parry every attempt of his enemies. But his astonishment was extreme, when Mughdum Ali Khan informed him that there was reason to suspect the fidelity of Mirza Ali Khan; since he had learned that the army of the Marathas, to the number of 150,000 men, was on its march from Pona, Madhorao, Nana, at their head, who was then beginning his first campaign; his march teeing directed towards Scirra, as Mirza could not but know, since he had envoys at Madhorao's court.

To conceive the trouble and astonishment of Haider at this news, it will be sufficient to know, that Mirza Ali Khan, his brother-in-law and cousin, was the most beloved by him of all his relations; he had educated him himself; and the young lord, endued with the most estimable qualities, had always appeared full of gratitude and tender attachment. The great confidence Haider had reposed in his virtues induced him to think that he could not, in spite of his youth, place the important government of Scirra in better hands. The only precaution he took was that which he commonly used with all his governors, namely, to give him a minister, or principal secretary, whose fidelity he could depend on; and who had orders to give an accurate account of the conduct of his brother-in-law.

This man, who, like most courtiers, had concealed his ambition, and the bad principles that actuated him, conceived the hope of making his fortune by means of Mirza. He undertook to gain the confidence of the young prince by flattery, and by condescending to all his wishes, or, in other words, to all his weaknesses.

Mirza Addicted to Pleasure : Mirza was young, generous, and addicted to pleasure, and dissipated the revenues of his government in his amusements, instead of reserving a part, according to the orders of Haider. The Brahman, his secretary, so far from advising the Nawab, as he had engaged to do, or at least remonstrating to his young master, flattered him that he would have time to arrange his accounts, in case Haider should demand them, and to amass a sum sufficient to cover the deficiency, before the Nawab, then engaged in the war on the coast of Malabar, would think of visiting Scirra. Mirza suffered himself to be persuaded by the adulation of his secretary; and, continuing his imprudent extravagance, reduced the finances of his government to the utmost disorder.

Haider, who thought it proper to keep his brother-in-law in some fear, and concealed his project of making war on Travancore, wrote to Mirza, giving him commission to renew the truce with the Marathas; and at the same time acquainted him of his intention to repair to Seringapattam at the end of the year, and afterwards to Scirra. He likewise gave orders to take, out of the money in reserve at Scirra, a sum sufficient to obtain the renewal of the truce with the Marathas.

This letter, sufficiently perplexing to Mirza in every particular of its contents, gave him much anxiety and trouble: but the Brahman, finding the occasion favourable for averting the storm that threatened him still more than his master, addressed him thus:

> "If you have skill to seize the opportunity that Haider presents to you, you will not only be out of all embarrassment, but may become an independent sovereign. Send me among the Marathas, under the pretence, and with a commission to renew the truce,

and I will treat with Madhorao, and the national council, in such a manner, that they will with pleasure acknowledge you sovereign of the country you command; and for a small tribute they will engage to defend you, as they desire nothing more than to diminish the power of Haider, who has taken this very country from them."

The insinuations of the Brahman's ambition, the pleasure of being independent, the fear of Haider's arrival, and, perhaps, more than anything else, that false shame which prevents young people from recanting an error, determined this prince to betray his trust. He suffered the Brahman to depart, giving him a commission to treat with the Marathas as he thought proper. This faithless minister found the Marathas very much disposed to listen to him. There was an English envoy at Poona, who proposed to them to attack Haider, at the same time that Nizam and the English attacked him on their side.

The arrival of the envoy determined the grand national council to make war on the Nawab; but Madhorao, though very young, possessed courage and greatness of soul, and would not consent to form any alliance with a traitor. "I will not, " said he, "consent to make war upon Haider, unless he refuses to pay the Chotay; and, in that case the Maratha army will be sufficient to compel him, without requiring an alliance with any one, much less with a traitor. " In spite of the generous sentiments of this young man, it was not in his power to determine the general council; and he was obliged to conform to their decision. The very day following that on which Mughdum had apprised him of the infidelity of Mirza, Haider received news of the arrival of the Marathas into the country of Scirra. It was in the highest degree afflicting to him, when he heard that his brother-in-law, to complete his gratitude, had joined his enemies with the very army that was entrusted to his charge; and that he had engaged to admit the Marathas into Scirra, and every other fortress in his government.

An event so totally unexpected overthrew all the projects Haider had formed, and reduced him to the most difficult plan of defence. For though, upon the false advice of Mirza, he had supposed the Marathas were ready to renew the truce, yet he had concluded that at all events, he should have time to meet them on the other side of Scirra; and, by joining his army to that of Mirza, he might give the battle with Scirra, and the other strong places of that government, behind him, to which he might retire, if necessary: an event he hoped to see decided before the Nizam could arrive with his army on the frontier of Bangalore, where of necessity he must make his first attack on him. But his dominions being laid open by the treason of Mirza, he could neither meet the Marathas nor the combine armies of the Suba and the English; but was forced to wait for them under the cannon of Seringapattam, the capital of Mysore: for the country between that city and Scirra being a plain, without one good fortress and his army much inferior to the Marathas in cavalry, he must have fought to a great disadvantage as he must have run the risk of a total defeat, without being able to secure his country from pillage.

The numerous Maratha cavalry, habituated to make incursions, and to subsist on the straw that covers the houses, would infallibly spread themselves over all Mysore, and might cut off his communication with the magazines of Seringapattam, and the mountains in its vicinity, which were thc only resource to support his army; and again, the army of Nizam would probably hasten its march, on hearing of the operations of the Marathas; of which concatenation of circumstances, the probable result would be, that, finding himself between two armies he might be forced to retire into Canara and abandon Seringapattam, and the kingdom of Mysore, to his enemies.

Division of Army

The genius of Haider, vast and fertile in resources, seems to have been formed to shine in critical and embarrassing situations of this nature. He immediately determined on a plan of action: he divided all his army into small parties, and dispersed them over all the country, with orders to all the chiefs to command and oblige all the inhabitants, as well of the country, as of the cities, towns, villages, and fortresses, to abandon their dwellings, and retire to Seringapattam, bringing with them all their property of any kind whatsoever. The troops were ordered, at the same time, to lay the whole country waste, without sparing anything but the trees; and to burn all forages, even to the straw that covered the houses. To facilitate the devastation, and the transport of goods, all the suiters, valets, and other dependents on the army, were permitted to share the universal pillage; and they went forth on this expedition, attended by every beast of burthen belonging to the army or the city.

It is scarcely possible to form an idea of the promptitude with which this extraordinary order was carried into execution; and in how short a time one of the finest and most beautiful countries in the world was changed into a desert, for thirty leagues round Seringapattam. It is difficult to determine who were the readiest to shew their obedience, the inhabitants or the army: the former abandoned their houses, leaving nothing they could carry away, and they were succeeded by the troops, one party after another, who finished, by leaving absolutely nothing.

Horsemen and soldiers were continually arriving at Seringapattam, carrying corn, rice, maize, and even wooden beds and earthen pots, no one choosing to return empty-handed; and what may seem still more surprising, all the inhabitants arrived cheerful and contented, some carrying their children, others their sick and infirm; the number of whom, in this happy climate, is always very small. As soon as any troop of people arrived, they were paid immediately the value of their effects, at so advantageous a price, that no dispute ever arose on he subject; and afterwards they were dispatched to an alloted part of the neighbouring mountains, where they were allowed a sufficient quantity of rice and other necessaries, at a price much below that which was given for what they sold at Seringapattam.

To remove the surprise, that a whole people cheerfully abandoning their habitations must occasion, we only need observe, that all the lands are the property of the sovereign, the cultivator being no more than an annual tenant. The Indians of this country, even those who dwell in towns, have no other furniture than a bedstead, without covering or tester, whose bottom is composed of withy, and the bedclothes of the richest is no more than a carpet; a few chests of pasteboard to enclose their linen, some mats, and utensils of pottery, without tables or chairs, whose use is unknown to them, as well as three-fourths of the moveables which the Europeans employ; and, as their houses are built of brick or earth, with very little wood-work, all the damage that the most merciless enemy can do, is quickly repaired.

While the troops were employed in laying the country waste, the utmost diligence was used in completing the fortifications of the camp which, on the left, terminated against the city ramparts, and on the right at a redoubt situated at the extremity of the canal, that, with the river Kaveri, forms the island on which the city is built. By this position, the back part of the camp was secured from every attack by the canal, which is very broad and deep, with steep banks: the front of the camp was defended by nine large redoubts, mounting twenty four, thirty three, and thirty six pounders, that commanded the whole plain. About 300 horses before these, on the banks of the river, were seven other redoubts, flanking those before mentioned, each mounting six or eight pieces of cannon, and served by five hundred men.

All these redoubts had ditches before them, planted with palisades; and as the river was everywhere fordable, and hard at bottom, twenty thousand coltrops were forged, to be laid as soon as the enemy appeared disposed to the attack. About one hundred pieces of cannon from the town ramparts, and fifty that were in a fortified pagoda situated on a very steep hill on the other side of the river, opposite the part of the island farthest from the city, would have flanked those who might have been disposed to attack the first line of redoubts; and the same artillery would have rendered the attack of the second line still more difficult.

In this camp, defended by three hundred pieces of cannon, it was, that Haider waited the approach of his enemies; and, as his cavalry would have been of no use to him, he divided it into two parties; the principal of which was given to Mughdum, who was sent to meet the Nizam in the country of Bangalore, where he made the same devastation as had been made in the plains near Seringapattam. As that country is interspersed with woods and mountains, and contains many very defensible fortresses, it was not so entirely abandoned: this circumstance furnished Mughdum with better opportunities of harassing the army of Nizam, and carrying off the foragers, who were of necessity much spread abroad on account of the waste situation of the country.

The command of the rest of the cavalry, a small body of infantry, and all the irregular troops, was given to Mir Fizulla Khan, ancient Nawab of Kolar, and principal general of Haider, with orders to repair to the kingdom of Bisnagar, and defend the passes in the mountains which separate that kingdom from Canara, and to prevent the Marathas from penetrating, by joining his force to the military establishment of that country. He had instructions to assist Bassapattam, the capital of Bisnagar, if the Marathas should attack it, and to harass the rear of their army, if they should advance towards Seringapattam.

While Haider was busied in these preparations, to which he was compelled by one of the most critical situations it is possible for a great monarch to find himself in, he rode out every day on horseback, without many attendants, and affected to shew himself often to the army and citizens. His countenance was not then enlivened with that gaiety that usually distinguishes him, because his mind was occupied with the danger that threatened him, and he has not acquired the habit of disguising his thoughts; on the contrary, a kind of mild languor or sadness appeared in his looks, that would have interested even his enemies in his misfortunes; his tent was open at all times, and he never was easier of access than at this juncture.

Prohibition of any Assembly and Amusement: Though every kind of assembly and amusement was forbade, he instructed his generals concerning the means he thought proper to use in his defence, with an air and manner not in the least expressive of embarrassment.

The Europeans of his army, who interested themselves with an anxious eagerness in the success of the prince, were impatient to know the post he would assign to them, in case of an attack; for Haider did not make public his order of battle, and caused the guards of every post to be changed daily, though, according to the news, the enemy was on the point of arriving. To satisfy their impatience, their commandant, with two other officers, waited upon Haider, and acquainted him that, as he had always conferred upon the Europeans the honour of the most important post, they were come to request that he would put the defence of the first line of redoubts into their hands.

The prince immediately answered, "I had already determined to appoint "you to the post you request; and the demand you make on an "occasion when my enemies are innumerable, is so much the more "agreeable to me, as it is a new mark of your affection: take the "command, plant your colours in the centre redoubt; and you may "be assured of being powerfully seconded, for I myself will command "the second line, and engage to send you the necessary succours.

"I am very much oppressed with the treason of Mirza, whom I have "always treated as my favourite child; and I have had no reason to "expect so numerous a combination of enemies, who, so far from being "provoked, have been loaded by me with benefits; but, notwithstanding "their number, I do not despair. It is the power of God that has "raised me, and I possess nothing but through him: as long as be "supports me, I shall look down on my enemies; and if he should "forsake me, I must submit with resignation to his pleasure."

The fidelity of the commandants of the fortresses of Mark Scirra and Maggheri, gave Haider all the time his preparations required; for these officers, when they learned that the Governor-General had joined his army to that of the Marathas under Madhorao, refused to obey him; but the general, desirous of possessing the whole country, thought proper to besiege these places, which held out longer than was expected, particularly the fortress of Maggheri, into which a battalion of grenadier Sepoys had thrown themselves voluntarily, simply on the requisition of the governor of the place, while they were employed in laying the country waste: they made a journey of fourteen leagues without once stopping, for fear of being too late.

When the fortress had capitulated, Madhorao was desirous of seeing those grenadiers, whose formation had made so much noise in India: he was astonished to find these brave troops dirty and ill equipped, "I am surprised," said he, "that so powerful a prince as your master "pays so little attention to such brave men." Their commandant replied, "Desirous of the honour of fighting against you, we hastened "away without any necessaries but the clothes on our backs; and we have marched a day and a night without eating or drinking. "I am charmed at your spirit," returned Madhorao, "and should be"concerned that your master, who sent you out well clothed, should "see you return in such a state;" and immediately ordered them two complete changes of clothes, adding, that

"Though the terms of" the capitualation require you to leave your arms and your colours, "yet I return your colours as a mark of esteem for your master, and "a recompense due to your valour." Thus it was that war was carried on by men we are so ready to think barbarous.

After thus displaying the merit of the Indians, it would be unjust to pass over in silence the spirited action of one hundred European cannoneers of different nations. They had marched, like the others, against the Marathas, supposing they were to fight them; but when they saw Mirza joined his army to theirs, they perceived the perfidy of the governor; and, repairing to their general, "Do you imagine," said one of their officers, "that we will fight against Haider, whose" pay we have so long received ? No, our intention is to fight for "him, and not against him. Adieu." At the same time they departed, leaving all their baggage, having no other arms but their sabres, because the cannoneers in Haider's army do no other service than that of the artillery. They arrived at Haider's camp, without having found any opposition; for Mirza, no doubt ashamed of his treason, gave orders not to oppose their departure. Haider received them with great pleasure, and gave the officers bracelets of gold, and money to the soldiers, paying them likewise the value of their baggage, upon their own estimation. This daring act of fidelity was perhaps the effect of the disgrace inflicted on the Europeans who adhered to Canero.

General Smith and Rocun Dowla were soon advised of the junction of Mirza with the Marathas, and announced it to Nizam as a certain presage of the ruin of Haider. This news frustrated all the efforts and intrigues of Haider's friends in the court of that Suba; and perhaps those friends, convinced that his ruin was inevitable, might grow cool to his interests. The Suba being always in want of money to support his expensive pleasures, General Smith found it not difficult to persuade him to hasten his march, without stopping to make any seige, lest the Marathas should take Seringapattam, and seize the greatest part of the spoils. This forced march, and the time consumed by Madhorao in his two sieges, were the causes that both armies arrived together near Cenapattam, about seven leagues from Seringapattam.

The absolute solitude and desert face of the country, which the enemies perceived in their approach to the capital of Mysore; the daily loss of their foraging parties, attacked by different bodies of Haider's horse; and the possibility of obtaining any advice concerning the situation and force of Haider's army, gave the different chiefs of the armies to understand that the brilliant hopes they had indulged, of sharing the dominions and treasures of Haider, were not likely to be realised.

As soon as the two armies were joined, different corps of horse appeared in the plain of Seringapattam. Many advanced so near as to reconnoitre the town, and the redoubts in which Haider's colours were displayed; as they met with no interruption from Haider, they rode about the plain, and viewed everything at their ease. The same ceremony was performed the following day: but on the third, at nine in the morning, the plain was covered with the cavalry of both armies, with the chiefs at their head on their elephants: this cavalry was followed by a body of infantry, who brought forward about fifty large cannon, that arrived about noon. The view was grand and striking: the number of horses was above one hundred thousand; and there were more than two hundred elephants.

General Smith, at the head of a large body of cavalry, among whom were distinguished various chiefs, though neither Nizam nor Madhorao were seen, advanced to reconnoitre the camp. When this cavalry appeared disposed to advance no farther, a signal was given from the redoubt in which Haider was, and the fire poured at once from all the redoubts, from the fortress at the head of the bridge, and from the mountain: this last did no great mischief, but terrified Nizam and his army, and convinced General Smith that the project of attacking Haider in his camp was impracticable, especially for an army whose chief strength lay in cavalry. Towards the evening they who commanded this vast multitude of men retired, together with their soldiers, in much disorder, to their respective camps.

The following day, a council was held with Nizam, at which the chiefs of both armies assisted. Every one being desirous of putting his own opinion in practice, no determination was settled on, though General Smith gave the only good advice, which was, to separate the two armies, and make feints, to draw Haider of his camp; but, notwithstanding the propriety of this idea, every one was dissatisfied with it, because it showed too plainly, that their elevated expectations were ill-founded, and required great abatements to reduce them to probability.

No More Conferences

The Maratha chiefs having returned to their camp, no more councils were held; but the two camps remained in the same situation, many messengers passing between them. The Marathas traversed the country, as well as different corps of Nizam's army they frequently met the cavalry of Haider, which almost always had the advantage; Mughdum especially, who is an excellent officer, had the most decided success. Forages every day became more scarce, and the capture of the foragers, of horses, elephants, camels, and oxen, continued to such a degree, that they at last could not be sold at Bangalore at any rate. At length, the provisions of rice brought by the merchants were exhausted, and the price of this indispensable article, as well as of every other necessary, increased every day.

Haider, who was informed of everything as it happened, remained at ease in his camp, where everything was in such great abundance, that subsistence cost scarcely anything. The inhabitants, supposing everything would fetch a great price, had laid in vast stores; every soldier had a hole in the earth near his tent filled with rice; the river afforded fish in abundance: and every kind of country provisions came from the mountains and valleys in the night, attended by a numerous escort of infantry, after four hours travel through a road intersected by hedges and ditches, where the cavalry would have had no opportunity of shining.

'The Marathas, under the pretence of being nearer to the forages, withdrew from Cenapattam, and encamped on the Kaveri, at five leagues from Seringapattam. It appears that they must have conferred with Haider previous to the movement; for two days after the change of their camp the truce was concluded on; and on receiving six lacks of rupees in hand, and six payable in six months, they engaged to retire out of his country, and to restore Scirra,: but the rest of the district entrusted to Mirza was abandoned to them, and they suffered that governor to remain in possession of it, on the condition of paying a small tribute; for the security of which they retained the fortress of Maggheri: the money was no sooner counted than the Marathas raised their camp, and departed, taking the road to Scirra.

This news gave the alarm in the camp of Nizam, and that sovereign, more alarmed than the rest, was exceedingly embarrassed, Haider, who knew his character, and judged it a proper occasion to impress him with still more terror, recalled his army from the kingdom of Bisnagar, marched his troops out of the island, and encamped in the plain on the road to Cenapattam. This manoeuvre produced its whole effect on the timid and enervated prince, and disposed him to listen to the suggestions of Basalatjung, his brother, Mahfuz Khan, and other friends of Haider: and there is no doubt, but he would have proceeded in direct opposition to his Divan, if that minister, seeing the impossibility of encouraging his master, had not been the first to give him the direct advice to treat with Haider; and offered to undertake the negotiation himself, as a business that he was confident might be concluded with the greatest facility. To remove General Smith, and the greatest part of the English forces, he informed that commander, that since, in the present situation of things, provisions, and succours could only be had from the country of Arcot, it was necessary that the English should get possession of certain places belonging to Haider, to secure a free passage for the convoys that might be sent from Madras and the other places dependent on the English and Mohammed Ali.

The English general had not been blind to the disposition that prevailed of treating with Haider; but he was happy at an opportunity of approaching his frontiers, to place himself out of the reach of the perfidy it was probable he might experience, and to remove himself from a country in which he might be shut up, and obliged to surrender, with all his army, if Nizam chose to deliver him up to Haider. He wrote an account to Madras of what had passed, and at the same time expressed his suspicions of Nizam and his minister; he proposed to make the best treaty they could with Haider, for fear the English should find themselves charged singly with a war so much the more burthensome as it would be in their own country; and, after having taken leave of Nizam, who loaded him with caresses from the satisfaction he had of seeing him depart, he set off, leaving, however, to the faith of Nizam, two hundred Europeans, one thousand Sepoys, and some pieces of cannon.

While the government of Madras received the dispatches of General Smith, Mohammed Ali received others from Rocun Daulla, his brother-in-law, which gave him the most positive assurances that Nizam would continue the war against Haider till he had forced him to yield at least all the country of Bangalore, and all Malleam, or the Karnatic; that is to say, the valleys of Coimbatore, Ceylon, Kisnagari, *etc.*: and while he magnified the forces of the Suba beyond the truth, he diminished those of Haider, who, he said, were incapable of presenting themselves before the army of his invincible sovereign.

The council of Madras, persuaded by Mohammed Ali paid no regard to the advice of General Smith, but ordered him to attack the places of Haider, and to agree with Nizam in everything, promising to supply him amply with provisions, ammunition, money, and even troops, if necessary. At the same time that this unprincipled Divan wrote thus to Mohammed Ali, he dispatched his other brother, Mahfuz Khan, to Haider, to offer to meet him at Seringapattam, and to assure him, that he was disposed to do everything that might be agreeable to him, as Mahfuz Khan would explain to him.

Haider, on receipt of Rocun Daulla's letter, in order to give some confidence to Nizam, caused his army to return to its ancient camp, and wrote to the Divan that he would be received as became a person of his rank and character: it was likewise permitted to the merchants of his camp, and the country people, to carry provisions to the army of Nizam. When this Suba had read the letter of Haider, he ordered a cessation of arms, which was likewise ordered on the side of Haider; and the Divan set out for Haider's camp.

Haider received him, and, after a short conversation, retired, and Rocun Daulla having seen the grand retinue of Haider, returned to his own camp. The day following, the Divan came to have audience of Haider in great ceremony; and, to lose less time in going and coming, he came and encamped between the two lines of re doubts: both parties being desirous of concluding, the treaty was made in a few days.

It was agreed that Tipu Sultan, the son of Haider, should marry the daughter of Mahfuz Khan, who, as eldest son of Unvarudeen Khan, was the lawful Nawab of Arcot; that Mahfuz Khan should give up all his right to his future son-in-law; that the two Subas should join their forces to reduce Mohammed Ali Khan, and those who took his part; that during the time the two armies acted in conjunction, Haider should pay six lakhs of rupees per month to the Nizam, and should have the sole right of putting garrisons in the several fortresses of the Nawabship of Arcot the command of which should be given to Mughdum Ali Khan, brother-in-law of Haider, who should govern the country in the names of his nephew, Tipu Sultan, and Mahfuz Khan; that the former should enjoy the whole revenue of that Nawabship, for which Mughdum should account, after deducting the charge of supporting the troops and administering the government.

To unite all the claims in the person of Tipu Sultan, Raza Ali Khan, son of Chanda Saeb, likewise yielded up to the young prince all his pretensions as well to the nawabship of Arcot as to Trichinopoli and Madura; and Haider and Tipu Sultan, on their part, engaged to give him all the country of Tanjore, after deposing the Raja as a punishment for the murder of Chanda Saeb, father of Raja; the country of Tanjore was understood as intended to be held by him under the same vassalage to the Nawab of Arcot as it had therefore been held by the former Rajas; and finally, the two Subas engaged not to separate, but to exert all their forces to carry this treaty into effect.

Retinue Prepared

Previous to the ratification of the treaty which Mahfuz Khan undertook to prepare, the retinue of Tipu Sultan was got ready; it was composed of six thousand of the best infantry, of which three thousand were grenadier Sepoys or Topasses, and four thousand chosen cavalry, with three hundred Europeans, and a regiment of hussars: he likewise had the greatest part of his father's Savari. Mahfuz Khan having brought the ratification, Rocun Daulla departed, loaded with presents, and Mahfuz Khan accompanied him.

It will hardly be credited that Haider, at the moment of parting with his son, was in the greatest perplexity and concern, and expressed it to his friends. "I am afraid," said he, of the perfidious and cruel Nizam; he has assassinated his own brother, will he spare my son ? or, at least, have I not reason to conclude that he will detain him, and compel me, by the apprehension of my son's danger, either to pay him a large sum, or to make great concessions to him ?

For, in short, I trust my son in the hands of a wretch to whom nothing is sacred. This discourse, and many other actions of his, prove that one of the greatest weaknesses of Haider is his extreme affection for his children and all his relations. However, on the assurances made by Raja Saeb and Meer. Fesoulla Khan (who were charged to accompany his son, and who protested they would themselves perish before the least accident should happen to the young prince), he suffered him to depart, being likewise much encouraged by reflecting on the bravery of the troops and the nobility that atteneded him. This little army arrived by a single march at Canapattam. The whole army of Nizam, and especially the English officers as well as soldiers, were extremely surprised at their appearance. Though they had heard of Haider's army, yet they could not conceive how Indian troops, who have always been ill-disciplined, could march in such good order, and perform their evolutions with such rapidity and exactness. The beauty of their arms and clothing was equally uncommon and strange to them; and they were astonished at the pomp of the Savari. The troops were no sooner encamped than the officers came to visit those of Haider, and continually spoke with admiration of the excellence of the troops.

The following day Tipu Sultan received a visit from Busalatjung, brother of Nizam: he was accompanied by Rocun Daulla and the principal lords of the court. The succeeding day the son of Haider repaired with all his retinue to the tent of the Suba, who rendered him the highest honours, and the voluntary cession of Arcot by Mahfuz Khan and Raza Saeb, the only legitimate pretenders to that territory, left no doubt concerning the rights of the son of Haider Ali Khan. The Nizam dismissed the few remaining English troops, acquainting them that the alliance he had contracted with Haider Ali Khan having terminated their differences he had no farther occasion for their services; and that he should write to the governor and council of Madras, to which place they might retire.

3

Tipu Sultan

Nawab of Arcot

As soon as Haider was informed that his son was acknowledged Nawab of Arcot, he wrote to his Vakeel, Menagi Pundit, resident at Madras, transmitting to him a memorial to be presented to the governor.

The substance of the memorial was, that Nizam Daulla and Haider Ali Khan, being well informed that Mohammed Ali Khan, by his continual usurpations and intrigues, was the author of ail the troubles that had so long agitated Hindustan, had resolved to make war upon him, till they had deprived him of all the territory he possessed to the exclusion of the proper and legitimate heirs; that in consequence they thought proper to warn the English against affording him any assistance; and required them to withdraw their troops out of any garrisons they might possess in the Nawabship of Arcot, or any of the countries usurped by Mohammed; that nevertheless, as it was known that these places were pledges for sums due to them from Mohammed Ali, Haider Ali offered to reimburse them in any sums lawfully due, among which he could not reckon those sums that were dispensed for the purposes of dispossessing the Nawabs of Vellore, Vandevachi, and other rightful proprietors, of their territories; but, on the contrary, he expected that these last should be indemnified from all the losses they had sustained.

It may be easily conceived that a memorial, or manifesto, totally new and uncommon in India, and declaratory of a war against the English, of which they were to bear the whole expense, must have caused the utmost astonishment to that people. This declaration was directed against the possessions of the English, Mohammed Ali Khan being a Nawab merely nominal, without troops or money, and the slave of the English.

It was the policy of the English in India to traverse the designs of the smallest potentate, who might wish to enlarge his dominions, for fear he might arrive to a capability of making head against them: their administration had long been alarmed at the rapid conquests of Haider, and the sudden elevation of his power. In consequence of Nizam Doulla's having ceded to them four northern provinces, they had engaged to furnish twelve hundred Europeans, and a corps of Sepoys, to the army of that Suba: General Smith, commander of this body of troops, was ordered to inspire Nizam with jealousy of the conquests of Haider, and to confer with Rocun Daulla concerning the projected war; offering the Suba all the English forces, and fixing his attention on the immense treasures Haider had found in the kingdom of Canara and the coast of Malabar; treasures which they affirmed could not but fall into his hands, as it was impossible for Haider to stand against the united forces of the Suba and the English.

The English government did not at that time indulge the hope of plundering Haider entirely, but they expected to stop the course of his conquests, and oblige him to abandon the coast of Malabar, among the inhabitants of which they proposed to excite a revolt. By this means their intention was to compel Haider to yield, either to them or to Mohammed Ali Khan, all the country dependant on Mysore that lies beyond the great *Gates,* or mountains; which, according to them, ought to be the natural bounds of his dominions. They proposed to leave him in possession of all the rest of his dominions, in the persuasion that it was of advantage to the security and tranquillity of their possessions, that so warlike and powerful a prince as Haider should be between them and the Marathas.

But at all events, whether the hopes of the English respecting the war with Haider were rational or not, it is certain that when they learned that the Marathas had declared war against him, and Mirza, his brother-in-law, had joined them, their expectations were unbounded, and they devoured by anticipation the treasures of Haider.

The council of Madras, who till then had envied the brilliant fortune of the Calcutta administration in the enjoyment of an immense territorial revenue, flattered themselves in a short time to realise their chimerical hopes, and to equal them in splendour and importance.

Their letters to the Court of Directors were filled with brilliant projects, that promised no less than the possession of all the coast from Cape Rama to Cape Comorin: the Court of Directors were thrown into a kind of delirium by their admiration of the profound policy of their servants; and every one being anxious to possess a large share of the Company's stock, the price rose to *£275 per cent* in the year 1768, though it afterwards fell at once to *£220*, on the news of the excursion of Haider's cavalry to the gates of Madras; a fall which, to the present time, has been constantly increasing.

Haider Ali Khan having by his address destroyed the formidable alliance on which the English company formed such pleasing dreams, because they knew so little of the character and power of their allies, and still less of the enemy whose ruin they meditated, it became incumbent on the council of Madras to justify themselves: for this purpose they could find no better pretence than to attribute the defeat of their projects, and the war that threatened them in the country of Arcot, to the intrigues of the French.

The despotism exercised in India by the English, against other European nations, was such, that there was nothing they hesitated to do against any power, whether native or European: they never pardoned other nations the crime of fulfilling their engagements, of whatever nature they might be, with any sovereign, though they themselves sold muskets and cannon to every Indian power; seven-eighths of Haider's arms being of English make. Their cruelty towards their prisoners, and the barbarity with which they destroyed Pondicherry, had reduced the greatest part of the French to misery. The unhappy situation they found themselves in after the establishment of the peace, compelled great numbers of them to seek employment and subsistence from Haider and other princes. When any of these unfortunate people fell into the hands of the English, a dungeon was the lightest punishment they were to expect. To accomplish their purposes they employed, as will be shown in the course of these Memoirs, promises, menaces, and even forgery, to cause them to enter into their service.

So far from the French government having had any concern in this war, declared by Haider, it is certain that no correspondence with respect to that Nawab's operations ever existed, either between him and them, or with any officer of Haider's army, till after the conclusion of the treaty between Haider and Nizam;—truth obliges me to make this last exception. The correspondence began by two letters, one from Haider, and the other from Raza Saeb, which these personages charged the commandant of Europeans to forward to the governor of Pondicherry. Here follows the substance of the letters.

Haider complained in his letter, that the English, without provocation, and after receiving many favours, had projected his ruin; and by every species of intrigue had formed a league with the Suba of Deccan, and the Marathas, against him; that they had attacked his places, without any other inducement than a desire to rob others of their property; but that he had dissolved the league made against him, by forming an alliance with Nizam Daulla, for the purpose of making war against the English and Mohammed Ali Khan, the promoter of their unjust aggression.

He observed, that by having formerly assisted the French against the same enemy, and having saved Pondicherry, he had every reason to hope that the French would return him the same good office in so just a war: that he was not ignorant of the peace then (1767) subsisting between the French and the English; but that, while the orders of the French king were expected, he might send concealed succours, for which Haider would be very thankful, and pay any price that might be charged for the service to be done: that, in short, he referred to the letter of the French commandant, on whom he had a perfect reliance, and whose proposals on Haider's part might be credited as if signed by himself, and to whom he might address himself on any subject that required secrecy.

Raza Saheb wrote, that his family had always been attached to the French since their first establishment in India: that in consequence of his inviolable attachment, his father had lost his life, his mother was prisoner at Madras, and he himself had lost everything: that an opportunity now presented itself of repairing his fortune in some measure, by the assistance of his friends: that he hoped to find his most ancient allies, the French, disposed to assist him against those who had unjustly robbed him, and were the cause of all his misfortunes: he concluded his letter, like Haider, by referring to the French officer for details, having, as he affirmed, the most unbounded confidence in him.

These letters were secretly carried to Pondicherry by the Persian writer of the commandant, a man deserving the most absolute confidence, and who had been long attached to the French nation, having been employed by M. Lally at Pondicherry, where his residence had been for above thirty years, and where his wife and children then were: the letters were put into the stock of a pistol, which this man wore at his girdle walking on foot, and leading an ox loaded with several wares of the country, like a petty merchant or pedlar.

To answer the trust these two princes reposed in him, and to fulfil his duty to his king and country, the commandant despatched a letter, together with those of the Nawabs.

Confirmation of Resolution

After confirming the resolution taken by the two Subas to carry on the war on the coast of Coromandel, he gave an exact detail of the forces of Haider, and those of Nizam; and, to shew that he spoke with a knowledge of the business, he likewise gave an account of the English forces.

He demonstrated that it was impossible for the English to secure themselves from loss in this war, because their former successes in India arose from their wars being carried on near the sea-coast, or on the banks of the Ganges, which gave them a facility of conveying stores and ammunition by sea, and receiving other assistance from their vessels; whereas, in their contest with Haider, they would be deprived of those advantages, the war being to be carried on in a country remote from the sea, without one navigable river; where the fortresses are spread at great distances from each other; and where every advantage would depend upon cavalry, of which the English were entirely destitute: that the army of Haider was totally unlike those of the other Indian powers, the duty being performed with regularity: and that, if the English placed any dependance on night attacks, surprises, or treason on the part of his generals, they would find themselves and mistaken: that he himself, being entrusted with the safety and preservation of the army, could, with the most absolute confidence, promise to insure it from any surprise; and that the treasons so frequent in the other Indian armies could not take place in Haider's, because the generals had no property in their troops, all the officers, horsemen, and soldiers, having but one master: and, concluding that Haider would have the advantage, he advised that an exact and absolute neutrality would not be the most prudent mode of action, because it would of necessity displease both parties.

But the medium he advised was, to send some small succours to Haider, promising to send more; the performance of which promise might be delayed at pleasure, by throwing the excuse on contrary winds, that prevented the arrival of shipping. As the force at Pondicherry was but small, no great force could be sent from thence, but it would be sufficient to send some officers and good gunners, who might join the army as deserters, without embroiling the nation, whose interest it was to see the power of the English in India depressed.

The officer added, that as a faithful subject of his king, and from the daring character of Haider when he is attended with victory, he judged it proper to advise the governor to fortify Pondicherry as early as possible, were it only by clearing the ditches, raising the ramparts with dry earth or the ruins of the old works, and mounting a few cannon on the bastions; because, if Haider should approach Pondicherry, and perceive it without defence, he might lay aside the respect due to the French colours, and take all the artillery, and other matters he might be in need of, as payment of his due for the succours formerly granted the French: at the same time the officer assured the governor, that if any violence or want of respect for the king's standard should be shown, he might depend upon the cooperation of about eight hundred Europeans, who were in Haider's army.

The letter was concluded, by advising the governor to purchase rice and provisions for Pondicherry, by taking advantage of the abundance then in the country, and the fear the inhabitants were in of being plundered by the Indian armies; because the resolution was taken to lay the whole country waste by the cavalry and irregular troops as was really done afterwards (the French governor profited by the advice, and was in consequence able, during the whole war, to keep the price of rice at Pondicherry at less than half its value at Madras): and lastly, the officer added, that to forward the good disposition of Haider and his allies, it would be proper to send M.B, or some other person esteemed by Haider, on an embassy, to compliment the two Subas.

Pleasures from Despatches

The receipt of these despatches gave the governor infinite pleasure, as they dispelled his fears concerning Haider, whom he justly considered as the natural ally of France. But, from experience, having a very low opinion of the bravery of Indian troops when they fight against Europeans, he could not adopt the ideas of the French commandant of Haider's army: besides which, Company's instructions, then subsisting, were so precise in commanding him to avoid every subject of contention whatsoever, and particularly with the English, that he thought himself obliged to answer these letters in a manner very different from what had been expected.

His letter to Haider began by felicitations on the glory he had acquired by his conquests, and the glorious peace he had made with his numerous enemies, who were become his allies: he observed that it was with concern he heard that war, which is always ruinous to nations, was about to commence on the coast of Coromandel: that he wished the Nawab every kind of prosperity, and would not fail to send an embassy to complement him when he came near Pondicherry; but that he was exceedingly concerned at its being out of his power to dispose of any troops against the English, because the two nations were at peace, which he could not infringe without new orders from the king his master, to whom he would write without delay: and, lastly, he referred to the French commandant, who had forwarded the Nawab's letters, and who, he said, would explain such matters as required detail.

The letter to Raza Saeb was to the same purport. In answer to the officer's letter, the governor advised him, that, by despatching the letters of the two Nawabs, he had subjected him to the risk of breaking with the English; that he earnestly begged he would spare him the consequences of such a correspondence, as he could not render a greater service to his country, in the then situation of the French in India, without troops, and without fortifications: that, in the mean time, he would not fail to represent his compliance to this request in its true light to the minister, and the East India Company; and he might depend on his informing them of the services he had rendered them by the important advices contained in this letter: that, from his own unhappy experience of the pusillanimity of the Indians, when they combat with Europeans, he had reason to fear that the future war would not turn out to the advantage of the two Subas: that he could not, in any manner, afford assistance either to Haider or Raza Saeb, his orders being too precise in directing to give no subject of complaint to the English, or to Mohammed Ali: that he begged he would explain these reasons to the two princes who had written to him, softening his refusal as he judged best: and, more especially, he begged him to write no more directly to him, but that he should be glad to hear news of his negotiation by a letter in cyphers, which he might send by way of M:

> There is no room to reproach this governor for his faithful and strict obedience to his orders. It is to be wished they had been less precise, as he might then have profited by this opportunity, that the ministry could not possibly foresee: by a correspondence with Haider, he might have animated him to a war against the English, that would have been ruinous to their Company; and, by answering the wishes of that prince in a very slight degree, might have prevented certain events that impeded his progress, and which obliged him to make peace, and reserve himself for another

opportunity of enforcing his son's just pretentions to the Nawabship of Arcot.

This governor gave advice to the minister and the Company of the approaching invasion of the coast of Coromandel by the combined armies of the two Subas: and at the same time he communicated his fears for the event of the war, which he considered as necessarily productive of the ruin of Haider: who would, he said, have been a very useful ally, if the French officer (commandant of Europeans), wanting experience, had not carried him to this extremity, but had reserved him for the time of war between England end France;—an expression dictated by the European prejudice, which leads us to imagine that the inhabitants of the other parts of the world have not received from nature the same portion of reason and judgement as ourselves, to determine for themselves according to their own interest, rather than to follow the most specious reasoning that can be offered to the contrary. It is to be presumed that, on the simple exposition of the facts, or from the copy of the French officer's letter, the ministry had taken those resolutions, upon receiving the news of the invasion; which were not determined on till the end of 1769; resolutions that would have been fatal to the English empire in India, if the differences relative to the Falkland Islands had not been made up.

Haider, after having determined to make descent on the coast of Coromandel with Nizam Daulla, took every precaution to prevent interruption from others parts: he was sensible of the importance of the war he was engaged in and which was to be transacted with enemies so much the more to be feared, as they knew how to fight. By the advice of his European commandant, he gave up the idea of forming a corps of European infantry, on account of impossibility of making them sufficiently numerous to face a single English regiment: he therefore determined to incorporate all his European soldiers either among his hussars or dragoons, or among his artillery, except such as were made officers of the grenadier Sepoys or

Topasses; which was the corps of infantry destined to face the English troops. The artillery of his army was likewise considerably augmented; and he took proper measures to have always an immense quantity of ammunition, such as it was impossible for any European army to convey after them, or indeed for any other army that was not perfectly assured of its rear.

The Indian armies have great quantities of baggage, carried by oxen and camels. Besides the baggage of the army, it is followed by a great number of merchants and workmen of every kind, who have many beasts of burthen. Haider gave orders that all these, not excepting those of the sovereign, should carry a ball, from twelve to six and thirty pounds, for which the proprietor of the beast should be answerable.

Horde of Bohemians

A horde, consisting of a kind of Bohemians, very numerous in India, of unknown origin, inhabitants of the woods (whom the prejudices of India have forbidden to dwell in walled towns, because it is said they eat every kind of animal or reptile,) was permitted by Haider, who is above prejudice, to follow the army, and sell milk, wood, and every thing their industry could procure. These men undertook to convey a considerable part of the powder, by means of their little carriages drawn by buffaloes: to assist them in procuring a subsistence, part of them were taken into pay as pioneers, and were of the greatest utility in sieges and the construction of intrenchments, or repairing of roads, as well by carrying earth as by making gabions and fascines.The harness of all the cannon and artillery was doubled; and, that nothing might retard their march, every piece of eighteen pounds or upwards was provided with an elephant. The ammunition wagons carried two hundred charges of powder, and an immense number of cartridges for the musketry. Every battalion of grenadier Sepoys had two four-pounders in its suit.

While these different preparations were making, Haider arranged every affair relative to his dominions, so as to be out of apprehension of any unexpected event happening in his absence. The truce with the Marathas, and his alliance with Nizam, delivered him from the fear of any foreign enemy and permitted him to employ his whole force against them, by depriving them of the means to create disturbances by their intrigues. He restored their dominions to the different Nayre princes, on condition of an annual-tribute, which he proposed to demand, or to let accumulate, according to the situation of his affairs; and withdraw all his troops from the coast of Malabar.

The French commandant at Mahe, and the Dutch at Cochin, employed themselves with effect, to terminate the difference between Haider and the Nayre princes; and to their efforts it is that the coast of Malabar is indebted for peace. An important discovery, totally unexpected by Haider, and which was made soon after the conclusion of the truce with the Marathas, occasioned an event that has induced many persons in India to speak against Haider.

It was discovered, that Nand Raja, ancient regent of Mysore, whom Haider called his brother, had joined with the Marathas and the English in the general conspiracy against him. Nand Raja then resided at Mysore, a fortress two leagues distant from Seringapattam; the capital of the lands he held *en appanage.* Haider was exceedingly embarrassed when he discovered this treachery: the great age of the prince made it improper to propose his marching against the English: to leave him in his residence, and to give the government of the kingdom of Mysore to another, would have excited his complaints, might have furnished him with an occasion to excite new troubles.

The pretence made use of by those ' who irritated Nand Raja against Haider was, that this last, after having conquered the kingdom of Canara, and fixed his residence at Nagar, ought not to have given the regency of Mysore to any one but

Nand Raja; but without considering the advanced age and incapacity of Nand Raja, which alone would have prevented him from taking that step, he was restrained by his promise to the old dowager Dayva, who had always been the mortal enemy of her brother-in-law, and was apprehensive of being subjected to his power.

Haider, in gratitude for the services rendered him by that lady, could not consent to displease her in this respect; but as she was the object of the pleasantry of all the court, on account of the irregularity of her manners, it was whispered that Haider made the old lady believe that Nand Raja demanded the government for the purpose of punishing her for the little respect she bore to the laws, and the name of her deceased husband; by which means he obtained large sums of her, either in the way of gift or loan; giving her likewise to understand that he was distressed for money to pay for the Maratha truce, and his alliance with Nizam.

Thus it was that Haider, from motives of interest rather than policy, took a pleasure in fomenting the discord between the brother and sister-in-law. An opportunity presented itself of doing this on the occasion of the death of the king of Mysore. Nand Raja wrote to solicit the title of king for the younger son, in preference to the elder, who, he affirmed, was weak, and incapable of the office; but his letter availed little with Haider, who was solicited by the widow Dayva in favour of the elder. He wrote, in answer to both, that not being able at that time to attend anything but the war with the revolted Nayres, he had given orders to Mughdum Ali Khan, to place on the throne that prince of the late king's sons whom he might think the most worthy to reign: he wrote, secretly, by the same courier, to Mughdum, to place the youngest on the throne.

This proceeding, which, as may be readily imagined, excited the complaints of the widow of Dayva, and of most part of the nobility of the kingdom, gave Haider an opportunity, on his arrival at Seringapattam, to make a parade of his equity, by giving the throne to the eldest. The whole business drew an additional sum from the old lady, and created many enemies to Nand Raja, and, perhaps, to Mughdum, who readily assisted in all these artifices, through his unbounded attachment to his brother-in-law.

It not being practicable either to give Nand Raja the government of the kingdom, or to remove him out of it, and still less prudent to leave him discontented in the absence of Haider, a council was held on the business; the general advice was to secure his person, at least during the absence of the Nawab, and in the mean time to remove from him a Brahman, his brother-in-law, who gave him bad advice, but to this Haider opposed the written promise he had made to Raja *never to make any attempt on his liberty, property, or life, besides* the difficulty of arresting that prince in his residence at the Mysore, a place capable of standing a seize, and where Naud Raja had upwards of two thousand troops, forming, it must be confessed; the whole of his little army.

This affair being of such a nature as to require a speedy determination, it was agreed, that Haider should go the following morning in grand ceremony to Mysore, to make an honourable visit to Nand Raja, and invite him to come and encamp with his little army in the island of Seringapattam, in order to make his public entry into the capital in quality of viceroy, as Haider was desirous of investing him with that dignity before his departure; the visit was accordingly made, and Nand Raja, at the height of his wishes, arrived with his family in the island, under the power of Haider, who, that very day, under pretence of exercising his troops in their evolutions, invested the little camp, and enclosed it in the night by detachments of infantry, who were ordered to suffer no one to pass them, without first conducting him to the Nawab, to be questioned by him. As it had been difficult to persuade Haider to secure the old man, it was easy for Nand Raja to perceive that he was under guard, which put him into such a rage against the Nawab, that he carried his views to an excess that might have been fatal to any other prince but Haider.

Sending a Messenger

The unfortunate Raja sent a messenger to the Persian writer, named Meer Saeb, secretary to the French officer, and who had been charged with the letters to the governor of Pondicherry; his pretence was to enquire whether he could not procure from Pondicherry some crude salt of tartar and other European drugs; the Raja being a chemist, or rather alchemist, who had worked many years to discover the transmutation of metals.

The Persian being alone with Nand Raja and the Brahman, the former proposed to him to acquaint his master, that if he would assassinate Haider, he (Nand Raja) would deposit the value of eight lakhs of rupees in gold, silver, precious stones, and elephants; the irritated old man being determined to strip himself of all his property rather than not satisfy his vengence against his supposed enemy: the project, he observed, was easy to be put in execution, because the Nawab, on his return from the excursion he made every two days, passed the night by the light of flambeaux before the camp of the Europeans; and nothing could prevent their seizing this instant, and shooting him by an aim taken from the inside of one of the tents.

The writer, according to his own account, not daring to shew the horror this proposition made in his mind, promised to speak on the subject to his master, and give an answer the following day to a Brahman, who was shown to him; and who promised to wait at the gate of a small pagoda indicated to him. The writer made haste to inform his master of the interview he had had with the Raja, and the abominable commission he was charged with: the officer, after recovering from the indignation this base proposition naturally produced, ordered him to keep the whole a profound secret. Fortunately, this officer had been one of the council, in which the affair of Nand Raja had been discussed; he knew, consequently, that on that very day the Nawab was to decide whether Nand Raja should be arrested, and to direct in what manner it should be done.

The storm that was ready to burst on the head of Haider, did not permit the commandant to defer any longer the waiting upon him; he therefore went with a determination either to conceal or relate what had come to his knowledge, according to the disposition he might find Haider in, with regard to arresting Nand Raja. When he came into the presence of the Nawab, that prince addressed him in private: " That old fool, Nand Raja," said he, " has sent for your Persian secretary to give him a commission to procure drugs from Pondicherry; has the man mentioned it to you?" "Certainly," replied the French officer, "he has given me an account of his interview, and I cannot but advise you, after what I have heard, not to delay a moment in arresting Nand Raja." "It is a decided step," returned Haider; "everything is arranged for that purpose; he is to make his public entry the day after tomorrow into Seringapattam, at the head of his troops.

The streets he passes through will be lined with grenadier Topasses, or Sepoys, and at the palace there will be placed an entire battalion: his troops will be arranged on the parade in readiness to relieve the posts as they are quitted by the grenadiers; Mughdum has undertaken to disarm the troops and all his people; and leaving him only his women and a few domestics, will confine him in his own palace; and, since the old man is without abilities, and, no one can rely on him, everything will be performed without trouble, before the cannon of the palace salute Mughdum, who will quit his government tomorrow. Send as many Europeans into the town as you a can, as cannoneers: let them enter by small parties, and through the several gates, and unite, as if by curiosity, about the palace of Nand Raja. Do not go yourself, but command your officers to obey punctually the orders of Mughdum, or his brother, Ismael Saeb."

Little Attention to the Manner of French Officer: The little attention paid by Haider to the manner of the French officer when he insisted on arresting Nand Raja, shows how far he is from being inclined to suspect those who have gained his confidence. This is not the only proof of the openness of his character, that Haider has given the same officer: for that very night, after returning from the Durbar, being gone to rest, he was informed from the prince that the chief usher and sword-bearer of the Nawab desired to speak with him on an affair of the last importance, which they could communicate to him in bed, without his getting up. Being introduced, they said:

> "The guard, which, as you know, is placed round the camp of Nand Raja, stopped one of your people, a short time ago, coming from thence; and, though he said he belonged to you, it was thought proper to conduct him to the Nawab, because his orders on that head are very precise. The man, in passing by your guard, called for help, and the guard, knowing him, took him out of the hands of his conductors, and set him free. The Nawab has therefore sent us to beg that you will send the man, that he may be known by those who arrested him: he has also charged us to give you his word, that as soon as it is certain that he is one of your people, he will send him back, for you to do what you think proper with him."

The officer, much astonished at this news, which he supposed to have some relation to the Persian writer, ordered inquiry to be made of the guard, concerning the man they had liberated: to which his valet-de-chambre answered:

> "He is a black Peon, whom I sent to the camp of Nand Raja before midnight, to procure some manna, as I was informed that a druggist of that camp had some. This Peon, having met an acquaintance, amused himself till after midnight, knowing that he was not wanted: on his return he was arrested, which he supposed

improper, on account of the protection of your bandolier he carried; he therefore called out as he passed the guard, and was set free."

The officer ordered the Peon to be sent for, and put him into the hands of the prince's officers, by whom he was conducted into the presence. The guards immediately knew him, and Haider was contented with asking him this question; "Did you come from Pondicherry with your master ?' And on his replying in the affirmative, he sent him back, and the affair was thus terminated.

On the day appointed, Nand Raja, without any mistrust, made a pompous entrance into Seringapattam, at the head of his little army, the cannon firing, and the troops beating to arms, and saluting him. Being arrived at his palace, his attention was taken up by the compliments of the great men of the city, who were admitted by a few at a time, on a pretended account of not making too great a crowd. Mughdum then entered the city, followed by a number of officers, and made a sign to the troops, not to pay him any honours: he went directly to the palace of Nand Raja, where every one supposed he was going to pay his respects, and dismounting, he caused the first company of the battalions of Sepoys who guarded the gate, to follow him.

As soon as he came into the presence of Nand Raja, who came to meet him, he acquainted him that Haider, being informed that he was surrounded by people who gave him bad advice, had sent him to remove them from about him: at the same time he commanded all present to leave the palace, which was done without uttering a word; the grenadiers followed them: and Mughdum remaining with Nand Raja, his two sons, and some officers, the conversation was carried on with the greatest politeness. Mughdum acquainted the two princes that they were to make the campaign; and that, instead of one father, they would find two in Haider and himself. During the short conversation, the women and all the family of Mughdum were announced. Mughdum took his leave, carrying the two princes with him, to whom he represented, that it became their dignity to wait upon the Nawab, and give him an account of all that had passed.

These young noblemen departed, accompanied by many of Mughdum's officers; neither they nor Nand Raja expressing the least astonishment or chagrin. After their departure, Mughdum spoke a word to Nand Raja's general, who ordered his troop to ground their arms, which was done with great silence. All the gates and windows of Nand Raja's palace, that looked towards the street, were afterwards walled up, except the principal entrance, which is no great disfigurement in an Indian palace, whose principal front lies towards the gardens. Then it was that Nand Raja, to the great satisfaction of the dowager Dayva found himself shut up in his own palace.

Haider paid the arrears due to his troops, which, for the most part, enlisted among his own. On the valuation of the Raja's income, it was found to be equal to four lacks of rupees: two of which were allowed him for his own maintenance, and the other two were given to his sons, who made the campaign with a brilliant equipage, under the conduct of their father's old general, who appears to have been in intelligence with Haider in the transaction just related. All the preparations for the campaign being made, the two armies began their march; that of Nizam took the road of Oscota, and that of Haider passed by the way of Bangalore.

When they had arrived, and encamped at the gates of this city, several councils were held, to determine on the operations, and take the necessary measures. Basalatjung, Rocun Daulla, and several other chiefs assisted at these councils. It was agreed, that the two armies should march always separate, but at such a distance as to assist each other in all their operations: that the army of Haider should take the avant-garde till they had passed the mountains: and that, when they had entered the kingdom of Arcot, it should again be considered, whether it was best to act separately or conjointly. Hitherto we have given no more than a superficial account of the different wars in which Haider Ali Khan has been engaged against the Marathas, the English, and other enemies, who envied his success or dreaded his power.

The true reason why the former actions of this celebrated conqueror have not been given in a more ample manner in the present work, is that the Author, not having joined the army of the Nawab before the time of the war on the coast of Malabar, did not think it necessary to speak largely concerning military operations he could only know from the communications of others. Every person acquainted with subjects of this nature, must be sensible how very imperfect an idea of the particulars of any war can be gathered from the accounts of officers, who, engaged in their own duty, cannot have much opportunity to contemplate the general scene of action.

Talents of Haider Regarding Art of War: To display the character, the genius, and the talents of Haider, with regard to the art of war, it would doubtless have been highly interesting to have described all the marches, sieges, and battles, in which he has exerted himself. But the curiosity of the reader will be amply satisfied by the details given of the facts that happened during the war between Haider and the English. The Author will at least relate what he has seen, and clearly come to the knowledge of; with the assurance that this, of all the wars in which Haider has been engaged, is the best adapted to make known the great abilities of that prince; because in this he had to contend with enemies who possessed the superior advantage of the military science and discipline. It will be easy to judge, from the war between the years 1767 and 1769, of the probable event of the present war, which commenced in 1779.

The war we are about to relate is so much the more interesting, as it forms an epoch in the history of the Europeans in India; since it is the first war the Europeans have finished by asking peace of the Indians. Before we begin our account of the operations of this famous war, it will be proper to give a display of the forces of the respective combatants.

Possession of Haider: The possessions of Haider in the year 1767, when he began the war against the English, consisted of the kingdom of Mysore; the country of Bangalore, that formerly composed part of Mysore; all the country called Malleam, or the Karnatic, in the charts, which words signify, in two different languages, the Country of the Mountains, and which comprehends all the vallies and mountains from Ambour to Madura, Travancore, and the cost of Malabar; the town of Scirra; the country of Ballapur; the little kingdom of Bisnagar; the kingdom of Canara, which extends from Cape Rama northwards along the frontier of Visapour; and lastly, the sovereignty of the coast of Malabar and the Maldive Islands, these countries being only tributaries. It may be seen, that the dominions of Haider have the advantage of being connected together, and of being defended, on the part of the English, by mountains and narrow entrances.

These countries contain, if popular report may be credited, above a thousand fortresses, of different magnitudes: however, as an eye-witness, I can affirm them to be very many. All the large fortresses or garrisons are guarded by the troops of the army, which are changed from time to time; and by garrison soldiers, who are a kind of militia, and serve for less pay than the regular troops.

The smaller fortresses are maintained only by this latter order of military; and, in case of any alarm, the inhabitants of the mountains take arms, throw themselves into the forts, and defend them with obstinacy sufficient to require a siege. These fortresses, which seem to have been constructed to defend the country against the incursions of the Marathas, have trenches, the bastions or towers; many of them have their revetement of stone; but the greater part, especially in the flat country, have their embankments of red earth, which possesses the property of acquiring, in a short time, the hardness of bricks baked in the sun. They are all kept in the best repair, or at least have been, ever since they became the property of Haider.

The dominions of this prince abound in rice, and every other necessary of life, as well as in cattle of every kind; that is to say, oxen, sheep, goats, and elephants. As to the horses and camels, they are for the most part brought out of other countries; and Haider, by making a proper use of his money, is always provided with a great number of horses and elephants, the most useful animals in war. He has always a reserve of these in the villages, to the number of six hundred elephants, and twenty thousand horse.

To be always provided with a supply of these very necessary animals, he never fails to purchase all that are offered to him, provided they be robust and strong, and the owners will part with them for the price he sets upon them, after a strict examination; and, as his offers are very equitable, dealers come to him from all parts, to present the finest of these animals for his inspection.

To all these means and inducements that might lead the prince to enter into a war with the English, we may add the assurance he had that the English, being almost without cavalry, could not prevent his army from being supplied with provisions from all parts of his dominions: and above all the immense treasures he possessed, which, joined to the considerable revenues of his kingdoms and states, put him in a situation to support with ease the most long and expensive war. In the year we speak of (1767) all the forces of Haider Ali Khan were estimated at about one hundred and eighty or two hundred thousand men, of which twenty five thousand were cavalry: but, as it was necessary to garrison all the fortresses, and leave some troops on the frontiers, the army he led against the English might be from fifty to fifty-five thousand men; of which eighteen thousand were cavalry, and about eight thousand Marathas, Pandaris, and others, that cannot be better compared than to the Cossacks who follow the Russian army, being fit for no service but to ravage the country, or rob the baggage of an army.

The infantry consisted of twenty thousand Topasses, or Sepoys, armed with sixteen thousand good firelocks, because all the officers, down to the corporals, have no muskets; the rest of the infantry were Carnates, or Calerots, armed with matchlocks and lances. The number of Europeans was about seven hundred and fifty. They were divided into two companies of dragoons or hussars, two hundred and fifty cannoneers, and the officers and Serjeants dispersed among the regiments of Grenadiers and Topasses.

There were likewise some troops, armed with arms either unknown or out of use at present in Europe, to the number of about three thousand men, mounted two and two on running camels, having each a firelock of a very great length, that threw a ball of about three ounces to a prodigious distance. These arms have an iron rest fixed to the barrel: and the soldiers, who are excellent marksmen, follow the cavalry, and plant themselves in covered places to flank the enemy, among whose cavalry they keep up a very destructive fire. This body of troops have the singular privilege of an ensign for every ten men; whether it be an honour, or a piece of policy to deceive the enemy into an opinion, from the number of standards, that they are opposed by a numerous corps of infantry. The troop is very ancient, being, according to all appearance, the first among the Indians that bore fire-arms.

The same number of men, carried rockets of iron, which are boxes of plate-iron, in the form of fusses, and attached to direction rods: they are of various sizes, some containing more than one pound of powder or composition, and fly to the distance of a thousand yards. Many of these rockets are charged to burst: others are sharpened at the end; and others are pierced at the foremost end, being charged so that the wind acts strongly on the flame, and sets fire to the matters it may strike in its course. This implement is, on the whole, far more expensive than useful; which, I suppose, chiefly arises from the want of care and attention in making them up; however they have been some times productive of dreadful effects, by setting fire to ammunition waggons. These rockets are very well adapted for setting fire to towns and villages in which the enemy have magazines.

A body of cavalry, not used to this kind of instrument, would be quickly thrown into disorder by it; for the rockets falling at the feet of the horses, emit a flame resembling that of a forge furnace, which frightens them and when they burst, they do considerable mischief. It is no small advantage, that they describe a curve line, and may therefore be thrown by people that are covered by a line of infantry. The English made use of them against the cavalry of Haider; but as it was habituated to he fire by various exercises performed with paper rockets, the horses, instead of being frightened, marched fiercely over them. A troop of Arabs, armed with bows and arrows, arrived at Seringapattam a short time before the departure of the army. The men were well-made, strong, and active; but as Haider did not suppose the arms they bore would have much effect on the enemy, he formed them into two companies; one clothed in red, which he joined to his Savari: and the other, in blue, he gave to the commandant of Europeans, to apply to any service he might think proper. They were very adroit in killing birds with their bows and arrows, which were large, and very much ornamented.

The army of Nizam Daulla, Suba of Deccan, *etc.*, was reckoned one hundred thousand strong; but he had not more than forty thousand fighting men, of which thirty thousand were cavalry, and ten thousand infantry. Scarcely two thousand of the infantry, were armed with firelocks; the rest had only that kind of musket that is called Cailletaux in India. The infantry was, however, commanded by a brave man, named Abderaman Khan, who had served under Messrs. Bourdonnaye and Buss. This last caused him to be promoted to the command he possessed. He was very sensible of the bad state of his troops, which was beside very ill paid.

The cavalry was good, but much better for show than service; every chief being proprietor and absolute master of his own troop. Following the army, for the most part, only as vassals of the empire, they were very little disposed to risk their life and their cattle in any war, except when animated by the desire of revenge, the hope of plunder, or some other passion. These chiefs were the most powerful lords of Deccan; such as Ram Schander, a Maratha, who bears the name of Alexander, his supposed or pretended ancestor; the three Nawabs of Sanour, Curpa, and Canour, *etc.*

The army was followed by a multitude of merchants working tradesmen, women, and servants, which occasioned the camp to be vastly extended, and would have rendered it an easy matter for the English to surprise it, if Haider had been possessed of less experience and vigilance. The army of the Suba, though capable of doing very little service in actual war, added vastly to the reputation of Haider, and might have procured him many allies; but the well-founded suspicions he entertained against Rocun Daulla, and even against Nizam, obliged him to be on his guard against a stroke of perfidy, that would have been of more consequence to him than the loss of a battle.

Besides, an indifference and coolness very soon arose between the two Subas, by reason of the continual wants of Nizam and all his chiefs; and Haider was not disposed to comply with their repeated requests for money, lest he should by that means lose both his money and his allies. He moreover repented that he had not previously agreed that Nizam, after having given the investiture of the Nawabship of Arcot to his son, should return to his states. It will be seen in future that these allies very soon separated from each other.

The united army possessed a very considerable train of artillery, consisting of at least one hundred and ten pieces of large cannon. That of Haider was more numerous, better provided with ammunition, better mounted, and served by good European cannoneers. The artillery of Nizam was all fine European brass cannon; and thirty, at least, were French pieces, cast in the reign of Louis XIV., being the remaining artillery of the squadron of M. de la Haye which was lost in a hurricane in the road of Masulipattam: this port then belonged to the Subas of Deccan, who recovered the cannon of the sunken vessels, which have come into the hands of Nizam Daulla. This beautiful artillery was ill provided with ammunition, badly mounted, and served by Lascars, or Indian gunners, who are virtually cowardly and unskilful.

Haider likewise employed in this war a small army of thousand men, returned from the coast of Malabar. He entrusted the command of this detachment to Mahfuz Khan, a man who he knew had no pretentions to military skill, but, in his opinion, able to cause the people of Madura, whose sovereign he was, to revolt. This able negociator and keen politician was, however, unfortunate in the attempt to become a warrior; for Colonel Beck, a German in the service of the English, pretending to fly before him, enticed him into the centre of Madura, and succeeded in taking him prisoner.

We do not reckon the fleet of Haider among his forces: it was then composed of a ship purchased of the Danes, pierced for sixty guns, but furnished with no more than fifty; three others of thirty two guns; eighteen palms, vessels both for rowing and sailing, and carrying fourteen guns; and about twenty large galliots, carrying eighty men, and two cannons. Three or four of the English company's frigates, that are always ready armed in the Indian sea. An Englishman, whom Haider had appointed his admiral, having carried the large vessel to Bombay to refit, it was seized and declared good prize as soon as the commencement of hostilities was known; an action that

Haider has always regarded as perfidious on the part of the English.

Power of English

The power of the English in India was in its meridian in the year 1767. That nation possessed the whole of Bengal, the richest, the most fertile, and the most populous of all the provinces in the empire; the number of its inhabitants being estimated at nine millions when it fell into the hands of the English; but since reduced to six millions, at most, by their vexatious and barbarous government.

Besides this province, they possessed all the coasts of Orixa and Coromandel, having no other limits inland than the gates or mountains; the large towns of Surat and Cambay, the former of which is the most trading port of all India the island of Bombay, and the country of Salsete, on the Maratha frontier; the forts of Tillicherry; Mondeli, and Anzingue, on the coast of Malabar; besides a number of factories and different establishments, such as are on the island of Sumatra, too remote to be of any advantage in the present war.

The territorial revenues of all these possessions exceeded two hundred millions of French money, as the Author of these Memoirs is well assured, having had in his hands the state of the English Company's affairs, which was given to the King of England and his Privy Council.

Forces of English

The forces of the English in India were more than ninety thousand men: namely, eight regiments of English infantry of one thousand men each, three on the establishment of Madras, three on that of Bengal, and two on that of Bombay, besides twelve hundred men forming the artillery companies on the several establishments, and one thousand or twelve hundred invalids in garrison at various places. The Indian troops consisted of sixty four regiments of one thousand Sepoys each, of which thirty were on the establishment of Madras. Their cavalry might be estimated at about four thousand horse, twelve hundred only being on the Madras establishment.

All this cavalry was Indian, except about four hundred Europeans. General Smith, after leaving the necessary garrisons, had at his disposal five thousand Europeans, two thousand five hundred Sepoys, two thousand five hundred horse, including two hundred Europeans; twelve hundred Indians, taught the English exercise, and commanded by European officers. The remainder of his army contained the cavalry of Mohammed Ali Khan, a troop not only much inferior in number to that of Haider, but even unfit to face the cavalry of that sovereign, by reason of their want of discipline, and the bad state of the horses.

The English have never yet succeeded in the attempt to form a good troop of European horse in India. As they have sent a regiment of dragoons from England, it is probable that their arrival may place the affair on another footing. Though it may not immediately be conceived, the reason of the want of success in forming their intended troop of horse, consisted in the good discipline to which they were desirous of subjecting them.

The excellence of the English cavalry is sufficiently acknowledged in Europe; and its advantages consist less in the goodness of the horse than in the choice of the horsemen. The pay of a horseman in England is such as renders his situation very eligible; so that the sons of rich farmers and tradesmen are very desirous of entering into the service. This being the case, it is in the power of the officers to select handsome, well formed men, of good character, and to keep them in good discipline merely by the fear of being dismissed.

The officers who were first entrusted with the formation of a body of cavalry in India, thought to establish and preserve the same discipline among them, without attending to the great difference of time, place, and persons. The recruits sent from England to India are in general libertines and people of bad character; and as the Company will not dismiss a soldier, all the punishment inflicted on a horseman is, to reduce him to serve in the infantry; so that a man is no sooner put among the cavalry than he is sent back again to his former station. The French have succeeded in forming very good cavalry in India, by attending more to their horsemanship, and less to their discipline and manners.

The English at Madras, in addition to all these troops, in number above thirty thousand, had the disposition of the troops of Mohammed Ali Khan, with those of some Palleagars, and of Morao, a Maratha chief, which altogether might be about twenty thousand men. The whole army to be employed in the defence of Arcot was consequently at least fifty thousand men; and Haider was likewise under the necessity of marching in person against eight thousand troops on the Bombay establishment, who attacked him at Mangalore, the centre of his kingdom of Canara.

General Smith had the advantage of possessing an army for the most part better disciplined, and more practised in their evolutions, than that of Haider; with a numerous corps of Europeans, capable alone, as was generally believed before this war, of beating the twelve hundred thousand men which Mohammed Shah, emperor of the Mughals, opposed against Nadir Shah, king of Persia.

His artillery was served by a sufficient number of officers and men, bred up in the services: in short, he had officers and engineers of every kind to second him, and was himself certainly much superior to Haider in military knowledge. With all these advantages, and a superiority of double the number of firelocks, he was certain of gaining every battle, in which the nature of the place, or the post he might take, was such as to prevent the cavalry of Haider from acting to advantage.

The advantage of General Smith over Haider were balanced by very great disadvantages: namely, first, the inferiority of his cavalry, which obliged him to reduce the theatre of war as much as possible to the mountainous country: secondly, the impossibility of his preventing the cavalry from ravaging the country and cutting off his convoys: thirdly, the very great difficulty of procuring a sufficient number of oxen for the conveyance of his artillery, ammunition, and baggage; a difficulty of such importance, that it reduced him to the necessity of having an inferior train of artillery, and to spare his provisions and stores beyond what would otherwise have been necessary.

But the greatest embarrassment he suffered consisted in his dependance on the Governor and Council of Madras; who, without having any well-founded knowledge of the forces of Haider, either with respect to number or discipline—and who, at the same time ignorant of the nature of the country, were incessantly giving orders contrary to his views, and every rational principle of war; and even went so far as to reproach him for the ravages made by Haider's cavalry, though in his advice to them previous to the commencement of the war, he had predicted this consequence to them. And as those gentlemen never lost sight of the occasions for enriching themselves, they supplied the army by means of contractors, with whom they were in league; treating the inhabitants of Madras in the most vexatious and odious manner, under pretence of furnishing the army with necessaries.

Though we have spoken of the departure of General Smith to take possession of several places in the dominions of Haider, we have not hitherto spoken of his operations; our intention being to unite all the military operations of this interesting war in one continued narration. The English General made several sieges during the time of the preparations and negotiations of Haider. He took Terpatoor, Vaniambari, and Singueman, without much difficulty; that is to say, each of these ill-fortified places held out some days. He likewise took Kaveripattam, whose fortress did not yield till seventeen days after the trenches were opened; and he besieged Kisnagari, a fortress on a steep mountain, where he was obliged to raise the siege, after having made two assaults; in the last of which he lost twenty four grenadiers, besides soldiers. This was the only place defended by an European officer.

It was during the siege of this place that the armies of Haider and Nizam began to move towards the enemy. Kisnagari is twenty two leagues from Bangalore, by the road that can be taken by an army; and, in order to arrive at this latter place, it is necessary to go through narrow passes, which are very easily defended.

Haider directed his march so that, at the end of the second day, he found himself four leagues from the foot of the mountains; being opposite the pass of Vellore, which opens about four leagues from Kaveripattam, a town and fortress on the Paler, seven leagues from the pass of Kisnagari, which was on the right, and about six leagues from the pass of Ventigheri, which is about two leagues and a half from Vaniambari. No precaution was taken to prevent the English general from being advised of the departure of the army from Bangalore; and consequently he was soon advised of that event, as well by his spies as by secret informers he paid in the army of Nizam. General Smith, on receipt of this advice, raised the siege of Kisnagari, and posted himself to defend the pass of Vellore; and that with so much the more reason, as it was the only passage through which artillery could be conveyed; and being in the centre, with Kaveripattam in his rear, he was better situated to repair to the defence of the pass Haider might attempt; or to retire in safety, if necessary.

Convening of a Council of War: Haider convened a council of war, at which Rocun Daulla assisted. Its object was, to decide which of the three passes they should attempt to force; and in order that every one might form an opinion with sufficient knowledge of the business, he produced charts of the different passages, in which every particular was exactly delineated. The council decided, that as the English were posted with all their forces to guard the pass of Vellore, it was proper to issue forth by that of Ventigheri, the pass of Kisnagari being absolutely impracticable for artillery: and though the army of Nizam, by reason of its being encamped to the left Haiders' forces, was nearer this pass, yet Haider, according to the agreement, undertook to form the advanced guard with his army. In consequence, orders were given to march at two in the morning, in a single column, leaving all the baggage in the camp.

Coronets and Other Irregular Troops: The Carnates, and other irregular troops, formed the head of the column; who were followed by all the Sepoys, each preceded by the grenadiers, and followed by the horse. They artillery came next, led by two thousand Topasses, their grenadiers, and the European cannoneers. And lastly, two companies of European cavalry closed the march, and completed the column. Haider, at the head of two thousand horse, marched on the right flank of the column.

The English being informed of the order and direction of this march, moved to oppose Haider, and to gain the pass of Ventigheri before him: a thing easily done, as they had but three leagues to pass over. But it was an unexpected manoeuvre to them, when, after an hour's march, the Europeans, the grenadier Topasses, and successively the artillery and all the other Topasses, made a turn to the right, and marched for the pass of Vellore with the utmost celerity.

As this troop was supposed to have no other destination than to escort the artillery, it was contrived, in the course of the march, that there should be a considerable interval between them and the cavalry that preceded the Topasses, in order that this counter-march might be less perceived; the chief of the Europeans, who had the command of this part of the army, being alone entrusted with the secret. The stratagem succeeded perfectly well. The hussars and dragoons passed full speed through the pass, which is long, narrow, and winding, but very even ground.

They were followed by the European cannoneers, and the grenadier Topasses, who ran with great expedition, though they had already marched quickly over an interval of four leagues. General Smith had been careful to leave some of the infantry of Mohammed Ali, and a party of Indian horse, at the entrance of this pass; but a body of Haider's cavalry, that had passed the strait of Kisnagari, having appeared in the plain, followed by the garrison of that fortress, the troops left by the English abandoned the pass, and retired with great haste to Kaveripattam. At the instant the European commandant cleared the pass, he met Bahoud Khan commander of cavalry, who came himself to acquaint him that he found no opposition. On this news he gave orders to fire nine cannon, three and three; the signal agreed between him and Haider, that the pass was free. On this signal, the Nawab caused his whole army to march to the pass of Vellore, where he arrived himself, at the head of his cavalry, and saw the artillery advance, under the conduct of the Topasses.

General Smith was soon informed that Haider's army was advancing through the pass of Vellore, and retired as quickly as possible to Kaveripattam; where he did not think it expedient to stay, but leaving twelve hundred of his best Sepoys, some Topasses belonging to the artillery, and thirty European cannoneers, he retired to Tripatour, to be nearer assistance, and at hand to receive the convoys he expected from Madras, as well as to join a body of seven or eight thousand men, commanded by Colonel Wood, who was then employed in besieging the fortress of Ahtour, a very ill-fortified place, defended by Carnates; against which, however, he employed fifteen days, from the opening his trenches to the time of its surrender. General Smith, when he retired, left one hundred Indian horsemen, to bring him intelligence of the events that might happen in his absence. The whole army and artillery of Haider cleared through the pass in the course of the day, but the baggage and provisions came through in the night; so that the Europeans in the army, who had marched from daybreak till night, and were fatigued, as well by that as by hunting (the country abounding with game), were not very well satisfied, at night, to be obliged to eat their game, roasted as well as they could, without bread or rice, to the great diversion of Haider, who in vain advised them to wait for the cooks.

Haider had no sooner passed the mountains with his cavalry than he despatched his brother-in-law. Mughdum, with four thousand horse, to pursue the English army, and invest Kaveripattam. This order was executed with so much diligence and address that Kaveripattam, was invested, as well as all the avenues leading to the English camp at Tripatour, without it being possible for General Smith to receive any advice by the hundred horsemen left in the neighbourhood of Kaveripattam, who were driven into the town. All the Hurkaras were interrupted, and the letters being carried to Haider, convinced him that his suspicions of the correspondence between General Smith and many of the chiefs of Nizam's army, were but too well founded.

Mughdum, after leaving the care of the investment of Kaveripattam to another commander, hastened to the environs of Tripatour, and arrived during the night behind the small mountains or rocks that lie about a league from that place. General Smith, who arrived at his camp the second evening of his march, supposed the inactivity of Haider to be the cause that he had received no news, either from the commander at Kaveripattam, or his friends in Nizam's army. In this persuasion he permitted the servants, with the greatest part of the oxen belonging to the army, to go in search of forage the next morning.

As soon as Mughdum saw them dispersed in the plain, he detached some cavalry, who quickly threw them into terror and disorder. This was, of course, observed from the camp and fortress and the piquets of cavalry, consisting of about one thousand horse, were despatched to chase the pillagers; who, according to their orders and usual custom, fled, on perceiving the enemy, and saved themselves by taking the road near which the ambuscade was.

The English cavalry were no sooner within reach than Mughdum fell upon them, and, having put them to flight, pursued them with so much spirit, that a party being prevented from reaching the camp, and endeavouring to take refuge in the town, the cavalry of Mughdum entered with them, and took the place, in spite of the fire from the fort.

General Smith, who, on sight of the enemy's cavalry, had hastened to draw up his forces in order of battle, was apprehensive of being surrounded by the cavalry of both armies, and consequently of being obliged to cut his way through, in order to procure provisions and reinforcements; he therefore collected as many oxen, and as much baggage, as the circumstances would permit, and marched in three columns, his artillery and baggage forming the middle column; and, leaving the fortress of Tripatour, hastened to Singueman, situated at the beginning of a chain of mountains, transversal to the great mountains passing by Tirnmale and abutting at Gingi.

He arrived in safety, though much harassed by Mughdum, who took many oxen, loaded with baggage, and two hundred horsemen, with their horses, of which six only were Europeans.

This irruption of Mughdum, and the total want of every kind of advice respecting the operations of Haider, ought to have given General Smith a very different opinion concerning the military skill and judgement of this Indian warrior, in comparison to those with whom he had hitherto fought: but, considering that Haider could not come to him without besieging Kaveripattam or Vaniambari, places whose garrisons might have interrupted his convoys, and being at Singueman, distant from Tirnmale only five leagues, by a road advantageous for infantry (besides possessing the advantage of his camp being defended by the fortress, a large tank or pond, and the river), he determined to wait the arrival of Colonel Wood; for which purpose he wrote to the council at Madras, to order the junction of the two armies.

Haider, the evening after he had passed the strait of Vellore, encamped about a league and a half from Kaveripattam, which was invested by his cavalry. He immediately repaired to a mountain at a small distance, from whence he could observe everything that passed in the town. It was easy to perceive, from the burning of the houses that would have favoured their approach to the fortress, that they intended to abandon the town, and retire into this last place. Haider, in consequence, gave orders to the commandant of his artillery, to get everything in readiness for scaling the walls by the Caleros, and Carnates, and other irregular troops, to prevent the English from carrying their effects from the town to the fortress.

This officer, who had brought thirty pieces of cannon behind the mountain, caused eight to be drawn across the plain, to the very edge of the ditch, in spite of the fire of three pieces of cannon the English had left on the ramparts of the town, after carrying the other pieces into the fortress, whose fire could not incommode them, because masked by the walls of the town. The English commandant was so far from expecting this attack, that, in order to see Haider's horse more at his ease, he had seated himself with his officers in a tent on the ramparts, at a table covered with bottles.

To engage his attention, the eight pieces of cannon, escorted by three battalions of grenadiers and some gunners, marched directly to the gate on the side remotest from the fortress; and, having placed them opposite the gate, they made their first discharge at the tent of the commandant, and immediately overthrew it: after which they directed them against the gate, and the towers that defended it. The troops that had escorted the artillery laid themselves flat on the earth behind the hedges and walls, and in the trenches of the gardens.

It was about two in the afternoon that this cannonade began. During this time, about ten thousand, and as many volunteers, out of all the troops of the two armies, appeared scattered in the plain, and hiding themselves among the gardens and houses that had been abandoned. The English officers, who had never beheld a scene of this sort before, supposed that this multitude, arriving without muskets, had no other intention than to rob or to seek for garden stuff round the town. They imagined that the attack would be made at the breach, and that there would be sufficient time to retire into the fortress at the beginning of the night.

The town of Kaveripattam is surrounded by an antique wall and rampart, with towers of hewn stone: the Palar washes part of its walls; but this river, which is very broad, was not then more than a foot deep; the rest of the walls was defended by a dry ditch of no great depth.

About three o'clock, the different chiefs of the troops destined for the attack having given notice that they were in readiness, two salvos of the eight pieces of cannon served as a signal; and on the second discharge, from eighteen to twenty thousand men issued from all parts, with loud shouts: some began to cross the river; others entered the ditch with wretched bamboo ladders; other again had only poles with hooks and numbers had fastened hooks to their turban-cloths, which they threw on the ramparts, and attempted to scramble up; and lastly, another party were extremely busy chopping the gates with hatchets: the whole scene was very striking and laughable; and the activity of the assailants was vastly increased by the astonishment of the English, who made no resistance, but hastened to the fortress, though not with celerity enough to save fifty Sepoys, an Indian captain, and an European serjeant, who were cut off in their retreat: these were instantly stripped, as were also the inhabitants, who were but few in number, the more opulent having retired before the English besieged the place.

It was not without difficulty that the town was cleared of these pillagers, who were slain in the houses and streets by the cannon of the fortress. In the night after the attack a battery of twenty pieces of cannon, of twenty four pounds, was constructed, which announced itself at six in the morning by a full discharge, all the embrasures being unmasked at once.

The construction of this battery was facilitated by a wall of earth belonging to a large house on an elevated ground, which the English had left standing after burning its roof. It is to be observed, that there is no trouble in Haider's army to make platforms of wood for the batteries; the earth is sufficiently solid, and nothing is to be feared from rain during the fine season: the pieces are always mounted on their carriages, and consequently ready to be placed in battery; the carriages are very solid: and the fellies of the wheels very broad, so that they do not cut into the earth. It must likewise be owned, that in sieges of no great consequence as well to satisfy the impatience of Haider as to quiet the murmurs of the gunners and deceive the enemy, the pioneers often give the earth an appearance only of solidity: but, what will appear most astonishing and perhaps incredible, is, that the battery was partly constructed with the same gabions employed in the battery made use of by General Smith, which was still in good condition, and ready to have mounted cannon, if it had not been judged proper to place another to better advantage.

The English commandant had raised two cavaliers of earth upon the bastions that fired on the battery, from whence he plunged with four small pieces of cannon, which killed and wounded many men, exclusive of those who suffered from the musketry, the battery not being more than seventy paces from the body of the place; but the officer of Haider, who conducted the attack, recollecting that the ancient Flibustiers took places without any other firearms than their buccaneers, which are long muskets of a large calibre, caused about two hundred of them, with their guns, to place themselves in proper positions behind some ruins. We have already observed that they are excellent marksmen; and their fire was so well directed that in less than an hour it silenced that of the ramparts and cavaliers: ten or twelve cannoneers and a number of Sepoys were killed at the first discharge; so that in a short time it became impossible for their officers to compel them to appear on the rampart: every discharge of a great gun from the place cost at least a cannoneer, who was either killed or rendered incapable of fighting.

It was this destructive fire that, according to the account of the English, compelled them to hoist the white flag at nine in the morning, after three hours cannonade at most, "without any breach, except.... a few stones that began to be, loosened. Haider was so surprised that ne could not persuade himself of the truth of the fact, but went out of his tent to a rising ground to see the flag: bestowing a disgraceful appellation on the English, he ordered the commanding officer, who had waited on him for instructions concerning the capitulation, to refuse nothing that might be demanded.

In consequence of this, Captain M— obtained, that himself and his troops should march out with the honours of war; that the Europeans should retire to Madras by the way of Tripatour, Vellore, and Arcot; that the Sepoys should be at liberty to go where they pleased, or to enlist in the army of Haider, which they almost all did, as well as the horsemen; that all the officers and soldiers should carry away what belonged to them; but that the arms, ammunition, stores, horses, and every thing belonging either to the king of England, the East India Company, or Mohammed Ali Khan, should be faithfully put into the hands of Haider.

Captain M—, observing the facility with which Haider allowed all his demands, was not afraid to ask payment for the provisions, which he said he had purchased with his own money, and was not sure of being repaid by the governor of Madras this proposition was so much more absurd, as all these provisions had been taken by force from the inhabitants of the country, which, however, did not prevent the English administration from paying him the value; besides which, as a recompense for his brave defence, the command of the garrison of Madras was bestowed on him. This facility of Haider to suffer the English to enjoy the fruit of their rapines, has apparently served greatly to facilitate the capture of places.

Haider having Caused the English garrison to evacuate the place the day after the capture of Kaveripattam, marched his army the following day about two in the morning; at noon he pitched his camp on the banks of the Paler where the camp remaining under the guard of the irregular troops, the army passed the river, and resumed their march in several columns, with the cavalry at their head, followed by the grenadiers and artillery, the rest of the infantry forming the rear.

March of Enemy: The army marched in this order till ten at night, at which time they rested about two hours in fields of carbi, a kind of pulse that horses and cattle are very desirous of, and which they were suffered to eat at pleasure. At midnight the moon rose, and the army proceeded; and at the break of day the hussars and European dragoons joined the cavalry of Mughdum, that was dispersed in the woods at a small distance from the English camp. This cavalry had been seven days in the open air, without tents or baggage, and Mughdum fared like the rest. It may be seen from this circumstance, how far Haider's troops are from being infected with that want of hardiness the Indians have been so continually reproached with.

The five thousand grenadiers, as well as the artillery that followed the cavalry, arrived at the same time, having traversed seventeen leagues in a march of twenty eight hours, without taking more than four hours' rest: the fatigue these grenadiers had been subjected to, in the exercises and evolutions at their formation, had put them into a condition of making such long and extraordinary marches. The rest of the infantry remained in the fields of carbi, and did not begin their march till daybreak.

It may with justice be a subject of admiration, that so numerous a train of artillery, drawn by oxen, could follow the troops with such rapidity. This surprise will vanish, when it is known that the oxen of India are very strong, and that those who are practised in drawing almost always go on a full trot; it is also known how sure-footed this animal is: the elephants assisted in cases of need, and a multitude of pioneers, that went before the artillery, made the roads practicable and even easy.

General Smith, as we have already observed, supposed he might remain without molestation in his camp at Singueman till the arrival of Colonel Wood, being persuaded that Kaveripattam would hold out at least as long against Haider as it did against himself; but Haider, who he believed to be at Kaveripattam, was already close upon him with his cavalry, his artillery, and his best infantry.

Mughdum had distributed his cavalry and Caleros with such judgement, that they possessed all the avenues to the English camp. It was Haider's project, when the rest of his infantry should arrive, to convey his forces to a small plain between Singueman and Tirnmale, and to take his post on the banks of a small river of considerable depth that General Smith would be under the necessity of passing in his way to Tirnmale.

By this position, Haider would have prevented the junction of the two English armies, which must have thrown General Smith into the utmost embarrassment; because it would have subjected him to the necessity of taking the road through Tripatour, Ami, and Arcot, and of traversing plains where he must have fought to disadvantage, on account of the numerous cavalry of his enemies.

But, contrary to expectation, Rocun Daulla arrived about ten in the morning, at the head of a large body of cavalry, announcing his arrival by the grand tumbles, doubtless for the purpose of advising the English; besides which, after his junction with Haider he sent advice of the capture of Kaveripattam, and the arrival of the army in the environs of the camp.

This is confirmed beyond contradiction by "the manoeuvre of the English, who raised their camp a little before noon. On the advice of this, Haider mounted all his cavalry, and the infantry repaired to arms. The hussars and dragoons having orders to issue out of the wood, and show themselves to the English army, found them in full march in a single column, coasting the river, and covering their baggages: their cavalry was at the head and rear of the column, and appeared desirous of gaining a hill that was before them.

The European commandant, who had been at the head of the European cavalry to reconnoitre the English, gave advice of what he had observed, and of the apparent designs of the enemy. Haider, in consequence, gave orders to his grenadiers, supported by his cavalry, to attack the English army; commanding the rest of his infantry likewise, who began to appear, to advance as quick as possible.

To judge of the disadvantages under which Haider's army fought, it will be sufficient to consider how much his infantry must have been harassed and fatigued by the prodigious march they had made without taking any repose. This did not, however, prevent the grenadiers from marching with such order and firmness to the attack, as astonished the English general.

Success to English Army: The English army had gained the hill. It was composed of three thousand Europeans, ten thousand Sepoys, and two thousand horse: all the infantry was in a single line, the English being in the centre; except six hundred grenadiers, separated into two bodies, and closing the line with twenty four pieces of cannon, that composed the whole of the English artillery. The artillery was placed in the centre and flanks of the line: every regiment had its own field-pieces. The cavalry, divided into two bodies, was at the front and rear of the baggage; it formed the two sides of a triangle, of which the infantry constituted the third; whose fire, as well as that of the artillery, would have flanked any cavalry that might have attacked them.

The slope of the hill was gentle, but it was covered with underwood that impeded the march of those Indian battalions who approached to attack the English. Notwithstanding this obstacle, they advanced to the distance of twenty-five paces, and fought many hours without losing ground, in spite of the enemy's musketry and cannon; giving the rest of the infantry time to come up, though not with the same courage and ardour as the grenadiers; except eight or nine hundred volunteers from the different corps, who, led on by the European Serjeants, attacked the left of the English line, and took two pieces of cannon. But a body of English, immediately sent to assist, repulsed them, and recovered the cannon, a little before night; which alone put an end to the firing on both sides: the two armies resting on the field, as if intending to continue the action.

The disadvantages under which Haider's infantry fought in this battle, and the good conduct of his grenadiers, must appear surprising to Europeans, who are accustomed to entertain a bad opinion of the bravery of the Indians: it appeared so to General Smith, who speaks in high terms of them, as well as of the European officers that commanded them. But to say the truth, this infantry was sustained by sixty pieces of large cannon, pointed by able gunners, who made great ravages among the English infantry, that was uncovered from head to foot; while the English artillery did little injury to Haider's infantry, on account of the difficulty of aiming well in pointing downwards. This difference of advantage compensated, in some respect, for the advantage of position, and the number of muskets, that were more than double those of the grenadiers, before they were joined by the rest of the infantry.

In this battle Haider lost nine hundred of his grendiers; a loss so much the more considerable, as they were brave men, accustomed to fatigue, and who never gave way. The Bakshi, or minister of war, who has the right of marching at the head of the infantry, though he does not command them, was killed by a cannon-ball; and the cavalry, which was of no use in this day's service, nevertheless lost some men and horses, the English artillery having good play among so numerous a troop. It was perceived, about eleven at night, that the English retired to silence. Haider gave orders to his troops not to attempt to molest them, the cavalry not being able to attack the English infantry in the night; and he was desirous of giving some repose to his infantry, who had distinguished themselves, and had need of rest.

Haste Employment of Cavalry: Before day-break, the cavalry, headed by the hussars and dragoons, set out in pursuit of the English army, who had abandoned their baggage for the sake of carrying of their wounded. General Smith himself set to example: the dragoons finding part of his kitchen utensils, and two valuable trunks belonging to Major Bonjour, a Genevan officer, esteemed by the English, and who did the duty of major-general of their army—these baggages afforded the hussars and dragoons excellent plunder.

In order more effectually to secure a conveyance for their wounded, the English threw their ammunition and stores into the river, from whence the Indians recovered the balls and sacks of rice; and, in order to conceal their loss, they buried their dead: but the night, and their haste, caused them to perform this duty with so little care, that the bodies were many of them partly uncovered. The avidity of the soldiers for plunder, when it is permitted, induced them to dig up the dead, in order to get the clothes they were wrapped in.

In spite of the haste employed by Haider's cavalry in pursuit of the English they gained Tirnmale, with no other loss than two small iron three-pounders they themselves left behind; and there was only one skirmish in sight of Trinmale, between the grenadiers, who formed the rear-guard of the English, and the hussars and dragoons one of whom only was wounded. Thus it was that General Smith escaped the risk he would have run, if Haider, with his army, could have taken his post beyond the river, as he had projected.

All the irregular troops had been left in the camp at Paler; because this kind of troops being without discipline, it would have been difficult to have keptithem out of sight of the English; and because the enemy's spies are generally of this body of troops. Haider, elated with the glory of having caused the English to fly before him, advanced, and encamped a league and a half from Tirnmale, in a place full of large rocks, and separated from Tirnmale by a plain; and, as he was encamped very near the enemy, to whose method of beating the Indians by attacks in the night he was no stranger, he took every precaution that could be required to secure his camp from any surprise.

A large opening between these rocks that might have been taken for a work of art, and behind which his camp was situated, was fortified by a redoubt. All the heights were occupied by guards, whose sentinels continually called *Khabardar* which signifies *Take care of yourself!* Guards of cavalry and Caleros were despatched close to Trinmale, with rockets to make signals: so that the English could make no movement to attack the camp of Haider, without his being immediately advised. But General Smith had no intention to run any risk till Colonel Wood should join him with his army, which had been augmented, and was eight or nine thousand strong, exclusive of a body of Caleros from Tanjore.

Haider, who ought to have sent a strong detachment, or the whole of his army, to prevent this junction, suffered it to take place, in spite of all the advice that was given him on the subject. He continued to keep his army collected, and to make war in a country where his cavalry was almost entirely useless; especially while General Smith remained in his camp at Trinmale, situated between two mountains on which there are fortresses; having his van covered by the town, and a tank, where no force could arrive but through narrow passes, defended by retrenchments with artillery.

His hope was to draw his enemy out of their camp. For this purpose he caused his infantry to make a kind of parade every day; sometimes coming within reach of the artillery with all his troops, and at other times with his infantry alone. He lost his time so effectually, that Colonel Wood joined his forces to those of General Smith.

Notwithstanding this junction, which made the English army amount to above five and twenty thousand good troops, four thousand five hundred being Europeans, General Smith did not think proper to expose himself in the plain against Haider; but, to give him an opportunity of attacking him in a country the most favourable to his infantry, he quitted his camp at Tirnmale, and marching to the left at daybreak, he pitched another camp two leagues from Tirnmale, that his army might be less confined.

Haider, informed of the design of the English general, was desirous of laying a snare for him, that he communicated to no one, and which might have been attended with fatal consequences. The fact is this: the English army had to pass through a plain, bounded on all sides by woods and small eminences: Haider gave orders, in the evening, to the chiefs of his artillery and infantry, to march into this plain at the dawn of day; entering it by a kind of valley that enlarged itself into the flat ground. He himself, in consequence of his project, departed at two in the morning with all his cavalry, which, by a very large circuit, he conducted into the close places that bordered the plain.

They who commanded his infantry being apprized of his departure, began their march at the appointed hour; not doubting but they should either find the cavalry at the plain, or receive orders relative to their disposition. They were highly astonished, on their arrival, not to see a single horseman, nor any other troops whatsoever. In proportion as the entrance grew larger, the infantry extended their front, and drew themselves into order of battle. The plain, though to appearance even, was divided in two by a rising ground. Some officers, who went before, were astonished, on mounting the eminence, to find the English army drawn up in order of battle behind it. As there had been no orders given for attacking them, and no news had arrived of Haider and his cavalry, a council, held hastily on the spot, decided that they should retire to the entrance of the valley, in order to post themselves more advantageously; while scouts were dispatched on all sides to obtain news, and the orders of the Nawab.

The English, who had been advised of the ambuscade prepared for them by Haider, remained in order of battle till the beginning of the night, when they entered their new camp. The infantry and artillery of Haider returned to theirs; and the prince returned very late in the night with his cavalry, much fatigued with having rode ten leagues in very bad ground, and without having taken any nourishment. Haider supposed that General Smith was ignorant of the march of his cavalry; and would have been tempted to attack his infantry, who apparently were not supported by any horse; by which means he expected to find an opportunity of falling upon the English army with his horse. We may easily imagine that things would have been conducted in another manner, if he had communicated his project.

Son's Role

As Tipu Sultan, who was then about seventeen years of age, is now the right hand of his father, and is the person who had the most brilliant success against the English,—we think it proper to mention his conduct on this occasion. Haider, who passionately loves his son, and is acquainted with his zeal and courage, was fearful respecting him on account of his very early age; for this reason, he usually entrusted him with the guard of the camp, when he supposed the day would prove too fatiguing or dangerous. The young prince, being charged with the guard of the camp on the present occasion, was in great plain when the infantry returned, and the night closed in, without any news concerning his father and the cavalry. Two hours after dark, that is to say about eight o'clock, he sent for all the generals, gave them a short account of the state of affairs, and demanded their advice.

The unanimous opinion was, that the English were too weak in cavalry to make any attempt against the Nawab: and that they could not come to attack the camp but by marching three leagues, and passing through straits where guards were placed. The prince replied to them, "As I have no orders from my father, I have need of your experience to direct my actions: I will wait here with patience and confidence according to your advice; and am much obliged to you for your attention and care." The whole company had not yet left the prince, when word was brought that Mughdum, his uncle, second commander of the army, had entered the camp, having taken the vanguard with some horse.

Haider always indefatigable, advanced at dawn towards Tirnmale, with four thousand infantry and twenty pieces of cannon. The town was open to him; but while he was making the proper disposition to attack the fortresses, he learned that General Smith was in motion to attack him. This intelligence obliged him to return into his camp; not choosing to fight in a position where his cavalry would have been of no service to him.

He removed his camp the next day, because he could not reach that of the English, but by narrow passes, or by marching above ten leagues, though the camps were not above four leagues asunder. After passing by the rear of Nizam Daulla's army, that had arrived two days before, and was encamped in a fine plain, he pitched his camp to the left hand of Nizam, but in advance, being then about four leagues from the English, with a plain before him, interspersed with some wood and a pond that covered the left of the English camp.

The very evening that Haider had changed his camp, the English at the close of day struck their tents; the news of which was quickly carried to Haider, and obliged him to keep his men to their arms all night. But the English contented themselves to pass the night in the open air; and at sun-rise they again set up their tents. This manoeuvre was repeated, for no positive reason that can be deduced, the four following nights, in spite of the frequent showers they were exposed to; and Haider, in consequence, fortified his camp with four large redoubts.

As the English camp was always surrounded with cavalry and light troops, as well on foot as on horseback, who had taken possession of all the passages, they could not receive provision and ammunition except from Tirnmale, where they had no other stores than rice. Their troops therefore suffered much, as Haider was well instructed by the capture of patmars or couriers passing between the army and Madras, and likewise by the reports of individuals.

The governor of Madras blamed General Smith for having given the soldiers their rations of arrack in money; saying that money being scarce, ought to be sparingly distributed, and that it would have been sufficient to have promised the men their due from the council of Madras. In a letter to the paymaster, he Blamed him for having refused to pay the troops their money in lieu of arrack, at the orders of the general; observing, that no one in the army can refuse obedience to the general, who is alone responsible for the consequences of his orders and dispositions. The governor likewise wrote to the doctor, who was commissary to the army, to continue to instruct him of all that passed, *etc.*

This knowledge of the inconvenience sustained by the English ought to have determined Haider to continue the plan of investing the army, and ravaging the country. The English, impatient, no doubt, and desirous of extricating themselves out of their disagreeable situation, either by a night attack or by removing their camp, began to march about ten at night, after having struck their tents as usual. Haider was soon informed of this unexpected march, by the repeated signals of rockets; and a short time after was apprized, that their course was directed to the camp of Nizam Daulla.

The news was extremely embarrassing to the Nawab. He had the best founded suspicions of a secret correspondence between Rocun Daulla and the English, and had sufficient reason to believe that Nizam himself had not the best intentions towards him. If Nizam was in concert with the English, his army, which was without defence on the side of his ally, was very much exposed to danger; and on the other hand, without considering the probability of actual treachery, if the English should attack Nizam, the little order that prevailed in his army might be dangerous to his own, where the fugitives would not fail to fly for shelter and protection. Having called a council in a small casemate where Haider usually slept, at the head of his camp, it was resolved, that his army should be in readiness to march and intercept the English in their course to Nizam's army; which it was easy to do, as they had no more than a league and a half of ground to pass, whereas the English had near six: and that in the mean time, the European commandant should march with all the irregular troops, and those dispersed in the country, to reach the front of the English army; and, by harassing them, retard their march, so that they might not be able to reach Nizam's army before daylight.

It was about one in the morning when this officer learned that the English army was advanced about three leagues on their way. He immediately assembled the greater part of the chiefs of the Caleros and Carnates, and commanded them to approach as near the English army as they could; extending themselves on their flank the whole length of the line, without fear of spreading themselves too much, and not to fire till within fifteen paces;—that they might fire at pleasure, though as quickly as possible, taking care every man to lie flat on the ground after making his discharge. This last piece of advice might have been spared; but it had its weight with them, as it was a tacit approbation of their manner of fighting.

They very exactly obeyed their orders; their approach, and the great extent of ground they covered, which was known to the English by the matches of their muskets, stopped the march of the English, and obliged them to call into the column the small detached parties that were on their flank, no doubt for fear they should be surrounded. The fire of the Caleros having commenced, the English, who ought to have despised them, faced about and answered by platoons, which made much noise, and did little mischief for the space of more than two hours, the Caleros returning their fire to the best of their abilities. An hour and half before day-break, the English marched to their left, and pitched another camp that was nearer Tirnmale, which covered their right; the bank of a large pond was on their left, and before them a mountain of considerable height (where they placed a battalion of Sepoys) and surrounded with rocks and underwood, impracticable for cavalry.

After reconnoitring the English camp, Haider raised his own, and took another station, that was within two leagues of theirs, and so situated as to prevent the enemy from attacking the army of Nizam, without first engaging himself.

Numerous Cavalry, Useless: By the new position of both armies, the numerous cavalry of the two Subas became still more useless and difficult to be supported; which induced Haider to attend to a piece of advice that had long been given him,—to send a large detachment from his army to take Godelour, an English factory two leagues from Pondicherry; and to return by following the sea coast as far as Madras, whose environs they were to ravage and lay waste: a step that could not fail in obliging the council to recall the army for their own defence, which would have produced the greatest discredit and real prejudice to the Company's affairs.

This detachment was on the point of departing, commanded by the European officer who gave the advice, and was assured of taking Godelour, from his intimate acquaintance with the place: but an English emissary, introduced into the camp of Haider, and who had acquired the confidence of Raza Saeb, ancient Nawab of Arcot, a man of a contracted understanding, and much given to suspicion and jealousy, took the advantage by means of this man, to make Haider believe, that the whole was no more than a contrivance of the French officer to return to Pondicherry with his troop, being recalled (as it-was insidiously affirmed) by the governor of that place.

If the answer of the governor of Pondicherry to the letters of the two Nawabs had been less precise, and had given some hope of assistance to them, as sound policy perhaps required, the imposture of the English emissary would have made no impression on the mind of Haider; and the commerce of Pondicherry would, by the ruin of Godelour, have been benefited by the lose of commerce the English would have sustained.

Haider Regarded French Officer: Haider had so much regard for the French officer who was to have commanded the expedition against Godelour, that he had caused the Nizam to grant him a jagir, or immediate fief of the empire, without any vassalship to the Nawab of Arcot, all the country along the coast between the rivers of Alemparvy and Divicoty, and a line drawn from one river to the other, touching and including Paniroti. The Paravana or patent recited, that this gift was made in return for the great services rendered to the empire by the said officer; and that it was without any other obligation than that of maintaining two hundred Europeans for the guard of the country, whose revenue was estimated at eight lacks of rupees; with a promise of enlargement of the territory, if it should prove less. Haider, and his son, as Nawab of Arcot, had confirmed and ratified this donation.

The French officer, who was firmly persuaded that the English and Mohammed Ali Khan would lose all the Nawabship of Arcot in this war, thought it expedient to profit by the favour of Haider, by obtaining a gift that would be so useful to his country. He did not wait till conquest had put that Nawab in possession of the territory; presuming, perhaps with reason, that he might not then be so generous. The investiture, which ought to have been a secret in the cabinet, was made public by the secretaries of Rocun Daulla, Divan and keeper of the great seal, who came in ceremony to compliment the officer, and receive his present on the occasion. This gift excited the jealousy of Raza Saeb and some others, and was doubtless one of the inducements that led Haider to suspect the French officer.

But, whatever may have been the cause, there is no doubt that Haider was fearful of suffering his Europeans to approach too near Pondicherry. He, therefore, informed the French officer, that as he could not then spare any infantry, it would be proper to defer the capture of Godelour till another opportunity; but that he would despatch a body of cavalry to destroy the country close up to the gates of Madras; " and as it is no more than a kind of course," said he, "and as my son has never yet had any command, it will be "doing him a great pleasure to give him charge of this operation, at "the head of five thousand horse." It may, perhaps, seem surprising that Haider should use so much address to make this officer acquiesce with a good grace in the substituting another general to the command of a detachment that had been promised him; but no prince can possess to greater advantage the art of softening his refusal;

so that he never appears to deny anything. In consequence of this conference, the young prince departed with his detachment; and advanced with so much speed and secrecy towards Madras, that the governor, Mohammed Ali Khan and his son, together with Colonel Call, and almost all the council, very narrowly escaped being taken in the country-house at the Company's garden.

Happily for them a small vessel, that by accident was opposite the garden, furnished them with the means of escaping, which otherwise would have been impossible. Their flight was so precipitate, that the governor did not stay for his hat and sword, which were taken by the soldiery, as well as the breakfast equipage; it being the custom at Madras to take the air every morning, and breakfast in the country.

The governor and his company would infallibly have been made prisoners, if a domestic of their French emissary in Haider's camp, sent expressly to apprise them of the incursion, had not arrived the very moment they were preparing to take their usual ride. The cavalry of Haider arrived full speed, and cut off their return to Madras: Mohammed Ali Khan, who alone took the high road, escaped being taken only by the swiftness of his horse.

If the governor had had the misfortune to have been taken, his own vanity and presumption would have been the cause: for his company had scarcely met, before a crowd of the country people ran past towards Fort St. George, crying *Maratha, Maratha*, the people of the coast never having, before the present war, experienced any incursions except from that nation.

The governor and other English, instead of paying arty attention to the cries of the fugitives, were much diverted with the circumstance. A second troop passing by, and some of the company observing that the business deserved attention, the governor answered, " The enemy's cavalry cannot "arrive here without first passing by fortresses where we have "garrisons, whose commandants would sent me advice: the terror "of these people is certainly a panic; and to put an end to it, I "will order the Chaubuc to the neat that comes to alarm us in "this manner." Every body applauded his discourse, according to the established custom of crying *Amin* to what is said by men in power. But in the instant arrived a crowd from St. Thomas, many of whom were wounded; they announced that the enemy were plundering that town. The whole company was seized with fear and had just time to save themselves by the sea-coast, in consequence of the advice so luckily given them.

While Tipu Sultan ravaged the environs of Madras, his father reconnoitred the English camp; which it was easy for him to do, without danger, from a plain on the top of a hill that commanded a view of the rocks and underwood we have described. The Nawab perceived that he could annoy a part of their camp with large cannon; and having taken his resolution, he caused his army to march the next day early, and conveying some large pieces of cannon to the top of the hill, he caused them to be pointed at the English camp, where they carried admirably well, and occasioned a kind of disorder and haste in striking and removing tents, *etc.*

Haider, delighted at having thus insulted the English, caused all his artillery, even the very smallest pieces, to be drawn up the hill for the purpose of making a vain parade, though the greater part of the balls could never reach the English. He imagined he should give the enemy a high idea of his forces, and intimidate them by shewing them all this artillery, and the vivacity and spirit it was worked with; and, in order that his intention might be answered, he encouraged the soldiers himself, by giving abundance of gold and silver money to the cannoneers of those pieces that appeared to be best served:—all which was matter of derision and laughter to the English; and, in reality, answered no other purpose than that of frightening the feathered inhabitants of the underwood that grew on the hill-side.

Exercise of Artillery by Haider: While Haider thus exercised his artillery, and kept his infantry in parade, his cavalry galloped about the plain to almost as little effect as the discharge of the greatest part of artillery.

Nizam, who did not think proper on this occasion to be an idle spectator, had marched with his army, nearly at the same time as his ally, and caused his cavalry to parade round the English camp; but about three in the afternoon, with his whole infantry, he attacked the Sepoys that General Smith had posted on the mountain. To defend themselves against this attack, the Sepoys were obliged to take position that exposed them to the artillery of Haider: seeing themselves obliged to give way, they made several signals to General Smith, who marched to their assistance with his whole army.

It was near four in the evening when his columns were observed to march out, Haider immediately caused his artillery and infantry to descend from the hill, and recalled his cavalry, in order to face the English with his whole force. His troops were scarcely drawn up, in order to march before the whole infantry of Nizam was seen in the most precipitate flight and disorder; while his cavalry appeared to advance bravely and in good order against the English, followed by his artillery; but instead of extending itself in the plain, to the left of Haider, the troop placed itself between the English and his army so as entirely to mask it from their sight.

The English advanced along the banks of the pond near the mountain, marching on ground covered with stones and shurbs, whose branches being very flexible, are no great inconvenience for infantry. They were formed into two columns, having their cavalry in their rear, and their artillery in front, which firing on the cavalry, caused them to give way, and in a short time put them to flight full speed by the shortest way, which happened to be through the camp of Haider, across which they drove, spreading terror and disorder as they went.

Haider perceiving the flight of Nizam and all his army, found himself exceedingly embarrassed, as he had every reason to suspect some treachery: he was likewise apprehensive, that, while he fought with the English, his camp would be plundered by the fugitives; and the approach of night added to the trouble that employed his thoughts. When the dispersion of Nizam's army had left the English army uncovered, it was seen advancing in one full line, with the cavalry in reserve.

The artillery of Haider, distributed along the front of his infantry, made a few discharges which must have slain a number of the enemy: but as the ridiculous cannonade from the top of the hill had exhausted his ammunition, his great guns soon became useless to him; the cavalry that formed the two wings having received orders to charge, the right wing, where the hussars and dragoons were made several charges, and advanced within pistol-shot, but could never stand against the fire of the English artillery and musketry. The left wing, for some unknown reason, made only one charge, and afterwards kept at a sufficient distance from the fire.

Haider seeing very little hope of beating the English, who had the advantage of artillery, and the night closing in being in favour of their infantry; yielded the field of battle and retreated in good order; the Nawab himself forming the rear-guard at the head of hism cavalry. He withdrew his army into their camp, without leaving the English any mark of their victory, except one of the iron three-pounders they themselves had lost before whose oxen were killed, and might have been easily replaced by the oxen from the empty ammunition waggons, if Haider would have consented.

No Prisoners English Made: The English made no prisoners, except a Portuguese officer of the Topasses, who, being wounded was given to be carried by four of his soldiers, and thrown by them into a ditch; and a Pandari, who was likewise wounded, all the other wounded were brought off. The number of killed in the army of the two Subas did not exceed four hundred men. The English followed Haider to his camp; but his situation between two mountains a large pond, and two redoubts, between which they must have passed, prevented them from thinking of the attack.

They contented themselves with firing some cannon across the pond, none of which reached the camp; and passed the night in the open air, a good cannon shot distant from the redoubts. Upon the arrival of Haider in his camp, he found it in confusion; the greater part of the servants and other people in the suite of the army, terrified at the flight of Nizam and his troops, having ran off, leaving the camp all standing.

After placing his infantry in the redoubts, and behind a retrenchment hastily thrown up, he ordered all his heavy artillery and baggage to march: the execution of this order was attended with great difficulty. Haider has a particular talent in choosing places where his camp can be in security, as well from the nature of the ground, as from the defences that art can add; in which particular he has gained the praises of general Smith, who himself possesses this talent in a superior degree.

The continual wars of Haider with the Marathas, who are far superior to him in cavalry, have no doubt obliged him to make it a particular study of the art of encamping in advantageous positions, which are without number in his dominions; all the country being intersected by mountains and valleys, and covered with towns, fortresses, ponds and woods. But he has the fault of not projecting easy sorties to his camps; though the inconveniences have been often represented to him, especially on the occasion of the retreat after the battle of Tirnmale; his camp having no other way out behind, but by a pass filled with rocks and underwood, through which was a winding, narrow road, scarcely practicable for a single carriage. This road was very soon choked up by the number of beasts of burthen, whose owners had anticipated the order for raising the camp.

The pass was divided into two, one leading to the camp of Nizam: all the baggage marched at their own discretion; a considerable number took the right-hand road and crossed the immense baggages of Nizam's army, that marched in the greatest disorder, intermixed with artillery. The consequence of all this disorder was, a stoppage that prevented the march of Haider's artillery, in spite of all the pains that were taken to get forward by the light of more than a hundred torches; for, as they compelled the loaded beasts to walk on the borders or the road, they fell and overthrew their burthens; which occasioned cries and a dreadful tumult, the noise being repeated by the mountains: so that nothing better could be done than to despatch some troops to stop the march, and give orders for every one to remain where he was till morning.

When the day appeared, regularity was soon restored, as Nizam's army was already in the plain. If General Smith had detached a small party of his infantry, by a circuit of two leagues, they might have entered the camp of Nizam; and by a few shots among the fugitives and conductors of baggage, they might have occasioned so much disorder, as would have rendered the consequences of the victory of the greatest importance; for, though he met with no molestation after his defeat, he left seven or eight pieces of large cannon in his camp: Haider caused the carriages to be repaired, and sent them to him with the harness. Even the silver plate, and other valuable effects of Nizam, were found in the roads.

Appeared of Haider at Day-break: Haider, instead of imitating the cowardice of Nizam, appeared at day-break with his troops drawn up in order of battle, at the entrance of his camp: all his infantry being in the first line, and part of his cavalry in the second. In this position he made the English respect him. When his artillery and baggage had gained the plain, he retired with his army, himself forming the rear-guard with his grenadiers, who did not quit that post of honour to the cavalry, till after the whole army had reached the plain.

The English, who followed them, durst not make any attack, but fired a few cannon, which slew four men, including a quarter-master of dragoons, who was struck by the last rebound of a ball.

It will readily be supposed, that General Smith hastened to forward the news of this victory to Madras, which extricated the government of that settlement out of the most tormenting embarrassment. The unexpected incursion of Haider's son had thrown them into the greatest consternation; the garrison of Fort St. George consisted only of two hundred Europeans, and six hundred Sepoys; so that the Black Town, which is property the town of Madras, was at the discretion of Tipu Sultan, a youth of eighteen.

This town contains a great number of inhabitants, not less than four hundred thousands according to the English calculation; and their number was then vastly augmented by the fugitives from the country. Though it bears the name of the Black Town, it is inhabited by great numbers of Europeans of all nations, who have warehouses furnished with the richest products of every country. Among others, there is a large colony of very rich Armenians, possessed of immense riches; and great numbers of Gujaratis, or wealthy bankers, dealers in pearls, precious stones, and coral: in short, this town is always one of the richest emporiums in the world.

The terror that spread itself among this immense population, when they saw the fugitives from the country enter, was so great, that they imagined the whole army of Haider, headed by himself in person, was on the point of entering the town. Men, women, and children, all ran to take refuge in Fort St. George, abandoning their houses and all they possessed. As the governor, counsellors, commandant, *etc.*, were not yet arrived, no one gave orders to shut the gates; so that in a short time the fort was crowded with a multitude of people, that filled the streets, the ditches, and even covered the glacis.

The governor, on his arrival, could with difficulty force a passage to his house; where he entirely lost all fortitude, and remained two days with his head resting on a table, suffering Colonel Call, the chief engineer, and a man of abilities, to take the charge of everything. This gentleman did his utmost; but has since confessed, that Haider's son had entered the Black Town, and pursued the fugitives, nothing could have prevented his taking Fort St. George. But this young prince was without experience; and his cavalry having approached the Black Town by the road from St. Thomas, passed of necessity under the cannon of the fort, a few discharges of which served to impose on him.

Tipu Sultan convened a council, where the advice of the grand almoner, who had been sent with him in quality of Mentor, was, that it was not proper to run the risk of entering the Black Town: but that the orders of Haider ought strictly to be followed, namely, to ravage the environs of Madras: and more particularly, not to hazard the life of the prince by exposing him to the cannon of Fort St. George, or any other fortress. Every one was obliged to submit to this opinion, which, it may be affirmed, was the cause of saving the English, and other inhabitants of Madras, the sum of more than one hundred millions of French money, that might have been lost to them by burning the Black Town, or forcing the governor and council to accept of peace on the hardest terms, by threatening them with this consequence.

The Author of these Memoirs had advised Haider to besiege and take the Black Town of Madras, and to burn it; though he did not imagine the thing to be so easy; yet his advice was partly the cause why he did not accompany the young prince, for fear of exposing him; and it is this advice alone that was the ground of the prosecutions of Governor B—against him, as well as the foundation of a legal process, in which no other evidence was brought than that of the English spies, who affirmed that they heard him give it. But this proceeding, contrary to every notion of justice and the laws of nations, was an ordinary act of that despotism the English have arrogated and exercised in India.

No Damage to Madras: Though the town of Madras suffered no damage, because Colonel Call, having armed all the Europeans he could collect, despatched some Sepoys and volunteers to defend the entrance of the Black Town, who prevented the pillagers from approaching; yet the damage sustained by the English was, nevertheless, very considerable. They have superb houses in the neighbourhood of Madras, richly furnished: and all the villages, which are very numerous and full of people, are inhabited by painters and manufacturers of every kind, who were all pillaged, or affirmed they were in order to take advantage of not restoring the works that were entrusted in their hands, or paid for in advance.

An English merchant named *Debonnaire,* of French extraction, was the only one of the inhabitants of Madras who did not suffer by the ravages made by Haider's troops round that city: not by way of gratitude for the services he had done Mahfuz Khan the friend of Haider; but by the effect of chance, which led Chaki Shah, grand almoner of Haider, and his real friend, to fix his residence in the country house of this merchant, which was situated at St. Thomas's Mount, a league and a half from Madras. On the appearance of Haider's cavalry seen from the mount, the servants of Mr. Debonnaire made their escape, with his children; leaving all the moveables and effects to the mercy of the enemy.

The situation of the house was agreeable to Chaki Shah, who chose it for his residence during the time Tipu Sultan remained in the environs of Madras. On his entering the house, he told the gardeners that he was a man of peace, and that his presence would secure the house from insult. He forbade his people either to take or spoil the smallest thing; and having assured himself that his orders were not infringed, he inquired the name of the proprietor, and sent one of his gardeners, accompanied by one of his own people, to carry him his children's clothes, with traits and herbs; assuring him that nothing in his house should be either damaged or stolen, but that he himself would overlook the gardeners, and see they did their duty; and would take care to send him the necessary produce of his garden every day, which he punctually performed.

The young prince, in a visit to the grand almoner, was desirous of taking a microscope; but that nobleman would not consent, but wrote to Mr. Debonnaire to set a price upon the instrument; and it was not till he had received the merchant's second letter, that he consented to offer it as a present, on his part, to the prince.

The fugitives from the environs of Madras having spread themselves all over the coast, carried the news of the capture of that town by Haider; and it came to Europe by the way of Pondicherry, Tranquebar, and the other European settlements. The caravans, and every possible conveyance, distributed this news with pleasure; for the jealousy and hatred that other nations have conceived against the English, smothered the account they themselves had given of their victory at Tirnmale.

The consequence was, that the price of the Company's stock, at London, fell at once from 275 to 222. General Smith, to convey the news of his victory with readiness and expedition to Madras, despatched a courier mounted on a dromedary, who, instead of avoiding the troops of Haider, addressed himself to them to demand news of the Prince, saying, that he was charged by his father to inform him of the loss of the battle at Tirnmale, and to order him to rejoin him. By means of this stratagem he succeeded in gaining access to the town of Madras, though the Prince was not above half a league distant. The governor, on receipt of General Smith's letters, announced the victory to the people by one hundred and one guns; and distributed the most exaggerated accounts of the advantages gained over Haider.

The young prince, astonished at so unexpected an event, consulted his council, who unanimously advised him to rejoin the armies of the Subas as early as possible; which he executed in good order, carrying with him four monks, and a priest, grand vicar of the Bishop of St. Thomas, who was then at Pondicherry.

On the reputation of Haider's lenity, these priests did not think proper to follow the example of the other inhabitants of St. Thomas, by abandoning their habitations. But as Haider had recommended to his son to bring away some person of distinction, who might instruct him concerning the forces of the English, and the succours they expected from Europe or elsewhere—for want of more important personages, he engaged these monks to accompany him; and conducted them with all possible care and attention, though by a disagreeable carriage, having caused them to mount two and two on the backs of camels, a beast whose pace is very fatiguing.

Their journey having lasted five days, they arrived worn out with fatigue, and in the most deplorable condition, especially the Jesuits, who wore their square bonnets, and who, to retain this headdress, and at the same time to defend themselves from the heat of the sun, bad been under the necessity of wrapping their heads in painted silks given them for that purpose.

Battle of Tirnmale: The battle of Tirnmale happening in the month of November, which is in the rainy season in that part of India where the theatre of war then was, General Smith thought proper to send his army to quarters, as they had already suffered greatly. He distributed it into Vellore, Arcot, Cangivaromarni, Gingi, *etc.*, after having strongly garrisoned Tirnmale, Vaniambari, Ambour, and other advanced places.

The loss of the battle of Tirnmale, though of so little importance, spread itself over all Hindustan with the greatest rapidity, and was variously related, according to the dispositions of the narrators. Haider was very little concerned at an event that he attributed solely to the fault of Nizam, whose alliance, instead of producing advantage, was a real burthen to him.

Nizam, on his side, perceiving that the conquest of the country of Arcot was by no means so near a conclusion as he had flattered himself, was desirous of returning to his own dominions; but he was desirous first of extorting money from Haider, as well as from the English and Mohammed Ali Khan. The different motives and intentions of the two Subas augmented the distrust that was between them; but, instead of its becoming apparent, they were both careful to redouble the public testimonials of mutual friendship Nizam Daulla, on the return of Tipu Sultan, invited Haider, and all the great men of his court, to a superb festival. He rendered the highest honours to that sovereign; and, among other things, caused him to sit on a kind of throne or sofa of massive gold, with cushions of cloth of gold, which he presented him with in the evening, when they parted. He likewise paid the highest respect and honour to Tipu Sultan, and bestowed honourable titles on several of the retinue who were most in Haider's favour.

A few days after, Nizam was invited by Haider in his turn; but, instead of causing him to sit on a thrown of wrought gold, a sofa was prepared with sacks of star pagodas and gold muhars, covered with fine carpets and cushions of velvet, with a gold ground—all which was likewise presented to him on his departure. It is agreed, at this last interview, that the two armies should separate, and that Nizam should return to his own dominions. This separation was not, however, to take place till after Haider had taken possession of Vaniambari and Ambour, which he had resolved to besiege. It was likewise settled that Haider should continue the war against Mohammed Ali Khan and the English; and that Nizam should attack the English on the Masulipattam, to oblige them to divide their forces.

To show the intimacy between Haider and his family, as well as his manner of conducting himself with respect to his relations, it will not be amiss to describe an interview he had with his mother about his time. This lady, who in quality of queen-mother has the right of commanding in the seraglio or palace, having received information of the check her son had experienced, and which, no doubt, she supposed more considerable than it really was, departed from Haider Nagar to see her son in the army, notwithstanding the inconvenience of travelling a hundred and fifty leagues in the rainy season. She made long journies, and arrrived at the camp in a few days. When the Nawab, who had been apprized of the queen's departure, was informed of her approach, he left the camp with his whole army, in Savari, or parade.

The army met the head of the queen's retinue at a league distance from the camp, at which time they halted; and Haider and his sons advanced alone on horseback, till they had joined the palanquin of their mother, which was close, and covered with muslin. They inclined as low as they could on their horses; and, placing themselves on the right and left of the palanquin, the lady continued her journey, guarded by her son and grandsons, and followed by the whole retinue of Haider. She passed through the middle of Haider's army, who saluted her as if she had been the prince himself.

The retinue of Haider's mother consisted of about two hundred ladies, mounted on horses; they were enveloped in large pieces of thick muslin, which prevented even the smallest part of their clothes from been seen. They all went before the palanquin of the queen-mother, which was followed by eight carriages, covered with scarlet cloth, and drawn by large Persian oxen. There were likewise ten elephants, and a great number of camels and beasts of burthen. Some European horsemen proceeded the women, and marched on one side. All the retinue was surrounded by about six hundred lancemen, having feathers and bells to their lances; and the horsemen who preceded and followed the retinue were about four hundred in number.

It is said that when this lady was conducted into her tent, Haider inquired what could have induced her to make so long a journey, especially at a time when continual rains rendered the roads almost impracticable; and that she answered—"I was desirous, my, "son, of seeing how you bear the ill-fortune you have sustained. "The prince having replied—"That if heaven should put him to no "greater trial, he should find no difficulty in supporting it." "Very "well, then," replied she, "since that is the case, I give thanks to "God, and shall immediately return, that I may be no impediment to "your operations. " Two days after, this lady, having wished her son every kind of prosperity, departed, accompanied by her son and grandsons, to the place where they had met her.

Encampment of Haider's Army: The first place of encampment of Haider's army, after the battle of Trinmale, was at Singueman. After having rested two days, they passed the Paler, which was much swelled by the rains, and encamped in a plain five leagues distant from Kaveripattam, and six from Vaniambari. It was in this camp that Tipu Sultan rejoined the army, that the Subas formed their last treaty, and that Haider received the visit of his mother.

The second day after the departure of that lady, the army marched towards Vaniambari: the cavalry and the greatest part of the infantry arrived in good time to reconnoitre the place, which was found susceptible of being approached by favour of the water, hedges, and trees, without the necessity of opening the trenches. For the purpose of the attack, a garden was chosen, in the midst of the inundation, upon a rising ground, an which was constructed, the same night, a battery of twelve pieces of cannon.

As this place is not more than three-quarters of a league from the pass that leads to Vellore, a body of troops, with artillery, were sent to take possession of the same. The commandant of Europeans being slightly wounded Haider would not permit him to attend the works during the night but insisted on his going to repose in his tent, while he himself undertook to superintend the workmen. In consequence of this determination, he passed the night in the battery, seated at the foot of a tree, in spite of the dampness and frequent rain—exposed to the balls and shot that killed many workmen and officers near him—and diverting every one by his pleasantries, till the return of the commandant permitted him to retire.

The battery began to fire about six in the morning, and though the service of the cannon was attended with much difficulty, the English fire was soon silenced, and Captain R— commander of the place, displayed the white flag, and sent Mr. D—, his second in command, to treat about a capitulation. This gentleman, being conducted to the European commandant, demanded the same terms as had been granted to the garrison at Kaveripattam. After much altercation, on the repeated orders of Haider to refuse nothing, the required terms were granted, on condition that the commander of the place, and the other European officers and soldiers, should not serve against Haider for the space of a year.

When these conditions were agreed on, Mr. D—, much chagrined at not being treated so favourably as he desired, demanded that Haider should affix his seal to the capitulation. Haider, being advised that the conference was broken off, and the officer was about to return to his place, came forward, and seating himself by the European commandant, upon a cannon, addressed himself to the English deputy: "I am not," said he, "commander of the siege. You demand my seal: I have not my great "seal here; but to put an end to all difficulties, I give my small seal "into the hands of my commandant:" and pulling his ring from his finger, he gave it to the commanding officer of artillery, saying— "Make what use of this you think proper."

The officer made an impression with it at the bottom of the capitulation; and this dispute of self-importance was thus, by the good sense of Haider, put an end to.

The garrison of this place consisted of one thousand Sepoys and thirty Europeans: fourteen iron cannon, that had been dismounted for the most part by the cannon of the besiegers, composed all the artillery. Besides these cannon, that were found by the English in the place, two other pieces belonging to the regiment of Sepoys were taken. The place made no great resistance, though it was well provided with ammunition and stores, though there was no breach, and a sufficient number of workmen to repair the carriages: but we have already hinted at the reasons that induced the commandants of these places to make so little resistance.

After placing a good garrision in Vaniambari, the army marched towards Ambour, a place famous for the battle gained by the French, and the troops of Mouza Ferring and Canada Saeb, against Unvarudeen Khan, father of Mahfuz Khan and Mohammed Ali Khan, who lost his life, at the age of eighty-two years, on the third day of the battle, after having repelled the enemy from his retrenchments for two successive days. This place, in which the English had amassed considerable quantities of ammunition and stores, together with artillery, muskets, uniforms, and tents, is composed of three different fortifications, inclosed the one within the other.

The first is the citadel, situated on a mountain of the most difficult access, on account of its steepness on all sides. This extensive fortress is capable of containing a numerous garrison, with all the necessary stores, not excepting even beasts of every kind: two very large basons, cut in the rock, contain much more water than it is possible to consume from one rainy season to another: and lastly, the ramparts are constructed with such strength and firmness, that for this reason, as well as the elevation of the mountain, very large cannon, and much time, would be required to make a breach.

At the foot of the citadel, and on the only accessible side, is a fort, which the English have strengthened by the addition of palisaded covered way, and a glacis: and lastly, a town of considerable magnitude incloses the fort, defended by a brick wall, with round bastions, and a dry ditch. Half the town is covered from any attack by a large pond; at the end of which the English have constructed a redoubt, which closed the road that led between the pond and the river, and commanded the road on the other side between the river and a high mountain.

As soon as the army had encamped about a league distant from Vaniambari, on the banks of the river they had passed at Vaniambari Haider went, the very same evening, to reconnoitre the town, in spite of a very heavy rain, that was partly the cause of his being in great danger; for, having advanced to the border of the pond, he found himself unexpectedly opposed to the cannon of the redoubt, which was masked by trees, and the end of the bank of the pond. This artillery, which consisted of three large pieces, made a discharge that killed fifteen horses, and covered Haider with blood, and the limbs of the unfortunate men that were slain. Notwithstanding this accident, Haider continued to reconnoitre the approaches; and resolved to cross the river again with his army, to encamp on the other side of the town; where he should be in a position equally advantageous for the security of his camp, and for prosecuting the seige of Ambour, which would be blocked up by his camp on the side of Vellore and Sattgheri and by the army of Nizam on the side of Vanimbari and Ventigheri.

In consequence of this resolution, the army traversed the river during the night, and passed under the fire of the redoubt before the break of day; so that a few stragglers among the valets and settlers were the only persons that suffered.

Encamped of Haider's Army: Between the river that flows on the side where Haiders army was encamped, and a chain of mountains that extend from Ambour to Sattgheri, is a plain about three leagues in length, and of an unequal breadth, from half to three-quarters of a league. One extremity of this is entirely shut up by the town of Ambour, the redoubt and the river. This part of the town, whose approach was much favoured by fields of a kind of millet, then very high, was judged capable of being taken by storm, without making any breach. Orders were consequently given to prepare ladders of bamboo: but as it was thought that the garrison, which was numerous, might make resistance, the grandiers and best infantry were ordered to make the attack.

The order of attack being settled, the chiefs of each corps were conducted, in open day, to reconnoitre those places they were destined to march against; and at the close of the evening, after supper, the troops spread themselves in the plain, carrying their ladders, and posted themselves opposite that part of the town they were to assault; with orders to lie down, and wait in silence for the concerted signal. Cannon were likewise conducted into some deserted houses, that formed a village in the midst of a great number of trees, fronting the part nearest the river; from whence it was judged they might favour the attack, by enfilading the rampart.

The English, who could not be ignorant of these preparations, as they were openly made, appeared very busy during the whole night; and kept a great firing on the village, whose houses they shot through, and through, without killing more than one man. They continually threw out fire-pots and fosses, to discover the manoeuvres of the assailants; but while the night lasted, Haider's troops remained at their ease. At the break of day they advanced in good order from all parts, carrying their ladders, with drums beating and colours flying, till they came to the edge of the ditch, into which they descended.

They mounted the walls and bastions so quickly, that Haider's colours were hoisted on the ramparts immediately after, in spite of the cannon and musketry of the enemy, which was not very sharp; whether it be that the commandant of the place did not think proper to make a longer resistance, or whether the English had retired, supposing the escalade would not take place. Some men were at first seen on the bastions; but the cannon placed in the village, or perhaps their fears, drove them away ; for the grenadiers in ascending found them abandoned, and immediately proceeded to plunder the town.

Some of them having ventured to pursue the fugitives as far as the glacis of the fort, found themselves exposed to a cannonade that destroyed considerable numbers; others were slain in the streets by the cannon of the fort and citadel, which obliged them to stretch curtains across the street, and to cut passages through the houses. Among those who were slain in this attack, was the brave and generous Caki Shah, Peerzada, or grand almoner, who was running from house to house, according to his laudable custom, to prevent the soldiers from committing any act of cruelty.

Haider himself formed the project of this attack by day; and conducted the left wing of his troops in person, on horseback, with his sabre drawn, to the edge of the ditch.

At the beginning of the night an English gunner, a deserter, gave information that the garrison of the fort would retreat into the citadel that night, and that they were employed in carrying off the most valuable effects, and destroying the rest. The commandant of Europeans proposed to Haider, immediately to attack the fort with all the grenadiers; having the Europeans, as well horsemen as gunners, at their head.

This being agreed to, every preparation for the attack was made in an hour; and at eight o'clock the troops sallied forth through the streets, and leaping into the covered way, scaled the fort, which the English made haste to abandon; however, they could not do this so quickly but that twenty five sepoys, an officer, and six Europeans were taken prisoners two of the latter being wounded.

The English had thrown a large quantity of cartouches into a pond in the middle of the fort, and had caused a fire to be made in the *place darmes* for the purpose of burning the uniforms, a considerable quantity of which were saved. The besiegers found eighteen brass cannon designed for field service, three thousand firelocks, a great quantity of shot, bullets, and gun-flints, and a considerable stock of rice and flour. There were likewise store-houses filled with tents, chests, and effects belonging, or intended to be sold, to the army; which was very acceptable plunder for the soldiers; and might easily have been saved, as Captain C—, commandant of the place, was in a situation to have defended the fort a very long time, his garrison being numerous, and well provided both with artillery and ammunition.

The Facility Met to Haider: The facility Haider met with in taking all the English places he attacked, encouraged him to undertake the siege of Ambour; though he had received advice, that the English were marching from all parts to assemble at Vellore. Firm and determined in his smallest resolutions, he refused to follow the prudent advice that was given him, to repair immediately to Vellore; as he easily might in a single march, the distance from Ambour being only ten leagues. At this last place he would have been in the centre of the English quarters, which were dispersed for more than forty leagues round, and might have prevented them from uniting; a step of so much the more consequence, as the English at Madras had lately received a reinforcement of troops from Bengal, which the position of Haider's army, at Vellore, would have prevented them from joining the other troops.

The difficulty taking the citadel of Ambour, which we have described as being situated on a steep mountain, was rendered much greater to Haider, by the circumstances of his being without either bombs or mortars. The ditches of the town, serving in some respects as trenches, favoured the approaches; and many guns were mounted in a short time, though with the loss of the best gunners, who were uncovered from head to foot, by reason of the elevation of the castle. Haider allowed but one night for constructing the batteries, and consequently the parapet could not be made of the requisite height and thickness, till after the loss of many brave men. Cannon were planted on a mountain that overlooked the citadel; but the English, in two days, erected a bulwark on that part of the citadel exposed to the ricochet, or rolling shot of the cannon, which rendered them absolutely useless. The great distance between the two places prevented the firing in battery from the mountain; so that after seventeen days' siege, with the loss of many Europeans, and much powder and ball, the work was no more advanced than at first, In this state of affairs news arrived that the English army was assembled at Vellore, and was preparing to march and raise the siege.

On this intelligence Haider took the resolution of anticipating the enemy, and retreated. The redoubt we have spoken of being entirely cut off from all communication with the fort by the escalade of the city, its garrison consisting of one hundred Sepoys, six European cannoneers, and an English serjeant, who commanded, was obliged to surrender at discretion. A number of irregular troops being introduced, at the close of the day, into the city and fort, who climbed up the sides of the mountain, and fired upon the guards—the cannon was drawn off under favour of this noise; and at midnight, an hour before the rising of the moon, all the troops quitted the trenches, and marched to join the rest of the army that had left their camp, at the beginning of night, and repaired to another on the road to Vaniambari. On the following day the army marched, and encamped on the banks of the river of Vaniambari; its right wing bearing against that fortress, and its front directed towards Ambour.

This retreat of Haider was the signal of Nizam's separation from him, that Suba retiring into the country of Curpa. The same day that Haider pitched his camp at Vaniambari, General

Smith arrived at Ambour with his army, consisting 28,000 men, of which 500 were English; for the Bengal reinforcement consisted of six hundred Europeans, and six thousand Sepoys, very much superior in appearance to the Sepoys of Madras, and esteemed by the English as the best infantry in India.

The English general allowed his troops a short time for repose and left Ambour on the very evening of his arrival directing his march to Vaniambari.

Haider was so confident that the English would not come to seek him, that he did not take the usual precaution of despatching advanced guards of cavalry and light troops on the side of the enemy. There were no other than large bodies of cavalry on the other side of the river, about half a league from the camp; and two redoubts, raised about one hundred paces from the same bank, on an eminence, that served as posts for the advanced guards of infantry. Each of these redoubts mounted two pieces of cannon: and it was not till seven in the morning that the approach of the enemy was known by the cannon of the redoubts, that gave the signal of alarm; at the same instant that the arrival of the horseman put the fact out of doubt.

That which induced Haider to suppose the English would not pass Ambour, a town on his frontier, was, his having dispatched propositions of peace to the army and to Madras. The bearer of these proposals was an Englishman, formerly factor or consul at Carvac.

As the chief preliminary was, that everything should remain in *status quo* (an offer so much the more convenient, as neither party had any restitution to make; all the places formerly taken by the English being recaptured, and Haider having evacuated the dominions of the English, or of Mohammed Ali Khan) he did not doubt of their being accepted. This mediator had promised to send advice, as early as possible, whether he had any hopes of succeeding in his mission. But General Smith, who had his instructions and his projects, did not think himself at liberty to suspend his operations, though he was of opinion that peace would be advantageous to his nation. The Englishman continued his journey to Madras, without sending back advice according to his instructions. On his arrival at Madras, he found the governor and council recovered of their fright, and elated With the hopes of success from certain intrigues they were carrying on. In this disposition they treated him as a young man, and derided his propositions; but the consequences gave them sufficient reason to repent.

On the news of the enemy's approach, Haider put himself at the head of the piquets of cavalry, and passed the river; after giving orders to strike the camp, to draw up the infantry in order of battle, and to march the heavy artillery the baggage to Kaveripattam; at the same time commanding his brother Mughdum to follow him with all the cavalry.

The Nawab advanced as far as the redoubts. The enemy appeared in good order, coming forward in three columns of infantry: their whole cavalry formed the rear-guard in a single line, except two hundred English dragoons who rode before the columns.

Drawing off Cannon of the Redoubts: The first care of this sovereign was to draw off the cannon of the redoubts, and cause the advanced guards of infantry to rejoin the rest of the army; and as he observed that the enemy continued to advance, he himself repassed the river, leaving Mughdum Ali Khan at the head of a large body of cavalry, and the commandant of Europeans at the head of the hussars and dragoons, with orders to observe the march of the enemy, and to harries them even so far as to attack the head of their columns; with the intention of causing them to slacken or stop their march, that Haider's army might have time to retire.

This cavalry, with the dragoons and hussars at their head, hastened to attack the enemy's columns to the centre and the left, which appeared in a situation to come up with Haider's army the soonest; because the column to the right was on an eminence, and could not pass the river without defiling, as the banks were very steep.

The European cavalry were advancing full trot to attack the centre, when several cannon discharged from the right-hand column on their flank, killed two horses; one of which was that of the commandant of Europeans, who falling, found himself immediately surrounded by the English dragoons, and abandoned by his own, through the treachery of the greater number, who, together with their officers, gave themselves up to the English.

The French commandant, in falling, received a contusion on the buttock and thigh, that formed an absecss; in the cure of which he kept his bed three months at Madras. This desertion slopped the Indian cavalry, who returned and General Smith ordered his army immediately to halt, suffering Haider's army to retreat unmolested. A few shots were fired at some cavalry that came to reconnoitre his army, that remained on the same ground till evening, because his equipage could not arrive sooner; at which time he turned back, and encamped on the road to Ambour, about half a league distant from the river.

It is impossible to exceed the politeness and respect that General Smith shewed to his prisoner, the French commandant. He caused him to sleep in his own tent; and informed him, than he march of his army had no other purpose than that of favouring the desertion of the Europeans, which was expected to be much more considerable, in consequence of a plot that had long been carried on, and which they were apprehensive could be no longer concealed.

The honour and integrity that the writer of these Memoirs has adhered to in the relation of the facts they contain, do not allow him to pass over in silence the odious plots that were made use of, in order to execute this infamous piece of treachery.

Capture of Kaveripattam and After Math: After the capture of Kaveripattam the permission was given to an adventurer, a surgeon by profession, to retire to the coast of Coromandel, taking the advantage of going in company with some English officers, who had been taken in that place. This permission was, no doubt, a great indiscretion; but as the proverb says, we can never think of everything; and there was, besides, a wish to get rid of a worthless man, from whom there was no reason to fear any thing. Nothing less than an unforeseen chain of circumstances could have given him the power of doing mischief.

This surgeon came to Haider at Coimbatore, where he announced himself as Chevalier de St. Louis, and ancient captain of artillery, travelling to Pondicherry. He found credit with the commandant of Haider's Europeans, to whom he addressed himself; because he had been recommended to that officer by the chief of the French factory at Calicut, who, in forwarding European news, added, *These things may be depended on, as they come from good hands: I have them from M. le Chevalier de, who is arrived from Europe by the caravans, and is on his way to Pondicherry, etc.*

This commandant did not indulge a doubt respecting the good qualities of the chevalier, who, together with the cross he had the audacity to bear, possessed likewise, to the misfortune of many, an engaging and seductive exterior. On this false appearance of candour and rectitude, the commandant of Europeans received him in the best manner, and presented him to Haider, who gave him the command of a battalion of Sepoys, with appointments to the value of £50 per month. The man was absolutely without common necessaries; and the French commandant supplied him with lodging, subsistence, a carriage, and every thing becoming a gentleman.

After these services, it may naturally be supposed that he would have felt the utmost gratitude and regard for his benefactor: but, on the contrary, his perfidy and want of principle were such, that in less than three months he was dismissed from all his employs. Being on the point of being reduced to beggary, he had the confidence to request permission to exercise his business a a surgeon. This request was made by the mediation of Haider's surgeon, who had been a fellow-soldier with him in Lally's regiment, and had recollected him perfectly on his arrival; though, at the request of the other, he did not expose him.

Our gentleman, thus becoming a surgeon, found himself to be a Chevalier de Christ, by the assistance of a cross that served every purpose; it was however a real cross of St. Louis, that side being untouched on which are the sword and laurel crown, with the motto *Bellica virtutis preamium;* but on the other, the enamel that represents St. Louis was taken off and a small cross substituted in its place.

He affirmed that he had caused this cross to be made in this manner when in Portugal in order to give it a French appearance. However he was forbade to wear it; but he adorned himself by an embroidery on his clothes, that was permitted him. A specimen of his usual tricks having procured him to be confined, he obtained his enlargement by means of his comrade with leave to repair to the coast of Coromandel, in company of some English officers who were to return to Madras.

Our adventurer spoke good English, and undertook to court the favour of Captain M—, by a string of narrations to which that gentleman either gave credit or pretended to do so. Among other things, he told him that all the Europeans in Haider's service, who constituted his chief force, were much disgusted with the service they were engaged in and still more with their commandant; and that if the government of Madras would employ him, he would engage to cause them all to desert; in the execution of which project, his friend, the surgeon of the Nawab, would engage to lend every assistance in his power.

Discovery of a Method to Turn Madras Administration: The English officer, charmed at the discovery of a method of turning the attention of the Madras administration from the cowardly defence he had made, presented our chevalier to Colonel Call, engineer in chief, and a man of great influence in the council. He had great abilities; but, considering the extent of his mind, he was blameable for attending more to the purpose or end he aimed at, than to the difficulties that might prevent his arriving at it. This colonel, who, like many others, was bigoted to the opinion that the Indians can do nothing without the help of the Europeans in their service, was delighted with the project of the chevalier; and presented him to the governor and Mohammed Ali Khan, by whom he was received as a guardian angel.

Thus it was that this man, from being a surgeon driven out of Haider's camp, suddenly found himself the friend and confidant of the governor and Mohammed Ali Khan. He was nobly entertained, and loaded with presents, in spite of the railleries of some Englishmen, who knew him from the reputation he had acquired by exhibiting his tricks at Bengal.

While the gentlemen at Madras were deliberating on the means of carrying their plot into execution, an ancient French officer, of the East India Company's troops of that nation, arrived there. He supposed himself to have been unjustly treated by that Company; and came to offer his services to the English against Haider Ali Khan.

The project of the chevalier surgeon was communicated to him. He did not hesitate to undertake the task of carrying it into effect. His offer was accepted, with a promise of making him lieutenant-colonel, with the command of a corps in the pay of the English Company; the basis of which was to be composed of the deserters from Haider.

To engage the confidence of the English government, this officer caused his trunks and valuable effects to be carried to the house of the governor, who placed them in his cabinet. Not to make himself suspected by Haider, this new emissary repaired to Pondicherry, where he communicated in confidence to all his acquaintance his design of going Into the service of that Nawab.

A number of officers and young men offered to accompany him. He was careful to transmit their names to the governor of Madras; and left Pondicherry secretly, at the time he expected the complaints of the English governor would arrive. The French governor, on receipt of the letter of complaint, sent for those who were nominated, and demanded their word of honour, that they would not leave Pondicherry without his consent.

The informer, who had the utmost facility in making his journey because the country he had to traverse was entirely under the government of the English, repaired to the camp of Colonel Wood in the environs of Ahtour. He remained there two days; when that army departing to join General Smith, he went to Ahtour, and declared himself to be French: guides and everything he demanded were consequently allowed to conduct him to Haider's camp. He arrived, accompanied by a single servant: and affirmed, that having met the army of Colonel Wood, he had passed two days in the forests, at the risk of being devoured by tigers; and that he had made the journey from Pondicherry to Ahtour on foot.

The reputation he had acquired, probably in consequence of the virtues and talents his relations had exhibited in India, prejudiced the commandant of Haider's Europeans in his favour. That officer thought himself happy in seeing him arrive, supposing that he had found a companion to share his labours; and consequently endeavoured to render him every mark of friendship and respect. The emissary at first seemed to meet the advances of the commandant with cordial regard. He waited afterwards on Raza Ali Khan, whom he had long known, and who reposed the utmost confidence in him on account of his family, which had always been highly attached to that prince's father.

Raza Saeb undertook to introduce him to Haider, who, to the surprise of all present, received him with evident marks of chagrin: which was so much the more strange, as that Nawab always received the commonest French soldier with pleasure. But he had been informed positively by Mughdum, his brother-in-law, who had seen the officer at the head of the French cavalry, when the escorted the convoys from Gingi to Pondicherry, that the man was a coward. It was not possible to persuade Haider to receive him with any mark of respect; as he had too much esteem and friendship for his brother-in-law not to give credit to his report. By this prevention he could not obtain the command of a company of hussars, that was without a captain and was commanded by a lieutenant who could neither write nor read. The European commandant, not having the least idea of its being possible that a man of family and reputation, as the newly arrived officer was could deserve such a character, was firmly persuaded that Mughdum Ali Khan had prejudiced Haider against him without reason.

To convince him of his esteem, he communicated to him in confidence, the secret of the expedition against Godelour; believing that he could give him good advice, because he had lately arrived from Pondicherry which is not more than two leagues distant from Godelour; and expecting that the success of the expedition would be productive of advantage to him. We have already shown how he made use of Raza Saeb to frustrate this undertaking; and how he prevented the governor, and the major part of the council, from being made prisoners: for as he knew of the intended expedition of Tipu Sultan by means of Raza, who had an entire confidence in him, he sent off his servant among the Pandaris that Tipu Sultan took with him because, having no other intention than that of ravaging the country, he could not take a set of men more capable of doing it.

The battle of Tirnmale happened a few days after the arrival of this English emissary; and the officers of cavalry, with the permission of their commandant, who attended his duty as general of the artillery, offered to place him at their head during the battle. But he refused, and kept constantly behind Haider, who seeing him mounted on a horse of one of the hussars, as he knew by the harness, caused a horse to be presented to him that belonged to one of the Pandaris that had been slain, which was the greatest affront he could show him.

March of Army

When the army marched from Singueman to encamp between Kaveripattam and Vaniambari, and had passed the Paler about three leagues from their new camp, the commandant remained with the artillery, on account of the passage being rendered difficult by the rains that had swelled the river.

At this time Haider sent to him, on account of sedition among the hussars and dragoons, who refused the pay that was offered them as usual, insisting on being paid in silver rupees instead of gold pagodas; which would have made a difference of about five shillings a month in their favour.

As this difficulty had never been made before, the commandant had not much trouble in persuading them to receive the money that was offered them; and taking occasion of the battle lately lost, in which their attack, and still less that of the other cavalry, was not supported so well as might have been expected, he reproached them for raising difficulties about their pay, without shewing any great readiness to deserve it. They who secretly excited them to murmur, were doubtless eager in urging them to resent this affront; for that very evening they went off in a body, with their regimentals and sabres, and repaired with offers of service to the camp of Ram Schander, a Maratha prince, who had received into his pay the Europeans that Haider had formerly disgraced and cashiered.

On the news of their departure, the commandant pursued them of the head of a body of grenadier Sepoys. Ran Schander, cautious of giving offence to Haider, and probably informed that the Europeans were pursued, ordered them to quit his camp. Being then totally at a loss what steps to take, they waited for the commandant, grounded their arms at his command, and suffered themselves to be conducted back without resistance.

They were kept bound and exposed to public view for some days; but at length were reinstated, apparently at the intercession of Haider, who did no think it beneath him to pretend to speak in their favour. All this may not seem very prudent in Europe; but it is necessary to attend to the situation of Haider and the commandant, Haider esteemed the Europeans perhaps far beyond their value, and the other existed only by their means. This sedition was thought to be a kind of business that would not be attended with any consequences; more especially as they did not know where to direct their steps, or to situate themselves better.

This affair happened some days before the capture of Vaniambari; and everything seemed quiet, when advices came to the Nawab from Vellore, and from St. Thomas, to the commandant, that some treachery was carrying on, and a desertion projecting, among the Europeans in Haider's army. Not being able to build anything upon such general advice, and the agents being such as were least suspected, the commandant supposed he could do nothing better than to assemble all the Europeans, and to require an oath on the cross and the holy gospels, by which they should promise to serve Haider Ali Khan with fidelity; to advise the prince and the commandant of everything they might hear to his prejudice; and not to quit his service without asking for permission. Before the oath was administered, every individual was asked whether he had received his pay, and was offered his dismissing, if he requested it. This precaution was thought sufficient and would have been so, if the government of Madras had not employed means to prevent its effect.

The English emissary found an excellent coadjutor in the surgeon, the friend of the Chevalier de Christ; for this man had a natural inclination for hazardous undertakings, and sought to render himself the subject of discourse at any rate. He offered to undertake every thing, on the assurance of being appointed surgeon-major in the English service. But the conspirators not succeeding with the soldiers, on account of the oath they had taken, wrote to Madras, informing their principals that it was necessary they should have the cooperation of two Jesuits then in Haider's camp; and that it would be expedient to forward a letter from the governor of Pondicherry to those fathers, ordering the French to quit Haider's service, by passing over to the army and through the country of the English, who would receive them, and suffer them to join their own standard at Pondicherry.

Jesuits in Absolute State: The Jesuits were in the most absolute state of dependence on the English; and having no other existence in India than they were pleased to grant, they thought themselves obliged to serve them according to the directions transmitted to them, They obtained passports from Haider for their domestics passing to and from their houses at St. Thomas's, and by that means became the agents of the correspondence of the English with their emissaries.

They were provided with a fictitious letter from the governor of Pondicherry, who had already written to Haider in their favour, supposing them to be prisoners, though they received every kindness, and only waited a favourable opportunity to return. To perform the commission they had from the English, they privately shewed the Europeans the pretended letter, affirming that they were forbidden to shew it to the commandant; but that the governor had sent to them to excite the Christians to leave the service of a Mohammedan prince: at the same time that, as divines, they informed them that their oath given to an infidel was null, and ceased to be obligatory, by reason of the order of the king's representative.

The producing a letter of this kind to the soldiers of Haider cannot be denied, as the fact is notorious, and can be proved by many witnesses now in Paris.

The letter was false, because the governor of Pondicherry could have no reason for concealing it from the commandant; on the contrary, that officer being in possession of letters entirely written in the governor's hand, it would have been in his power to have prevented any suspicion of its forgery, if it could have stood that test: and as the governor was not ignorant that a counsellor of Pondicherry had a correspondence in cypher with the commandant, by which all despatches were communicated to him, he would certainly have informed him of the contents of this letter, which was addressed to all the French in Haider's army. The Jesuit fathers who served the English in this business, as well as the three Portuguese priests, were sent back in company with the English factor, who went to Madras with propositions of peace.

When the Portuguese priests arrived at Vellore, and saw the Jesuits give their letters to General Smith and the governor of the place, they were in the highest astonishment to find that those reverend fathers had charged themselves with a mission of such a nature; and so much the more, as the news they brought appeared to be not casual, but early and important. The priests never spoke of this event without trepidation and fear; protesting they were innocent and totally ignorant of the intrigues and manoeuvres carried on against a prince who had loaded them with favours.

In fact, Haider bad given each of them, at parting, the sum of three hundred rupees to bear their travelling charges; a sum which is equivalent to thirty guineas; and if he had been so disposed, it was in his power to have inflicted on them the punishment the worthless Jesuits had so well deserved.

Haider having retired to Kaveripattam, General Smith took possession of Vaniambari, which had been left without a garrison; but he could no longer follow Haider, because he was obliged to wait for the convoys of ammunition and stores that had a great distance to travel: and the difficulty of collecting a sufficient number of oxen for draught and carriage was such, that he was under the necessity of detaching a part of his army to bring forward the convoy. The capture of the stores and ammunition laid up at Ambour, was the cause of all these delays in General Smith's operations.

Formation of Light Troop by English: The government of Madras, according to their promises, formed a body of light troops, composed of cavalry and infantry, under the name of the foreign corps; of which their French emissary in the camp of Haider was made commandant, and the Chevalier de Christ commissary. To put a finish to the relation of these detestable proceedings, we think it necessary to mention, in this place, the fate this new troop experienced in spite of the intrigues of the commissary, who employed not only subornation but assassination.

To augment the foreign corps, he was always reduced to little or nothing; those who were sent to Pondicherry and elsewhere to enlist men, were discovered; almost all the horsemen deserted, and took refuse either at Pondicherry or with Haider, who paid them for horses they brought, as if they had not stolen them from himself. The commandant of this unfortunate corps was punished, according to his deserts, by those very men whom he had served at the expense of his honour. An English court-martial declared him a coward, and unworthy to continue in the service; and condemned him to be degraded from his rank, and expelled from the army. We have already mentioned the fate of the Chevalier who first projected this scheme.

Nizam Ali Khan, who, as we have before observed, quitted Haider, and departed for the country of Curpa, was no sooner arrived there, than his Divan and worthy minister Rocun Daulla wrote to Mohammed Ali Khan, his brother-in-law, to acquaint him that he had at length prevailed on Nizam to abandon Haider; and that if he and the English desired it, he would repair to Madras, with full power to make such a treaty as they might wish for or expect.

The governor and council of Madras hastened to signify their desire of seeing him in their capital; and, in consequence, Rocun Daulla and Ram Schander, a Maratha prince, one of the principal confidants of Nizam, repaired with great pomp to Madras, where they made a magnificent entry, being saluted by the cannon, and the English troops lining the streets they passed through. They were every day entertained with new spectacles, and conducted to see the shipping, and everything that was deserving their attention: but what gave them the most satisfaction was, the valuable presents that were made them Nizam had the least share; the presents sent to him were of inconsiderable value; but the deficiency was made up by promises of vast magnitude: and, on the other hand, these great and magnificent ministers signed a treaty, by which Nizam confirmed Mohammed Ali in the Nawabship of Arcot, and in all the country he possessed or might obtain. Nizam Ali likewise ratified the gift to the English of the four sirkars or provinces to the north of Masulipattam, as well as the gift of that great city.

Two counsellors of Madras afterwards departed, in quality of ambassadors, to Nizam Ali, who sent them back with the greatest honours, and loaded with presents for themselves and the governor. Thus it was that Suba, who, twenty years before, held the destiny of India in his hands, became a kind of beggar among other powers, and daily lost that credit and consideration which gave him his superb titles.

Morarao, a Maratha, possessor of a small territory beyond Scirra, joined the English army, bringing with him about two thousand five hundred horse, and three thousand foot, the whole in bad order; but the English sought for succours from all parts.

General Smith perfectly acquainted with the nature of the country, and the kind of war he was to carry on, endeavoured without success to prevail on the council at Madras to accept the offers of peace held out by Haider. He therefore offered it as his opinion, that would be more advantageous, instead of losing time in making sieges, to pursue and press Haider's army as much as possible; and, if he could not be come up with, to besiege some place of consequence. He proposed, for the object of their efforts, Bangalore, the capital of a fine country. But the government of Madras, determined to conquer all the country on the exterior side of the grand Gates, obliged the general to divide his army into two parts, and to give the command of one part to Colonel Wood, for the purpose of besieging and taking all the small places that lie in the valleys, while General Smith was employed in keeping Haider's army in employment.

General Smith having complied with these orders, the project appeared to be attended with the greatest success. Colonel Wood took a great number of places, and that with so much the more facility, as three-fourths of them had no other garrison than the militia of the country. These conquests wonderfully elated the governor and council, who, as the crowning stroke of their success, received the news that an armament of about eight thousand men from Bombay had landed at Mangalore, and taken that city; whose feeble garrison, not being assisted by the inhabitants, had made their escape.

Haider's vessels, being then at Goa, were not captured; but three hundred pieces of cannon were found in the place, including quantity of very indifferent iron guns, designed for the shipping, and for the most part unserviceable: but this is of no consequence, as the number of guns is always a great ornament to a relation. The commandant of this army wrote word, that he intended, as early as possible, to march to Haider

Nagar, not imagining he should find any difficulty in penetrating so far, and still farther from indulging a doubt of taking it, together with the immense treasures Haider had laid up in the place.

This important piece of news was announced to the people by one hundred and one cannon fired from Fort St. George; and the relation of the capture of Mangalore was spread into all the European settlements, and every other part of the country. The news of the landing of the English at Mangalore had been instantly forwarded to Haider: he was consequently under the necessity of hastening to oppose this army, that had taking footing in the centre of Canara, a kingdom lately subjected to him, and which he supposing, from its situation, to be out of reach of insult, had not provided with any considerable number of troops.

The troops that had been left at Bisnagar, Scirra, and Seringapattam, received orders to march immediately for the kingdom of Canara. The son of Haider had the advanced guard at the head of three thousand cavalry; and Haider himself marched with three thousand of his best grenadiers, part of his artillery, and about twelve hundred of his cavalry, leaving the rest of his army under the command of Mughdum, with injunctions to harass the two English armies for the purpose of retarding their operations, but to hazard nothing.

General Smith, as soon as he was apprised of the departure of Haider, proposed again the siege of Bangalore. The council, elated with the high expectations they had built on the news from Mangalore, were for once of opinion: but as they regarded the siege of Bangalore as an affair of the greatest importance, it was resolved that Colonel Call, chief engineer, should have the direction; and to emancipate him from the orders to General Smith, it was ordered that there should be a committee in the army, composed of the Nawab Mohammed Ali Khan, Colonel Call, and Mr. Mackis; the two last being of the council.

This committee were, conjointly with General Smith, to decide on all the operations; and in order that such grave personages might not have the mortification to fail in an enterprise of such importance for the English nation, it was determined that the greatest preparations should be made. In consequence, they were furnished with sixteen mortars of different calibres, thirty-three and thirty pounders, fifty cannon, with a profusion of powder and ball, and every other ammunition: and since all these things had a tract of eighty leagues to pass over before they arrived at Bangalore, and the original difficulty of procuring oxen still remained, several stations were appointed to be waited at till everything was in sufficient forwardness to begin the siege.

General Smith employed himself in securing a passage for the convoys, by the capture of a number of fortresses he found in his way. He even succeeded in taking one small place by stratagem. His scouts had taken an Hurkaru belonging to Mughdum, who carried a letter, advising the commandant of that place, that at the close of the night he would receive a reinforcement of five hundred Sepoys; at the same time informing him, that he was in danger of being besieged. General Smith having an Hurkaru, who was perfectly acquainted with the court and army of Haider, gave him the charge of this letter of Mughdum, with orders to carry it to the commandant, and assure him of the arrival of the succours. The letter produced its desired effect. At the close of night they received a body of English Sepoys, who did not fail to take possession of the place.

Mughdum being informed of this event had his revenge a few days after, and retook the place by another stratagem. He caused some Indian horsemen to appear on the plain, among whom were a number in blue uniforms, like the English dragoons. One of them was detached to advise the commandant of the place, in good English that they were pursued by a large body of Haider's cavalry, and that he was sent by the commanding officer of the detachment, to desire the gates might be kept open for their reception.

This man was an English dragoon, who had newly deserted with his horse, which prevented any suspicion from arising. A large body of cavalry appeared, and the pretended English detachment came full speed into the place, took possession of one of the gates, and admitted the whole troop. The horsemen in blue were clothed with the habits of Haider's cannoneers.

Besidge of Places by Colonel Wood: Colonel Wood besieging great numbers of places, according to his instructions, found himself very soon in a considerable embarrassment for want of troops. He accordingly wrote to the council at Madras for reinforcements, observing that his troops were dispersed in garrisoning the different places he had taken; adding, that if it was their pleasure that he should destroy these places instead of garrisoning them, it would be necessary to supply him with a large quantity of powder for that purpose. While he was in expectation of the answer of the council, he besieged Darmapuri, a place somewhat more considerable than those he had hitherto attacked.

The commandant was a brave man, named Pinda Khan, highly esteemed by Haider, and formerly in the service of the French. This active commander made a vigorous defence, and did not hoist the white dag till the breach was made, and the ditch filled. His deputies having waited on Colonel Wood, he offered them no other capitulation than that of surrendering at discretion.

The deputies not being authorised to accept such hard terms without consulting the commandant, returned to the place, almost all the garrison being then on the rampart and in the breach. When they saw the deputies return, they crowded about them to enquire what success they had met with; and at the same instant the English grenadiers leaped out of the trench, mounted the breach, followed by the Sepoys, who had been commanded for the assault, and all the garrison, the commandant, his son, and every officer, were inhumanly massacred, except twelve European cannoneers, who were saved by the English grenadiers.

This assault was made while the white flag was on the breach. It is reported that Colonel Wood's army was enraged to find no plunder in all the places they had taken: for Haider had commanded all the inhabitants of any place in danger of being besieged, to leave the same with all their effects; and had strictly forbidden the officers and soldiers from having any plate or valuable property, but only the small quantity of linen which is absolutely necessary in India. In this order he observed, that the Europeans make war on the Indians only in hopes of plunder; and that it was not proper to indulge their avidity.

It is not easy to determine why Colonel Wood and his officers did not repress the cruelty of the soldiers, since they avowed that the grenadiers made this attack without their orders. To revenge the sufferers at Damapuri, Mughdum afterwards massacred a considerable body of Sepoys in the plain of Ovilour; and as for Haider, he conceived so violent a hatred for Colonel Wood that he always afterwards endeavoured, in preference, to attack his army, and to lay snares for him; and it is probable that the consequences would have been very disagreeable to that gentleman if he had unfortunately fallen into the hands of Haider.

After the capture of Damapuri, Colonel Wood joined his army to that of General Smith, according to the orders he had received from Madras. That general, after securing the passage of his convoys, marched towards Bangalore, and took several neighbouring places: among others were Kolar and Oscota; and with the intention of making this last place the storehouse for the siege, he caused it to be fortified.

On his approach to Oscota, General Smith received a deputation from the inhabitants of Divanelli, who came to offer him a contribution. They informed him that the small town, and its fortress or castle, were the places that had the good fortune to see the birth of Haider Ali Khan, a circumstance that had assured them of the favour of that prince, who had bestowed many privileges on the town and territory. General Smith replied that he should be the first in giving the example of respecting the birth-place of so great a sovereign and granted safeguards as well for the town as the territory of Divanelli. He refused to accept their contribution, and strictly forbade any individual of his army from entering the place without his permission.

This proceeding augmented the esteem Haider had long conceived for General Smith; and on this occasion that sovereign sent two superb horses, splendidly caparisoned, and the trappings studded with precious stones, to him, as a present he begged him to accept.

The commander of the army from Bombay, who supposed, after the capture of Mangalore, that nothing now remained, as he wrote to Madras, but to march to Haider Nagar, found his expectations not a title abated, when he was informed that he had sixty leagues to travel in a country intersected by woods, mountains, and rivers, and more especially that the approach to Nagar would be attended with the greatest difficulty. He did not, however, give up his intention; but continued his preparations, though very slowly. His army was then encamped without the gates of Mangalore, in the greatest Security.

March of Haider's Son: The son of Haider marched from Bangalore with all the ardour of a young man, who burns with a desire for glory. He quickly arrived in the kingdom of Canara, whose people, alarmed, but full of confidence in the son of their king, ran before him as the man of whom their safety depended. Animated by the acclamations of the people the young prince continued his way to Mangalore, causing all the troops to follow him that he found in his way, and who assembled from all parts. His march was so rapid, and the fidelity of the Canarins was such, that he came in sight of the English camp before they had received any advice. He perceived the tumult and fear his sudden appearance had made.

Without waiting for repose after his fatiguing march, he advanced, drove back the guards, attacked the army, totally routed and pursued them to the gates of Mangalore, where his cavalry entered pell-mell with the fugitives. Three thousand infantry, just come up, were astonished to find the English camp abandoned. They plundered the camp and the town of everything they found, which the prince allowed, to punish the inhabitants for refusing to assist in the defence of the city. The rout of this English army was so great, that very few had time to make their escape on board the ships, to which they communicated their fears. Their flight added to the ardour of Haider's Europeans and Sepoys, who immediately embarked and took three transports.

In this manner was the whole English army taken, consisting of the general, forty-six officers, six hundred and eighty English troops, and above six thousand Sepoys, together with all their arms and baggage. This glorious event for Haider happened the eighth day after the capture of Mangalore. It is difficult to conceive how a victory of this nature could be gained; or how, during the space of thirty days, the English general could neglect the taking possession of some advanced posts, which would have given him advice of the approach of the enemy.

Haider arrived the evening after the victory; and his son had nothing to say but, with Caesar, "*Veni, vidi, vici.*" It is said he wept for joy when he embraced his son. Some Portuguese merchants, established for several generations at Mangalore, entertained the opinion, that from the fortunate disembarkment of the English army, and the great successes that the English attributed to General Smith and Colonel Wood, it was probable that the English would conquer the greatest part of Haider's dominions, or at least remain masters of Mangalore.

They had therefore the imprudence to treat with the English general, and to contract with him for supplying the army with provisions. As soon as Haider was informed of this circumstance, he caused these merchants to appear before him, with the chief of the Portuguese factory, and several Christian priests belonging to the three churches at Mangalore. He then demanded of the Portuguese chief and the priests, what punishment the Christians inflict on those who should presume to betray their sovereign, by giving assistance to his enemies.

The Portuguese officer having without hesitation answered that such a crime deserved death, Haider replied, "I do not "judge in that manner, for our laws are milder. Since they have "made themselves English by engaging to serve them, their property "shall be adjudged to belong to Englishmen; and themselves shall be "thrown into prison till I make peace with that nation." Haider, after this decision, hastened to return to the kingdom of Bangalore, taking care to leave a strong garrison at Mangalore.

Receiving of Artillery by General Smith: During Haider's expedition and return, General Smith had sufficient time to receive his artillery and ammunition. Mohammed Ali, and the other commissioners of the council, were likewise arrived with a numerous suite, and with a new kind of luxury, unknown till then even in the armies of the Indians; this, however, consisted in nothing else than a number of large covered wagons, loaded with a provision of all sorts of wines. But, after all these preparations, it was discovered that the rice and provisions were in so small a quantity, that they could not possibly hold out the time the siege might probably last; while Haider and his troops would not fail to recover part of the fortresses that were to secure the convoys from the country of Arcot. And it was, besides, impossible to send escorts strong enough to defend them against the army of Haider; General Smith having need of all troops, as well for the siege, as for the defence of Oscota, where his stores were deposited, and to keep an open communication between the two places.

Morarao proposed to make the seige of Little Ballapore, a strong fortress about ten leagues from Bangalore, and three leagues from the country of the Patane Nawabs; as he affirmed that, when they were masters of Ballapore, he could obtain, either from his own dominions, or from Sanour and the neighbouring countries, any quantity of rice or sheep that they might desire. This advice being approved of by the, committee, General Smith left Oscota with his army, and every necessary for making the seige of Ballapore. He left a strong garrison in Oscota, where Mohammed Ali Khan, Colonel Call, and Mr. Mackis were to remain.

Haider, who had followed General Smith, and continually harassed him with his cavalry, and sometimes with his artillery, perceived that he could not prevent his opening his trenches before Ballapore: he therefore raised his camp, and marched for Oscota, where he arrived a little before day. As soon as dawn appeared, he attacked and carried the suburb of the place, which was defended by the single retrenchment of earth, and a ditch the English had made: he took a considerable number of soldiers and Sepoys the English had placed in an hospital there: and desirous of intimidating Mohammed Ali Khan, whose pusillanimous character he was well apprised of, he ordered his troops to prepare ladders for scaling the ramparts of the place, himself animating and giving money to the workmen, and promising the highest rewards to his army if the town should be taken, and Mohammed Ali Khan made prisoner.

The view of all these preparations, and the reports of some prisoners who were suffered to escape for that purpose terrified Mohammed Ali Khan in such a manner, that, in spite of everything that Colonel Call could urge, it was decided that an order should be sent to General Smith, to raise the siege of Ballapore, which was already far advanced, and come to the relief of Oscota. The General to whom the danger of Oscota had been magnified, was obliged to comply with this order, though so very prejudical to his operations. Mohammed Ali Khan was encouraged by the return of General Smith but was determined to run no more risk of falling into the hands of Haider, but to return without delay to Madras.

Colonel Call's colleague was of the same opinion; and General Smith alone not being a committee of the council, was obliged to follow them; and that more especially, as nothing less than his whole army was necessary to escort them. They were under the necessity, at their departure, of leaving at Oscota all that immense quantity of artillery and ammunition that was intended to overthrow Bangalore.

Haider gave himself very little trouble to retake the number of places that were garrisoned by the English, but content himself with following their army, and harassing it; which he did in so vigorous a manner, that the terror of Mohammed Ali was not a little augmented.

It was during the time that General Smith marched against Ballapore, that Haider had the satisfaction of beholding the return of his brother-in-law, Mirza Ali Khan, whose defection had so sensibly afflicted him. This young man, whether from the natural goodness of his heart, or from the attempt shown him by Madhorao, the Maratha General, and the other chiefs of that nation,—was continually agitated by remorse for his past conduct; and had long reflected on the means of regaining the friendship of his brother-in-law.

But when he saw him abandoned by Nizam, attacked by General Smith on the side of Bangalore, and obliged to hasten with his son to defend the centre of his dominions, attacked by another English army; when he reflected that all the misfortunes of his brother-in-law, the friend and protector of his youth, might with justice be attributed to his ingratitude, his remorse was too keen to admit of long deliberation. He made levies of troops, quickly placed himself at the head of twenty thousand men, and traversing the kingdoms of Scirra and Mysore, arrived within two leagues of Haider's camp.

Attended by a few horsemen, he advanced to the outposts, where he announced his name, and requested to speak with Mughdum. Mughdum, astonished at so unexpected a message, hastened to meet him. "What has brought you here ?" demanded Mughdum with an earnest emotion, when he saw the young prince.—"Repentance," replied Mirza; "I come to repair as much as in my power the injury I have done to our brother. I bring a much better army than I deprived him of; and I offer my head to his mercy: bring me to him." It was in vain that Mughdum represented that it would be proper to advise Haider of his arrival.—"No," exclaimed Mirza; "bring me to my injured brother: I fear no consequences but those of not seeing him."

Mughdum told him to follow him, and they soon arrived at the tent of Haider. The young prince threw himself at Haider's feet, who raised him, and embracing him—"This is no surprise to me, Mirza,"' said Haider; "I have long expected thee." The two armies joined; and every one esteemed this return of Mirza as a happy presage of the return of Haider's good fortune.

Change of War Method by Haider: Haider, after following the army of General Smith as far as Vellore, changed entirely his manner of making war. He divided his cavalry into three bodies; of which he himself took one, and gave the command of the other two Mughdum and Mirza, his brothers-in-law: he kept no other troops but his grenadiers, his Caleros, and Canutes, which he likewise divided into three, between himself and his brothers-in-law, so as to form three flying camps.

These light armies traversed the whole country, spreading terror and disorder everywhere, and throwing the council and all the English settlement into the greatest consternation.

This was a subject of great pleasantry and satisfaction to all the other Europeans in India, most of whom they had insulted in the short period of their prosperity. By their quick movements the three armies seemed to be multiplied; and the hews of their appearance arriving from all parts, it was impossible to determine which way to face; and General Smith's army made a number of useless movements, that harassed his troops without finding the enemy.

Division of Army by Council: The council determining to divide their army after the manner of Haider, a body of troops under Colonel Frichman, a Swiss, who had never yet been engaged in service against the Nawab, was entirely cutoff; he himself, as it is said, alone escaping by the swiftness of his horse. This colonel was marching in a plain, surrounded on three sides with wood: his army, at most about four thousand men, of which six hundred were Europeans, marched in a long column, when some horsemen appeared at the bottom of the plain. Several of the officers represented to the colonel, that Haider's cavalry was habituated to make sudden attacks at full speed; and that it would be proper to close the column, and approach the wood, in order to support them selves against it.

The colonel laughed at this advice: "Be easy," said he, "you shall see how I will serve these Negroes." The number of horsemen increasing, and no one daring to speak to the colonel, all on a sudden a cloud of dust appeared: the colonel then attempted to give his orders, but there was no time. Three thousand horsemen fell on his little army, and every thing was in disorder in an instant. The colonel, in the general confusion, hastened to fly: he was pursued, and the goodness of his horse alone preserved him. Mughdum, enraged at the massacre of Darmapuri, suffered his horsemen to act within unrestrained fury.

Above fifty English officers were slain, or made prisoners. Captain R—, who had surrendered Vaniambari, and had engaged not to serve for a year, was taken. It was more than ten months that he had signed the capitulation. He was, as it were, compelled by the governor of Madras to go with his garrison of Sepoys to garrison in Madura, and was on his march with Colonel Frichman. Mughdum Ali Khan, on whom these reasons made no impression, having found him marching in the body of the army, caused him to be hung on a tree, after having refused the other officers the permission to ask his life of Haider. All these events happened in 1768.

In 1769 Haider, on his side, being employed following Colonel Wood, who commanded a body of eight thousand men, and in being very near Thiagar, succeeding in falling upon his rear-guard, and forced him to retire into a wood. This colonel was then endeavouring to throw a garrison into a place named Elvanisore. The commandant he had nominated was the captain who stood first in the order of seniority; a brave man, but subject to the vice of drinking to such an excess, as often to render him incapable of giving any orders; however, not to disgrace him, and with the persuasion that Haider would never undertake the siege, Colonel Wood suffered him to possess the charge.

It so happened, notwithstanding that the Prince came, before the place with some cavalry, grenadiers, and cannon, without either the means or the intention of making a siege. The captain commandant, absolutely intoxicated, mounted his horse, caused the gate to be opened, and rode directly towards Haider's troops, demanding to see his highness the Prince. Being conducted to the prince, he represented to him that he was governor of the place, and regarded it as an honour to be besieged by so great a sovereign; that he hoped to deserve his applause by making a brave defence; but that he and his garrison having neither wine nor arrack, he had come, in reliance on his great reputation, to beg he would either give or sell them a provision of both that they might be enabled by their brave defence to give him a new occasion of acquiring glory.

Haider, supposing him to be insane, and not believing him to be the governor of the place, promised to supply him with wine, presenting him with various sorts to taste; so that the captain in a short time was under the necessity of being carried to bed. While he slept off his wine, he was shewn to several people of the town, and they all knew him. On his waking he was informed, that, as he had entered their camp as a spy, it was a decided thing that he should be hanged; but that, if he was really governor of the place, he might give an order to surrender it to Haider, it being left to his choice, either to give the order or to be hanged.

The poor man obeyed, and signed the order; and, what is still more extraordinary, the commanding officer under him obeyed the order, and opened the gates. In this manner Haider took a place, with a regiment of Sepoys, by the ignorance of him who obeyed the order, by the drunkenness of him who gave it, and still more by the imprudence of Colonel Wood.

During the time these affairs were transacting, the son of Haider and Mirza Fesoulia Khan, under whose command the greatest part of the infantry and artillery were, busied themselves in retaking those places the English had garrisoned; and in fact they retook them all, except Oscota, in which were a strong garrison, and a fine train of artillery, that Haider hoped to obtain by a treaty of peace.

While the ravages, the success, and the rapid movements of the Nawab held the governor and council in perplexity, a vessel arrived from England with Mr. Dupre, ancient counsellor of Madras, and esteemed a man of great sense and understanding. He was sent out to take the government of that place on the first of January, 1769, and arrived early in March, 1770. He had orders for the governor and council of Madras to make peace on any terms.

The Company was weary of attending to the flattering hopes of conquests that were promised in the letters from

Madras. Instead of the diamonds and treasures of Haider, they saw nothing arrive from Madras but bills of exchange, drawn on them by the government of that place: they therefore thought it their interests to make peace with Haider at any price, if for no other reason than to prevent the fall of their stock. But it is the great defect of all companies, that even their most essential deliberations cannot be kept secret. The resolution that any power takes to solicit peace, ought above all things to be concealed; and the axiom, *Si vis pacem, para bellum,* deserves the utmost attention.

The Company's envoy signified and declared, that a messenger must be despatched to Haider to request peace. The person charged with this mission received for answer, "I am coming to the gates of Madras, and I will there listen to the propositions the governor and council may have to make." This answer was taken for declaration, that the Prince was determined to besiege the town. Preparations were consequently made, and orders given to the two armies to unite and encamp near Madras.

Haider Ali Khan continuing his movements, came near Pondicherry and Godelour, and advanced as far as Colientz, seven leagues from Madras on the Pondicherry road. The English army prepared to defend the passage of the river of St. Thomas, when Haider suddenly disappeared, and while all the world was at a loss to determine where he was, he all at once showed himself at the gates of Madras on the Paliacat side, and despatched a flag of truce to demand what propositions they had to make. The whole town was instantly in an alarm, the English army being a league and half on the other side.

The council deputed Messrs. Dupre and Boschier, the one appointed governor for the year 1770, and the other brother to the then governor. They were received with great politeness. A suspension of arms was agreed on for the environs of Madras only. Haider promised to establish his quarters on St. Thomas's mount; and on the 15th of April 1770, two treaties were signed to the following effect:

> In the first, which is in the name of the king of England, it is agreed, that there shall be peace and friendship between George III, king of Great Britain, *etc*.. and Haider Ali Khan, Bahadur, Suba of Scirra, *etc*., and their respective subjects; that all the prisoners shall be given up on both sides; and that there shall be an absolute liberty of commerce between the subjects, and in all the dominions of the two sovereigns, in the same manner as before the commencement of hostilities.

Second Treaty

The second treaty between Haider and Mohammed Ali implied, first that Mohammed Ali should immediately evacuate the town and fortress of Oscota, which should remain in the same state as at the signing of the treaty; that all the artillery, arms, and ammunition whatsoever should be delivered to Haider; and the garrison should retire into the country of Arcot by the shortest road. Secondly, that Mohammed Ali should annually pay a tribute of six lacks of rupees, of which the first year's revenue should be paid down. Thirdly, that all the families of the princes, and other persons of distinction, formerly established in the country of Arcot, and the prisoners, should be set at large, and be at liberty to reside where they pleased.

The other articles of this treaty are not interesting. The English Company engaged themselves for the performance of this, and promised to present Haider Ali Khan with a fifty gunship, instead of that which had been seized at Bombay, and was become unfit for service. The Company likewise engaged to supply Haider with twelve hundred Europeans to serve in his army as often as he should demand it. An engagement of the same nature was already subsisting between the Company and Nizam Daulla, Suba of Deccan.

Presents to Haider by Council of Madras: The council of Madras made the most superb presents to Haider; and that prince, in return, presented them with much more valuable effects, both in gold and silver.

The two treaties were made to save the honour of the king and English nation; and consequently the first treaty only was made public by authority. But as there is always an opposition wherever there is an English government, the second treaty was soon made public in England and elsewhere; with such annotations as the interests or opinions of individuals might lead them to make.

Colonel Call, the principal author of the last war, was one of those who most formally opposed the present treaty. General Smith, who had given his opinion for peace whenever Haider proposed it, being persuaded that it might be concluded on with credit to his country was, however, against the present peace. He urged, that it was out of the power of Haider to do any future injury to the English, since it was in his power to prevent that Nawab from undertaking any siege and he added, that there was no doubt but Haider would be the first to give up a war he could not continue with any advantage; more especially as his truce with the Marathas expired at the end of the current year; and the prince was too intelligent not to be desirous of finishing the present war before he engaged in another.

So that by holding out a short time longer, and refusing his propositions with the same haughtiness as they were made with, he would be forced to recur to those he had made after the siege of Ambour. To all these reasons he joined, that, in signing a shameful treaty with Haider, they would dishonour the English name, that had never yet received a blemish in any of their wars with the Indians.

We shall finish the history of this war by describing a print, that Shows, with considerable accuracy, the different sentiments of those who were then at the head of the Madras government.

There was fixed to the gate of Fort St. George, called the Royal Gate, a design, in which was seen Haider Ali Khan seated under a canopy, upon a pile of cannon; Mr. Dupre and the other ambassador being on their knees before him. Haider held in his right hand the nose of Mr. Dupre, drawn in the form of an elephant's trunk, which he shook for the purpose of making him vomit guineas and pagodas, that were seen issuing from the mouth of this plenipotentiary. In the back ground appeared Fort St. George; and on one of the bastions, the governor and council were drawn on their knees, holding out their hands to the Nawab.

On one side of the council, was a large mastiff growling at Haider, the letters J. C. (for John Call) being marked on his collar; and behind the mastiff stood a little French dog, busily employed licking his posteriors. This last animal was adorned with a star, such as the Chevalier de Christ, Colonel Call's confidant, wore. At a distance were seen the English camp, and General Smith holding the treaty of peace in his hand, and breaking his sword.

By this peace, Haider Ali Khan Bahadur gloriously finished a war, which all India supposed would terminate in his ruin.

When Haider quitted Madras, he marched by the way of Oscota and Bangalore, to dispose of all the artillery and ammunition which the garrison of the former place were commanded to deliver to him. After taking possession of the whole, he dispersed his troops into good quarters, that they might refresh themselves, and be of good service to him in the approaching war with the Marathas, which he knew to be inevitable.

The Marathas supposed that they have a legitimate right to one-fifth part of the revenue of certain parts of Hindustan, by virtue of a gift made them by Aurungzeb. Haider, as we have already observed, does not acknowledge this claim. He gives money to the Marathas when the necessity of his affairs does not permit him to refuse it; but he never makes any other treaty with them than a truce for three years, not choosing to own the legitimacy of their demand; and the Marathas themselves are better satisfied with this mode of adjustment, than to continue the war at the risk of being forced to abandon their claim.

Madhorao, who was not then arrived at his two and twentieth year, and already possessed all the qualities that form the hero, was far from wishing to consent to anything that could prejudice the honour and interests of his nation. He burned with the desire of opposing himself alone against Haider. In consequence of the different sentiments of the two warriors, the greatest preparations were made on both sides; and the Marathas, as usual, came into the field in November, and approached Scirra in the month of December.

They found Haider Ali Khan encamped near that city; and in spite of all the ardour and courage of Madhorao, the position of the prince appeared so respectable that he durst not attack him. But the Marathas being in possession of Maggheri and Mark Scirra, places acquired by the defection of Mirza, had the facility to spread themselves in the plain of Mysore. Haider was obliged to follow them, and to encamp on the island of Seringapattam, which he had newly fortified, and put under the command of Mir Fesoulla Khan, with a good body of infantry. As he returned from Scirra by Bisnagar, and kept near the mountains that cover the kingdom of Canara, he covered that kingdom, and could not be surrounded in his march to Seringapattam, though the Marathas harassed him continually.

Very early in the year 1770, Haider arrived in the island, and was in perfect security from the Marathas. He suffered them to traverse the country, which he had not laid waste as he did when their nation had joined the English and Nizam Ali. He had no apprehension that the Marathas would employ themselves in sieges like the English; and he relied on the generosity of Madhorao, whom he knew to be incapable of destroying for the sole pleasure of doing mischief; that general suffering his troops only to forage, and plunder the flat country, according to their custom.

Strength of Maratha Army: The Maratha army was composed of two hundred thousand men, of which above one hundred thousand were cavalry. Against such an army Haider risked much if he lost a battle, and could gain little by destroying a part of them. The Nawab therefore continued in his camp, notwithstanding many feints and temptations that were held out to him by the Maratha general. At length this young warrior pretended to retire, and take the road to the kingdom of Bangalore.

Haider thought he might with advantage follow the enemy in a country that was very favourable to his infantry, who were much superior to those of Madhorao. He had already marched nine leagues, and hoped that very evening to gain a covered country, where it would be in his power to gain advantageous positions, as well for the purpose of harassing the Marathas in his turn, as for the easy subsistence of his army. But the Marathas having briskly returned, obliged him to encamp in a place, where indeed he was in no danger of being attacked, but where the enemy entirely invested him, and cut off his communication and means of subsistence from all sides; so that he was obliged to quit his camp, and retire towards Seringapattam.

The Maratha army appeared to direct their care and attention to prevent him from following the road to the kingdom of Bangalore and the neighbouring mountains, while they left the road to Seringapattam free. Haider choosing the night, as the most favourable to his infantry, deposited the greatest part of his artillery and baggage in a fortress, against which he had pitched his camp, and at about eleven at night he began his march in a square battalion. His infantry was formed into two columns, and his cavalry at the head and rear closed the square, in the centre of which was the baggage, and the artillery at each end. This order of marching did not admit of much expedition; but he had already advanced more than three leagues by four in the morning, when it appeared that they were not pursued, and that probably the Maratha army was unapprised of their march.

There were not then more than two leagues to be traversed, before they would arrive at a camp where they might safely remain till night; and one single night would have been sufficient to have brought them to Seringapattam. Every one supposed that nothing was to be feared, when a numerous corps of cavalry, consisting of about twelve thousand horse, appeared drawn up in order of battle, not behind them, as expected, but in front to oppose their march. Haider ordered the march to be continued, making use of the artillery only to oblige the enemy's cavalry to give way.

The cannonade appeared to succeed, and the army marched forward, though slowly; when at day-break the whole Maratha cavalry appeared, and in a short time surrounded Haider's army. The enemy made several charges, which were well sustained and repulsed; but Mirza, who commanded the cavalry in the van, suffered himself to be hurried away by his eagerness to follow the enemy he had repulsed. He quickly attempted to return, for fear of leaving the infantry without defence; but the cavalry he pursued were close at his heels, and entered the battalion with him. In an instant everything is in the greatest disorder; the army is beaten and dispersed; Haider Ali Khan is himself wounded, and many of his friends slain, and among others Ali Jami Khan, Nawab of Vendevachi.

Almost all the troops threw down their arms. A single battalion of grenadier Topasses formed themselves into a close column, and made way by their fire to an eminence, where their commander died of his wounds. This battalion was led to Seringapattam by a young officer, who was wounded in the shoulder, and was the only surviving officer of the corps.

Arrival of Haider at Camp: Haider, after running the greatest risks, arrived at his camp with the entire loss of his army, artillery, baggage, ammunition, and colours. As it is not customary in India to make prisoners of common soldiers, or even subaltern officers, the greatest part returned to him, though without horses or arms; but, by means of his resources, Haider established his army, in a short time, in a better state than before.

It will scarcely be credited that he purchased again of the Marathas themselves the greatest part of the arms and horses they had taken from him; but this arises from the nature of their government, which is purely feudal, every man having a right to dispose of his share of the plunder as he thinks proper.

Madhorao, however, embraced this occasion to begin the formation of a body of Sepoys, with the muskets that fell to his share after the defeat of Haider's army.

Many French officers lately arrived were present at this battle, simply as volunteers: they were almost all wounded, and one was killed. M. Hughel, who had formerly served Haider as commander of the French cavalry from Pondicherry, was wounded, and afterwards died at Tranquebar in consequence of his wounds.

There were likewise several English officers present: and among them Colonel Stewart, who arrested Lord Pigot, and who was reported to have been slain in the present war, in the first battle between Haider and General Coote.

After this battle, Haider kept constantly within his camp at Seringapattam; and the greater number of the Maratha chiefs having left the army, on account of their six month's service being expired, Madhorao renewed the truce with Haider, who was obliged to open his purse upon the occasion, though he had promised himself the contrary. This truce was made in July, 1771: but it was for no more than a year.

Mirza Ali Khan, who, as we have observed, was the cause of the loss of this battle, was taken prisoner, and conducted to Madhorao, who addressed him thus:

> " Since you have made war upon us with the power we have given you, we should act properly if we were to take everything from you, and confine you for life; yet, however, if you will swear never to bear arms against the Marathas, I will restore your dominions and your liberty."

Mirza took the oath without hesitation: and Madhorao having set him at liberty, he departed to his small estate, where he made an absolute donation of all his property, dominions, and troops to his brother-in-law, Haider; and a few days after became a Fakir, which, in Persian, signifies a mendicant, a man who voluntarily embraces poverty.

This class of men make no vows, in which respect they differ from monks, who cannot quit their state; neither do they, like them, live in communities. He wrote to his brother-in-law the reasons that induced him to take this resolution, informing him that he saw no other means of preserving what he had consecrated to his service; and assuring him that if circumstances should in future point out occasion for him to be useful, he should always be ready, however dangerous the service. And, in fact, when Haider is at war with any other enemies than the Marathas, Mirza takes arms and follows the camp, as he does in the present war against the English.

Haider employed this short time in producing divisions among the Marathas; and from thence arose the catastrophe that deprived young Madhorao of life, to the extreme grief of Haider.

Raghoba, uncle of Madhorao, having performed the functions of general during the minority of his nephew, beheld himself, not without great pain, reduced to the state of an individual, after he had secured the dignity that devolved of course to his nephew. During his regency he had filled all India with his fame, and obliged the emperor of the Mughals to fly from Delhi, his capital, which he had destroyed and plundered in such a manner as perhaps never to recover its former splendour; while the emperor himself, by that event, became reduced to a mere phantom, possessing no more than the shadow of the power, the riches, and the grandeur of the ancient emperors.

Madhorao, young, ambitious, and elated with his increasing reputation, disdained to listen to the counsels of his uncle Raghoba and the other chiefs of his party, which induced the old general to contrive plots for his destruction. Madhorao having determined to carry the war into the environs of Delhi, and on the Ganges, found much opposition in the national council: his opinion however prevailed, and he marched with a powerful army at the end of November, 1772, leaving a considerable force in the hands of a Maratha general, named Goupalrao, to carry on the war with Haider Ali Khan.

The army of this general was not at all comparable to that of Madhorao when he made war in Mysore; he therefore suffered Haider to recover Mark Scirra and Maggheri, which produced a suspicion that he was intimidated by the arms, or gained by the bribes, of that potentate, Madhorao did not meet with all the success in the north of Hindustan that he had expected, and marched his army back into the Maratha country.

Many Seditions during March: During his march there were many seditions among his troops, most probably in consequence of a plot contrived against the young prince: he was found assassinated in his tent in the year 1773, before his arrival at Poni, the usual residence of the general of the Marathas. As he left only one son, an infant, his uncle Raghoba assumed the regency by his own proper authority. The cruel and unexpected death of the young Madhorao, who was beloved by his soldiers, gave rise to suspicions among the principal chiefs that Raghoba was either the author or accomplice of the assassination of his nephew. A conspiracy almost universal being formed against him, he attempted to collect and form an army of the troops in which he could place most confidence; but he had scarcely began his march against his enemies, when the greatest part of his soldiers left him.

Perceiving himself abandoned, he had only time to take refuge among the English at Bombay, who received him with open arms, and promised him assistance. In return for this support, he thought proper to make a treaty, by which he granted very advantageous concessions to the English nation; and among others, never to demand the fifth part of the revenue of all the lands the English might possess in Hindustan.

On the news of this treaty being forwarded to the government at Bengal, General Goddard was despatched from the banks of the Ganges with an army of eight thousand men, twelve hundred being Europeans. With this force he crossed the peninsula, marching about six hundred leagues, in spite of all the petty princes whose dominions he traversed, and at length arrived at the banks of the Sindhu or Indus.

He found that the Marathas, after having surrounded the Bombay forces, commanded by the governor of that island, had forced him to capitulate; and that the governor had promised to abandon Raghoba, to interfere no more in the affairs of the Maratha nation, and had annulled the treaty made with the fugitive general. This last event happened in 1774.

General Goddard, without waiting for any orders, declared the capitulation, as well as the consequent treaty signed by the governor of Bombay, to be null and void. Thus the war commenced again; and this general, who, if he had belonged to any other power would have been criminated, had the good fortune to see his audacity crowned by many victories, which however finished by obliging him to act only on the defensive, his successes even destroying his army, and the Marathas seeming to multiply in consequence of their defeats; because they were defending their own homes, and their country is exceedingly populous.

Haider, who, as we have observed before, had fomented the troubles that agitated the Maratha nation, took, at the beginning, the part of Raghoba (which assuredly he would not have done, if he had had only that war to support). In consequence of this proceeding, after the defeat of the regent and the Bombay army, several Maratha chiefs, who supported the party of Raghoba, and among them Goupalrao, were forced to throw themselves into his protection. He furnished them with troops, and taking advantage of the distraction of the Maratha nation, in consequence of the victories of General Goddard, he took a number of their strong places, which now form a second barrier beyond Scirra, Maggheri, and Mark Scirra.

Though the greatest number of these places are of great strength, and advantageously posted, yet the most part were taken by simple blockade; which occasioned Haider to employ several years in the war. He did not think proper to take more vigorous measures, for fear of obliging the Maratha nation to accommodate their difference with the English; which, however, was a very difficult thing to be brought about, on account of the horror and aversion that people had conceived against Raghoba.

In the year 1775, Haider profiting by the employment the English gave the Marathas in the defence of their own possessions, embraced the opportunity of sending a small army, under Cina Serrao, a Maratha lord, who had served him from his infancy, to punish the Samorin and other princes of the Malabar coast. This prince refused to pay the tribute he had consented to give, when Haider, in 1767, restored his dominions. The Samorin, fearing the anger of the Haider, thought to secure himself by offering to become a vassal to the crown of France. The commandant at Mahe accepted the gift of the Samorin and came with a few troops to take possession of the fortress of Calicut, where he hoisted the French standard. This was a most imprudent and inconsiderate step, for many reasons.

First, the commandant of Mahe had not forces sufficient to sustain the consequences of this act; the number of troops on the Mahe establishment being insufficient.

Secondly, he ought not to have made an agreement in the name of the French king, without first being authorised by the commandant general of the French establishments in India.

Thirdly, he could not but know that Haider Ali Khan was reputed the natural ally of France; and that the Prince had claims on the whole country of the Nayres, by a authentic treaty, concluded by the mediation of his predecessor at Mahe.

Cinao Serrao, Haider's general, paid all the respect to the French colours which his positive orders to take possession of Calicut permitted him to shew. But he gave advice to his master of all that had passed; and the latter having written to the commandant-general at Pondicherry, the commandant at Mahe was recalled, and Haider's troops took possession of Calicut, which, as well as the rest of the Malabar coast, has ever since remained under the power of that prince.

Commencement of Hostilities between England and France: Haider being informed, in the month of August, 1778, that hostilities had commenced between England and France, made a trace of six years with the Marathas, by which they suffered him to retain all his conquests.

The time required for the conclusion of this treaty, and the great distance between the Maratha frontier and the Nawabship of Arcot, did not permit Haider to arrive in time to prevent the capture of Pondicherry, which surrendered in the month of October. The Prince not having arrived on the frontiers before the month of November, laid siege to Chiteldrough, whose lord being a vassal of Mysore, was encouraged by the promise of support from the English to refuse obedience to the orders of Haider. This place surrendered at the beginning of January, 1779.

During the siege, Haider announced to all India the project he had formed of attacking the English. His principal invitation was to induce Nizam Daulla to attack them to the north of Masulipattam, in order to recover the four provinces they had extorted from him. The Suba promised to make the attack that was proposed to him; but, whether from timidity or the intrigues of the English, he did not keep his promise, but calmly suffered Haider to bear all the dangers of the war, and to enjoy, without the participation of any other sovereign, the glory of being the liberator of India.

It is proper to mention here, that while the lion-hearted Haider thus threw terror and dismay into the country of Payanghat, the Nizam, under pretence of sickness, did not stir from his capital, and the Marathas also, after some movements, having by treaty obtained possession of the person of Raghu (the usurper Raghunath) from the English of Bombay, remained where they were, and gave no assistance whatever to Haider.

In the year 1780, Haider Shah descended by the Ghat or Pass of Chungum, and pitched his tents in the environs of Kilpauk, and from the same encapment detached his youngest son Kareem Shah, with the Kuzzak horse or cavalry, towards Mahmud Bundur, while he himself, with his army, marched on and took the small hill-fort of Turnamul. He then besieged the fort of Jeet Peeth, and gave orders to his conquering soldiers to attack the town.

After the commandant, who was a Sikh, named Guru Buksh, had held out with great spirit two or three days, he was killed at one of the gates of the fort, and the fort was therefore taken. From hence Haider, after leaving a detachment at the fort of Dhobi Garh, dispatched his son Tipu, with a strong body of troops, to reduce Ami and Tumri; and then turning his victorious standards towards the capital of Arkat, encamped near Nimukpeeth and Ghalidpura, and next invested the fort and town of Alam Panah, against which he ordered batteries to be raised.

The chiefs in the fort, namely, Achna Pundit, a Brahman (otherwise called Raijee Naib Souba, and who had also the title of Raja Beerbar, Bahadur, the founder or builder of the Alam Panah), and Nujeeb Khan Salar Jung, Bahadur, with 5000 regular infantry, 2000 horse, and 400 dismounted Ashraf (that is, men of good families), held themselves in readiness to repel their enemies, and filled the capital with stores of provisions, arms, ammunitions, and materials for defence, and then arranged themselves for action. Two or three thousand ashraf or noblemen, inhabitants of the place, of all tribes, who rose in arms merely to defend their families and preserve their honour, were conciliated by a daily allowance, or subsistence, in money, and the show of a great deal of deference and respect, and the gates and bastions of Alam Panah also being confided to the inhabitants of the Muhlas, they fought desperately.

Kareem Shah, meanwhile, when he moved off to Mahmud Bundur, met with no resistance, and having by night marches arrived at the town, he surrounded, and, at the first assault, bravely took possession of it, and plundered the houses of all the wealthy merchants, bankers, and traders of bales on bales of merchandise, and bags on bags of gold and jewels. The next day, the whole of the wealth and commodities taken from all the merchants, who had expended millions of rupees in commissioning or procuring them from different parts of the world for the purpose of barter, were collected in one place.

Amongst the rest was the whole of the property of a certain Muhammad Mukrim, a man of the Bohra tribe (the Bohras are a tribe of newly converted Musalmans, residing mostly in the North Western provinces of India, they are chiefly merchants and traders), the chief of all the merchants, and the owner of three or four merchant ships, who about this time had purchased thirty five young elephants of eight or nine years old, sixty taukun, or ponies of Manilla and Pegu, and also cloths of great value, and dresses of honour from the countries of Bengal, Benaras, China, Kashmir, Burhanpur, Masulipattam, *etc.* All these articles were taken, and laden on elephants, camels, bullocks, and carts, and with the merchant to whom they had belonged, and his dependants, as prisoners, were sent to Haider.

The prince (Tipu) after he had taken leave of his father, proceeded to Ami and encamped there, and gave orders to attack the fort. Budruzzuman Khan Bukshi accordingly raised a strong battery to the westward of the fort, and in one day fired a number of cannon-shot into the place. The killedar, or commandant, whose name was Hussain Ali Khan, who even in his dreams had never heard of battle or fighting, much less witnessed anything of the kind, lost all heart, and ornamenting himself with his unworthy arms, and taking the keys of the fort, he sought the presence of the khan above mentioned, and through his mediation was presented to the prince, and delivered up the keys as a peshkash to his servants. He then represented, that in the fort there were many houses inhabited by Syeds, or descendants of the Prophet, and being in fear lest the Syedanian, their women, might be insulted or violated, he had given up the fort and its dependencies, but that otherwise he would have defended them as long as he had life.

The prince, at hearing this foolish story, laughed outright, and having placed a garrison in the fort, Sidi Imam, an experienced officer, according to the orders of Haider, was appointed its commandant. Taking with him the former killedar, the prince marched towards Tumri, the chief of which also gave up his honour to save his life, and without a shot from either gun or musket surrendered the fort. Still advancing, therefore, Tipu took possession of the small forts of Trivatoor, Gulwa, Kaveripauk, *etc.*, and placing strong garrisons in each, returned to join his own army.

We can give no details of the operations of Haider in the present war, having no other materials than the relations of the English; and on these we can place no dependance, because they are fabricated in India to deceive the English government, and afterwards arranged in Europe according to circumstances, and the necessity of imposing on the people.

So that the only thing that bears the appearance of truth, is a letter from General Coote, in which we see that Haider is master of the Company; that in November, 1781, he blockaded four places at once; that General Coote marched with his army from Madras to supply those places with provisions, without accomplishing his purpose as effectually as the necessity of the case demanded; that the difficulty of subsisting his army obliged him to bring it back into the environs of Madras; that in his marches his troops had always been harassed by the cavalry and artillery of Haider; that he had fought four obstinate battles with Haider, and gained the field, without speaking of his having taken either prisoner, colours, or standard: to all which he adds, that he sends Colonel Crewford, who will explain the true state of affairs.

It may be concluded from this letter, that the English are engaged in a most ruinous war, and that, with the assistance of the French, it may be hoped, this prince will succeed in taking possession of the whole Nawabship of Arcot, to which his son has so just a title.

Detail about Capture of Chittaldurgh: The direct news from Haider's army gives an account of the capture of Chittaldurgh, and the particulars of a council held before they entered the country of Arcot. It was deliberated whether he should attack the English, or wait till the landing of the French forces. The latter it seems was the general opinion, and even that of the European officers; but his son Tipu Sultan was of the contrary opinion, and remonstrated that the Prince had threatened so much to attack the English, that his reputation necessarily required him to proceed.

Tipu Sultan spoke with so much spirit and animation, that he was joined by the whole council. It was this young prince who decided the battle that was attended with the deaths of Colonels Bãillie and Fletcher, by taking advantage of the disorder the English army was thrown into by the blowing up of their ammunition wagons, to fall on them with his cavalry. The total defeat of a detachment commanded by Colonel Brawlie is likewise an exploit of Tipu Sultan; who having began, like Alexander, to gain battles at the age of eighteen, continues to march in the steps of that Grecian hero, whom he may one day resemble as well by the heroism of his actions as by the multiplicity of his conquests. As to Haider, we may compare him to Philip of Macedon, who formed the troops that procured the numerous victories of his son, and subdued the Greeks his neighbours, who were the enemies that were the most difficult to conquer.

4

Marathas and Mysore

The State of Mysore, situated at the junction of the Eastern and Western Ghats, was ruled over by the Wodiyar dynasty from the fourteenth century. Between 1731-34 the Government of Mysore was usurped by two brothers—Devraj and Nanjaraj, who left to the King Chik Krishnaraj only the exterior appendages of royalty Devraj was the Dalwai or Commander-in-Chief and Nanjaraj was the Sarvadhikari or Controller of revenue and finance. But from 1746, Devraj, grown old, allowed his brother to lead distant expeditions, himself taking charge temporarily, during his absence, of revenue and finance.

Early Career of Haider

In the service of Nanjaraj there was a young volunteer horseman named Haider, serving in a detachment led by his own brother Shahbaz. In 1749, he caught the eye of Nanjaraj in a shooting competition at Devanhalli, was promoted to the command of 50 horse and 200 peons. Between 1750-60 Haider, known in the early days of his military career as Haider Naik, came steadily into prominence and rose from prominence to power. Circumstances were favourable.

Peshwa Balaji Baji Rao began to pursue a policy of southward expansion, without abandoning his forward policy in the north. Mysore was invaded by the Marathas in 1753, 1754, 1757 and 1759. Nizam-ul-Mulk regarded Mysore as Mughal territory and his successors also considered that Mysore was a part of their territorial legacy.

Thus Mysore was drawn within the circle of the conflict between the Peshwa and the Nizam. To add to the complications, Nanjaraj conceived the project of seizing Trichinopoly with its dependencies by taking part in the struggle between the French and the English in what is known as the Second Karnataka war. Muhammad Ali offered him this bait and he eagerly swallowed it. From February to December, 1752, the Mysoreans and the British fought as allies against the French at Trichinopoly. But later Nanjaraj changed sides and through 1753 and 1754 he was the ally of Dupleix as against Muhammad Ali, backed by the English.

The Mysorean had to become the ally of the French when he found that Muhammad Ali would not hand over Trichinopoly to him and the British associated themselves with this "Fraud of Trichinopoly". Nanjaraj was recalled by Devraj in April, 1755 to meet an invasion of Mysore by Salabat Jang, guided by Bussy. The heavy expenses estimated at 3 to 4 crores incurred in the Trichinopoly venture, the drafts twice made by the Marathas, a sum of 56 lakhs that had to be paid to Salabat Jang—all combined to make the very solvent Mysore State of 1752 almost bankrupt in 1755. The Government was unable to pay its soldiery and defray its expenses. Thus were created those conditions that brought about the subversion of the existing authority.

Haider was with Nanjaraj throughout the Trichinopoly campaign. There Haider was not merely conspicuous for his intrepidity and daring, but was also successful in securing rapid promotion, as also a considerable share of plunder. Towards the end of his stay there, he was officially at the head of 1,500 horse, 3,000 regular infantry and 4 guns. He was now appointed as the faujdar of Dindigul, a rock fort belonging to

Mysore, 65 miles southeast of Trichinopoly. It is relevant to note that at Trichinopoly Haider learnt his lessons in the art of war. He was an eyewitness of the attacks and counterattacks of Clive and Lawrence as also their French opponents. Ambitious, able to take advantage of his opportunities, he learnt what the art of war meant in those days in the western sense of drill, discipline, attack and defence.

While he was consolidating his position at Dindigul during the years 1755-57 Devraj and Nanjaraj quarrelled and Devraj withdrew from Mysore to Satyamangalam, leaving Nanjaraj as the undisputed usurper. But Nanjaraj could find no opportunity of consolidating his position. The Marathas again invaded in 1757 and Nanjaraj agreed to pay them 32 lakhs, but could pay only six, and for the payment of the balance handed over fifteen taaluks as security.

Shortly after this, Haider came to Mysore and advised Nanjaraj to expel the Maratha garrisons from those taaluks on the approach of the rains. Nanjaraj acted according to this advice and this made inevitable another Maratha invasion of Mysore. When the Maratha army came in 1758, as the Mysore troops were still in arrears, none of the old veterans agreed to take command of the army; Haider took personal responsibility for arrears and was placed in charge of the field army. He somehow held his own, remained on the defensive, hoping thereby to wear the Marathas out.

The Marathas agreed to withdraw if they were paid thirty-two lakhs. Half of this was paid by raising forced contributions. For the remainder, Haider gave his personal security and he took the thirteen ceded districts under his control. His next step was to oust Nanjaraj. This he managed very adroitly with the assistance of his Diwan Khande Rao who had won over the nominal King in the interest of Haider. Deserted by the soldiers at whose head he now found Haider, Nanjaraj decided to retire. He was given a jagir and he promised to withdraw to Coonoor; but on the way he entrenched himself at Mysore.

He failed, however, to maintain his position because the Portuguese Officer commanding his white troops proved to be a traitor. He had to capitulate and withdraw to Coonoor. The King now found that he had only exchanged one master for another. Haider had now in his direct possession more than half of the kingdom and the King discovered that under the new dictator he continued to be a figurehead as he had been in the previous regimes of Nanjaraj and Devraj.

Consolidation of Authority

As the de facto ruler in Mysore Haider had now to consolidate his authority. But in the meantime the Court party in league with Khande Rao came to an understanding with the Maratha Chief Visaji Krishna and tried to launch a concerted attack on Haider. On 12 August, 1760, a cannonade was opened from the ramparts of the fort of Seringapatam on Haider's residence near the modern Darya Daulat Bagh. Haider was taken by surprise.

The Marathas could not arrive in time. Haider ran away leaving his family at Seringapatam. He reached Bangalore. His brother-in-law, Makhdum Ali, had been sent to help the French at Pondicherry in the Third Karnataka war. He was not asked to return. But the Marathas defeated him on his way back at Anekal. A relieving force sent by Haider Ali from Bangalore to his aid was also defeated.

Haider's career appeared to be approaching its close when suddenly the Marathas expressed their willingness to withdraw on his paying 51 lakhs and ceding Baramahal. Visaji Krishna had to withdraw because of the serious aspect of Maratha affairs in the north which culminated later in the disastrous Maratha defeat at Panipat. When Haider heard about it, he refused to hand over the Baramahal districts. Khande Rao, left alone, was unable to cope with the wily Haider, who had even induced Nanjaraj to join him and bless his cause. When Haider besieged Seringapatam, the King made an abject surrender and handed over Khande Rao. Nanjaraj was sent back to Coonoor to fade into complete obscurity. Khande Rao was kept a prisoner in a cage in which he languished for a year and died. Haider could now feel that he was safely established in Mysore.

Between 1761-63 Haider succeeded in conquering Hoskote, Dod Ballapur and Sera with its dependencies. The Poligar of Chik Ballapur exasperated Haider by his, tough resistance and was despatched as a prisoner to Bangalore while the Poligar of Raidurg for his willing submission was generously treated. Haider next took up the cause of Chen Basavaiya, who was believed to be the fugitive boy king of Bednur, adopted son of the deceased Bednur Chief Basavappa Nayak. The queen of Bednur could offer but feeble resistance. After the conquest of Bednur was completed in the name of the boy-king, Haider declared him an impostor and threw him into prison. According to Wilks the loot of Bednur alone brought Haider 12 million sterling. Haider next conquered Sonda, the king of Sonda, Savai Immadi Sadasiv, flying to the Portuguese for protection and surrendering to them his territory below the Gnats in return for an asylum and a stipend.

Haider had now to reckon with the Marathas with whom he had to fight at very frequent intervals from 1764-1779. He was unable to cope with Peshwa Madhav Rao and it was only the premature death of that great ruler that saved Haider from annihilation. Haider's recent conquests, his plan to extend his frontier up to the Tungabhadra and even beyond, brought him into collision with the Maratha power, recovering from the stunning blow of Panipat, under the wise guidance of Madhav Rao. Haider Ali was defeated in an engagement at Ratehalli, 70 miles southeast of Dharwar on 3 May, 1764. He had to fall back to an entrenched fort at Anavatty. But here too, he found his position untenable and suffered a complete defeat.

The Peshwa made a triumphant march towards Bednur. At this stage, Raghunath Rao, uncle of the Peshwa, thought it necessary to intervene and a treaty was concluded by which Haider paid 28 lakhs as tribute and restored all the territory of Murar Rao of Gooty beyond the Tungabhadra as also the territory of the Nawab of Savanur between the Krishna and the Tungabhadra, because these two chieftains were in Maratha interest.

The Peshwa marched against Haider again in November, 1766. He succeeded in persuading the Nizam, Nizam Ali, to join him in a scheme of offensive alliance against Haider. But Nizam Ali soon after concluded an alliance with the British and he hoped to dictate in any scheme of the partition of Haider's territory. But this at once made Madhav Rao determine to act on his own. He marched very quickly, realizing tribute from most of those places south of the Tungabhadra that had recently submitted to Haider. Haider sued for peace. He agreed to pay a tribute of 33 lakhs to the Peshwa and got back most of this territory including Sera, Chik Ballapur and Kolar, but the Marathas retained Dod Ballapur, Hoskote and some other places. Nizam Ali was outwitted and Peshwa Madhav Rao without waiting for his ally went away. Nizam Ali thought it proper to come to terms of accommodation with Haider.

Madhav Rao invaded again in 1769. Haider's persistent and systematic encroachment on the Maratha sphere of influence could only be countered by a relentless offensive against him. Haider had even compelled Savanur and Gooty to pay him tribute. The campaign of 1769-70 kept Haider on the defensive. But the Peshwa became so ill that he could not lead the campaign of 1770-71. Trimbak Rao, who was left in command, defeated Haider completely in the battle of Chinkurli or Moti Talao on 5 March, 1771, almost within the sight of Seringapatam.

Haider lost his entire equipment, his store and all his artillery. He and his son Tipu narrowly escaped being taken prisoners. But so tough and stubborn was Haider that this defeat was not followed by a collapse of his military power.

The Marathas were so much intent upon plunder that they let ten precious days pass before they laid siege to Seringapatam. After besieging Seringapatam in vain for a month and ten days, Trimbak Rao withdrew to Bellur, in view of approaching rains. He began campaigning again in September, 1771, but the Peshwa's condition worsened and the campaign had to be abandoned. The Marathas retained Sera, Hoskote, Dod Ballapur, Kolar and Gurrumkonda and gave up the rest. Haider promised to pay sixty lakhs. During the prolonged campaign of the Marathas Haider was expecting British aid because he had concluded a defensive alliance with them. The British did not come to his aid and this partly explains the strong anti-British turn which Mysore foreign policy took later.

Death of Madhav Rao

Fortunately for Haider Peshwa Madhav Rao died in November, 1772, and the chaos that now began in Maratha affairs, helped Haider Ali not merely to regain his lest ground but also to conquer and consolidate his sway up to the Tungabhadra, and extend his conquests up to the Krishna. He took the fullest advantage of the chaos and confusion in Maharashtra caused by the murder of Narayan Rao, opposition to the regime of Raghunath Rao and the resultant civil war. Haider recognised Raghunath Rao as the Peshwa and agreed to pay him an annual tribute of 6 lakhs.

The territory conqucred by Madhav Rao in his three expeditions was ceded to Haider. Between February 1774 and April 1776, Haider not only recovered all that Peshwa Madhav Rao had taken but also annexed Bellary, Cuddapah, Gooty and Kurnool. He also annexed Coorg in 1780. With the fall of Gooty Haider got under his control all that was included within the Maratha sphere of influence south of the Tungabhadra. The Poona Ministry learnt to their dismay that Haider began in 1776 to conquer Maratha territory between the Krishna and the Tungabhadra.

They could not, however, organise an expedition before 1777. Hari Pant was commissioned to oust Haider from Maratha territory in concert with Nizam's general Ibrahim Khan Dhausa. But the troops of Hari Pant were in arrears, Dhausa was lukewarm, the emissaries of Haider were at work and nothing very effective could be done during the year 1777-78. In the meantime, at Poona Nana Phadnis, who seemed temporarily to be eclipsed by his cousin Moroba, resumed his former power.

Haider took advantage of these complications in Maratha affairs to seize all the important places in the Krishna-Tungabhadra Doab. In view of the British supporting the cause of Raghoba which resulted in the first Anglo-Maratha War, Nana was on the look out for allies, and that great Maratha statesman had to recognise all these acts of aggression in order that he might enlist the support of the Mysoreans against the British.

Relations of Haider with British Government : Haider's relations with the British prior to the outbreak of the second Anglo-Mysore war are best studied separately. It would be a mistake to think that Haider was anti-British from the very beginning of his career. No doubt Haider gave the French some help in the Third Anglo-French War but that was because the French supported him in his usurpation and promised him valuable territorial cession in case of a favourable termination of their conflict.

At the time of the Khande Rao impasse the British carried on some negotiations with the king of Mysore, no doubt with the object of temporizing at the end, but this left a trace of bitterness behind. French influence in Haider's Court began to increase and French officers like Chevalier Du Mouhy, De La Tour and others joined him.

Haider gave shelter to Mahfuz Khan, the elder brother and necessarily an enemy of Muhammad Ali, Nawab of Arcot. He also entertained in his service Raza Saheb, son of Chanda

Saheb, Muhammad Ali's mortal enemy. There were also territorial disputes between Arcot and Mysore. But all this would not possibly have led to open war between the British in Madras and Haider Ali in 1767 if the British had not made the mistake of concluding a treaty with Nizam Ali in 1766 and helping him with a detachment of their troops in his operations against Haider.

It is relevant to note that in May, 1766, Haider had offered to the British a defensive alliance against the Marathas and the Nizam. His exasperation naturally knew no bounds when he found the Nizam backed by the British engaged in operations against him in apparent concert with the Marathas. He concluded a separate treaty with the Marathas, won the Nizam over and persuaded him to join an offensive alliance against the British and Muhammad Ali. Together they carried the war into the territory of the Nawab of Arcot.

In the first battle of the war, Colonel Smith won a nominal victory over Haider Ali and Nizam Ali at Changama. It was on the whole a very indecisive affair. Strong in cavalry, the confederates had no difficulty in getting into Karnataka. The next engagement was at Trinomali, where also the confederates were defeated. Thereupon Nizam Ali withdrew from the conflict. But Haider Ali continued to maintain his offensive. There were engagements at Vaniambadi (December, 1767), at Mulbagal (4 October, 1768), at Ariyalur (22 November, 1768). Haider was not successful in any of these, but neither was he worsted. He was unable to cope with Col. Smith but he was more than able to hold his own against other commanders like Wood and Lang. His cavalry gave him greater mobility and he made excellent use of rapidity of movement in the closing stages of the war. Having successfully screened his movements from the British field army, he appeared before the gates of Madras.

The panic stricken Madras Government was induced to sign a treaty on 4 April, 1769, that provided for mutual restitution of conquests and a defensive alliance. The Court of Directors later remarked that the Company's interest and influence suffered much diminution and discredit as a consequence of this war and the treaty that ended it.

Government of Madras and the Defensive Alliance : This defensive alliance with the Madras Government was regarded by Haider as the sheet-anchor of his foreign policy. But in January, 1770, when the Marathas invaded his territory, the British would not go to his help. He solicited the assistance of the Company again and again. In the twenty-fourth month of this long protracted war, the Madras Government at last asked him what money and provisions he could provide if they were to assist him and they informed him sometime afterwards that the Home Government had forbidden any assistance. Besides this infringement of the treaty of 1769, there were other sins of omission and commission that ultimately made Haider Ali conclude that it would be a mistake to depend upon British friendship.

The British would not supply him guns, saltpetre, lead and such other things that he required, but the French from the port of Mahe supplied him liberally. He repeatedly attempted to renew the violated conditions of the Treaty of 1769 but met with prevarication on the part of Muhammad Ali. Between 1775-79 many events happened that stiffened Haider's attitude. When war began between England and France, the British led an expedition against the French possession of Mahe which fell on 19 March, 1779. Haider's vakil had earlier protested that his master regarded all trading settlements on the Malabar Coast as under his protection. Haider's troops actually assisted in the defence of Mahe and his flag had been hoisted over it.

The Madras Government had also foolishly assured Basalat Jang of Adoni, a brother of Nizam Ali, unconditional defence of the place. They even advanced detachments to his place through the territory of Haider Ali and Nizam Ali. This aroused the antagonism of both. Basalat yielded to their joint pressure and the march of the British detachment had to be countermanded. Besides these episodes there were boundary disputes. In July 1780 Haider launched his war flooding the Karnataka with immense armies. Their activities have been described by Burke in his famous speech indicting Warren Hastings.

> "A storm of universal fire blasted every field, consumed every house, destroyed every temple. The miserable inhabitants fleeing from their flaming villages were either slaughtered or swept into captivity."

An English brigade under Baillie was surrounded and cut up. Munro, the victor of Buxar, smirched his reputation by abandoning his artillery and retreating in panic to Madras. However, on 1 July, 1781, a very important battle was fought at Porto Novo which Coote won by consummate generalship. Coote turned Haider's entrenched position, forced him in the open field, and against odds, made the best possible use of the echelon formation. It was a great tactical victory for the British, but it had no important strategic effects. In 1781, Coote defeated Haider on two other occasions in the second battle of Pollilore (27 September) as also at Solingar (27 October).

These two defeats in succession gave a great shock to Haider's prestige. Vellore, besieged by Haider, was relieved by Coote and this closed the campaign of 1781. But early in 1782, a disaster befell the British. Col. Braithwaite, while encamped with a detachment of the British army south of the Coleroon, was surprised and cut down by an army led by Tipu. Braithwaite was taken prisoner. Admiral Suffren, one of the best seamen that France ever produced, arrived off Pulicat on 15 February at the head of 12 ships. Five naval engagements took place between Admiral Suffren and Admiral Hughes, without any decisive result. But Suffren succeeded in seizing Trincomali in Ceylon which, as a base for French maritime operations, was immensely superior to distant Mauritius.

Haider's heart was growing sick and his trust in the French was evaporating. He was, however, reassured by this brilliant French admiral that Bussy would soon arrive with reinforcements. But Bussy did not actually arrive until after Haider's death. The most important action in the campaign of 1782 was that of Arni, which in the words of Fortescue, "produced no result beyond the heightening of Coote's reputation in the eyes of Haider".

Haider had also to detach Tipu with reinforcements to Malabar where the British were trying to create a diversion by sending a detachment under Humberston and McLeod. But on 7 December, Haider died and Tipu had to hasten back to join the main army. He was quietly proclaimed and his succession was accepted without any opposition. Brigadier-General James Stuart, who had now succeeded Sir Eyre Coote as the British Commander-in-Chief on his death in April 1783, failed to take advantage of the consternation in Mysore caused by the rumours of the death of Haider and the possibility of a disputed succession.

On 28 June, news arrived that peace had been concluded between the English and the French in Europe. The British were now free to deal with Tipu. General Matthews, Commander-in-Chief of the Bombay Presidency, was leading the British army in Malabar. He was asked to abandon operations on the coast and push on to Bednur. This he did successfully and took Bednur. On the western coast Mangalore was also taken by the British. But Tipu now advanced with his full force, invested Bednur and compelled the British to capitulate. It is said that safe conduct was promised to the British but Tipu violated the terms. Almost all the conquests of Matthews were retaken by Tipu, and Mangalore alone held out.

Tipu besieged Mangalore and the siege lasted from 20 May, 1783 to 30 January, 1784. Campbell, who defended the place capitulated on condition that the English garrison should be transported to Tellicherry. The terms were faithfully observed. Negotiations had already been begun by Macartney, Governor of Madras. Tipu at last agreed to make peace. There was to be a mutual restitution of conquests. The prisoners were to be restored. The Treaty was signed on 11 March, 1784.

Treaty of Mangalore

After the conclusion of the Treaty of Mangalore, it might have been expected that Tipu would remain quiet for sometime and try to make friends with the Marathas and the Nizam. But it was very difficult in the existing circumstances for these three Indian powers to cooperate. The Nizam had not, in any sense, played the part he had agreed to play as one of the confederate anti-British powers. The Marathas had concluded even before the death of Haider the Treaty of Salbai (May 1782) which was, of course, ratified after Haider's death. Nana Phadnis was anxious to get back the region between the Krishna and the Tungabhadra and Nizam Ali was further alienated and alarmed by Tipu's assertion of claims over Bijapur.

Tipu, lacking in moderation, created fresh grounds of dispute. The Desai of Nargund, connected by marriage with one of the leading Maratha chiefs, had been compelled to transfer his allegiance from the Marathas to Mysore when Haider annexed the Krishna Tungabhadra Doab. The Maratha government was assured by Haider Ali that all the chiefs in the Doab area, who had been dependent upon the Marathas, would be fairly treated by him. But Tipu is said to have seized the Desai of Nargund by treachery and the whole family was put in the Mysore State prison.

The Desai of Kittur was also overwhelmed. Three years tribute at the rate of 11 lakhs a year remained unpaid to the Maratha Durbar. Nana Phadnis knew very well that the circumstances leading to the Treaty of Mangalore and the treaty itself were regarded by Englishmen as humiliating. As Nana and Nizam Ali drew closer together they presumed that in case Tipu proved to be very much superior, in case he was effectively helped by the French, they might even get English help.

In 1786, Tipu's answer to this Maratha-Nizam coalition was to complete his preparations and to read the Khutba in his own name because "Shah Alam in whose name the Khutba was so long read was the prisoner or servant of Scindia". In the war that ensued, the confederates took Badami. But while they, were being watched by a Mysore army, Tipu by forced marches advanced from Bangalore to Adoni, the most important fort of the Nizam, south of the Tunga Bhadra.

Tipu could not carry the place by assault and had to raise the siege as the confederates marched to its relief. But as no arrangements had been made for a prolonged campaign, south of the Tungabhadra, the confederates evacuated the place which fell into the hands of Tipu.

Immediately after they recrossed the river, it was in spate and they expected that they would have a free hand in the Doab. But Tipu performed the very remarkable feat of crossing the river which was in flood in basket boats and rafts. The Sultan succeeded in repulsing the confederates near Savanur which he entered without opposition. He next made a very successful night attack in which he got possession of the camp equipage of Tahavar Jang, who commanded the forces of Nizam Ali.

Tipu, however, expressed an anxious desire for peace because he was apprehensive, in spite of the pacific professions of Lord Cornwallis that the English would most probably join the confederates. English military establishments were being reorganised and this perhaps made the Sultan believe that they were preparing for war.

Tipu agreed to pay arrears of tribute. Badami was ceded. Adoni, Kittur and Nargund were to be restored. Wilks distinguishes between the political and military conduct of the war. The generally accepted opinion was that Tipu concluded a successful campaign by an inglorious peace. But Malet, British Resident at Poona, thought that the treaty was highly advantageous to Tipu.

> "He has dissolved a formidable confederacy and dissipated an immense army, the members of which, embittered against each other by mutual distrust, disspirited by ill success, disgusted by disappointment, were not likely to be so formidable again".

It is only relevant to note that the rapid and accurate fire of Tipu's artillery, directed by French officers, very much impressed the Maratha Chiefs and can be said to account for Maratha eagerness for British help in the later stages of the war.

Lord Cornwallis arrived in India in 1786. He perceived from the beginning that a war between the British and Tipu was inevitable. Malet, ambassador at Poona, told him "Tipu is prompted to conquests by the ambition of a despot and the wild enthusiasm of a bigot, supported by a consciousness of superior military talents, founded on frequent success". Cornwallis wrote to Malet in December, 1787: "As the French policy has been generally extremely ambitious and as there appears to be no bounds to the designs of Tipu, the violence or injustice of either of these powers, may soon remove the present political restraints of this government and leave us free to form the closest alliance with the Marathas".

The settlement of the Guntur Sarkar with the Nizam provided Cornwallis with an opportunity of winning him over against Tipu. He elucidated ambiguous articles of the British treaty of 1768 with the Nizam in a way that really led to the formation of an alliance against Tipu. Tipu's diplomatic manoeuvres, on the other hand, failed. He had sent an embassy to Constantinople in 1784 and another in 1785. Only 68 men out of 1100, sent to Constantinople in 1785 actually returned.

He also sent an embassy to the French King in 1785 with valuable presents of jewels, and the bonds given by the general officers for supplies to the French troops during the last war were cancelled, as a proof of his esteem for the French. But nothing tangible could come out of these diplomatic feelers. After the termination of the war of 1786-87 an attempt was also made in 1788-89 to bring about a union between Nizam and Tipu, the two powers to pledge on the Quran to form a strict and indissoluble union.

The Sultan proposed an intermarriage between the two families, but Nizam Ali was unprepared for this social degradation. Thus Tipu was left politically isolated as the British, the Marathas and the Nizam drew closer together.

Causes of War

The immediate cause of the war was Tipu's attack on Travancore lines on 29 December, 1789. The Raja of Travancore was included in the Treaty of 1784 among the friends of the English. The Travancore lines were 30 miles long, extending eastwards from the island of Vipeen. A part of these lines was within Cochin. But Jaikottai and Cranganore belonging to the Dutch in Cochin were situated close to these lines and were necessary for their defence. Alarmed by Tipu's attitude the Raja induced the Dutch to sell these places to him. Tipu regarded Cochin as a tributary state and gave out that this was the purchase and sale of a part of the kingdom of Mysore.

Isolated and apprehending a concerted attack, Tipu's plan was to secure every part of Travancore, if possible in December, 1789, invade the southern provinces of the British and by the time the British would be prepared, he would be able "to begin his war with the Kaveri as his frontier towards Coromandel, a boundary anxiously and incessantly desired by the rulers of Mysore since 1751".

Tipu's first attack on Travancore lines failed. He gave out that he was searching for fugitives. His next attack came in

April, 1790. He carried everything before him and the Travancoreans retreated to their fortresses in the south. Cornwallis made his treaty with the Marathas on 1 June, 1790 and with the Nizam on 4 July, 1790. The war had actually begun in May, 1790.

This war lasted two years. The British plan was that the Madras army under General Medows would seize Coimbatore and thence invade Mysore from the south after an ascent via Gazalhatti pass. Colonel Kelly with three brigades would guard the passes leading from Mysore to the Karnataka, and if possible, penetrate to Baramahal. General Abercromby with the Bombay army would subjugate Malabar. General Abercromby would perform his part of the task quite easily. Medows succeeded in capturing the posts extending to the Gazalhatti pass. The British army did not meet with any opposition so far. Tipu's corps of observation under Sayyed Saheb was driven across the Bhavani by Floyd who took Satyamangalam. But the British troops were dispersed in three divisions at Palghat, Coimbatore and Satyamangalam.

Tipu saw his opportunity and inflicted swift blows in quick succession on the three dispersed detachments. Floyd had to retreat precipitately. Medows advancing, was for sometime unable to establish any contact with him and a repetition of the Munro-Baillie affair was barely averted. Kelly's detachment, commanded by Maxwell also barely escaped disaster. Tipu next made a raid on Trichinopoly, turned back after plundering Srirangam and, in the style of Haider, kept the British army under Medows dancing about him in the Karnataka. The Governor-General, who was also the Commander-in-Chief decided to take the command himself.

New British Plan for Campaigns

The new British plan of campaign was to evacuate all the posts captured by Medows in the last campaign except Palghatcherry and Coimbatore, to divert a part of Tipu's forces from the main army under Cornwallis, and with that end in view the Bombay army under Sir Robert Abercromby was to advance from Tellicherry upon Seringapatam by the pass of Periapatam. The Marathas and the Nizam besieging Dharwar and Koppal, were to invade Tipu's dominions from the north. Cornwallis himself advancing with the main army towards Seringapatam succeeded in deceiving Tipu as to the exact route he would take, and ascended by the Pass of Moogli, thus opening the campaign very skilfully.

There was really no opposition until the British reached Bangalore, which important place they succeeded in taking without much difficulty. But as Cornwallis marched in the direction of Seringapatam, Tipu's plan of campaign was revealed. On 13 May Cornwallis was at Arikera, nine miles from Seringapatam. Tipu made it impossible for Cornwallis to secure supplies and forage.

Tipu's excellent intelligence service kept concealed from Cornwallis all news about Abercromby's movements as also those of the Marathas coming to join him. In an action at Arikera Tipu could not maintain his ground and had to withdraw to Seringapatam. Rains fell and the "utter failure of all the equipments of the English army" compelled Cornwallis to retreat and his cup of misery would have been full but for the opportune arrival of the Marathas with plentiful supplies. His siege train having been destroyed, Cornwallis was not in a position to renew his attack on Seringapatam and fell back to Bangalore.

Tipu recaptured Coimbatore. After the rains, Cornwallis began his preliminary operations. A line of posts was established preparatory to a final advance upon Seringapatam. With an army of 22,000 together with 18,000 horse furnished by the Nizam and a detachment of the Marathas, Cornwallis began his advance towards Seringapatam. Tipu trusted too much to the defences of Seringapatam, where his father had so often defied his enemies, but, as Wilks says, unlike his father who extracted some advantage from every discomfiture, he was intoxicated with success and desponding in adversity. When the most important of his redoubts, called the Sultan's redoubt, was taken by Cornwallis and Abercromby formed a successful junction with the main army, Tipu offered terms. Half of his territory he surrendered, to Mysore—Haider Ali and Tipu Sultan be divided equally among the three allies. Maratha dominion extended to the Tungabhadra.

The Nizam got territory extending from the Krishna to beyond the Pennar with the forts of Ganjikotta and Cuddapah. The British got Baramahal, Dindigul, as also Malabar. Tipu had also to give independence to the Raja of Coorg, and had to pay an indemnity of three crores and thirty lakhs of rupees. Tipu was still left with sufficient territory "to make him respectable and still in some degree formidable to his neighbours", thus leaving unaffected the balance of power in the south.

End of Anglo-Mysore War

The fourth Anglo-Mysore War seven years later ended in complete collapse of Tipu's power. The situation is best described in the words of Wellesley:

> "Tipu has preserved without abatement implacable sentiments of revenge since the hour of his last defeat. It has always been well understood that Tipu Sultan's resentment was not to be appeased by any conciliatory advances on our part, nor by any other means than the recovery of lost power, the disgrace of the British army, and the ruin of British interests in India. His intrigues at the courts of Hyderabad and Poona, together with his embassy to Zaman Shah, were sufficient indications of an hostile mind."

But the immediate reason for this declaration of war was that he sent an embassy to the Isle of France which according to the Governor-General, proposed an offensive and defensive alliance against the British in India and levied a military force which was actually landed in Tipu's country. Wellesley admitted that the succour received was inconsiderable but he thought that this must be regarded as "a public, unqualified and unambiguous declaration or act of war".

Wellesley apprehended that Tipu's earliest hostile movements would lead to the general hostile movements of the French adventurers in the Indian Courts and more effectual French succour might arrive.

Wellesley's aim was to bring such a reduction of Tipu's power as would establish a permanent restraint upon his future means of offence, to seize his whole maritime territory, to compel him to defray the expenses of war as also to compel him to admit permanent Residents at his court from the British and their allies.

Tipu in reply said that "forty persons, French and of a dark colour, of whom ten or twelve were artificers and the rest servants paid the hire of the ship, came here in search of employment". As Mill says about this Mauritius episode, it really disclosed that the connection between Tipu and the French was very trifling and their mode of intercourse childish. There may be some difference of opinion as to the nature and extent of the French menace.

But it cannot be denied that in the existing circumstances war was inevitable. Tipu was an enemy of the British, beaten on his own ground yet able to hurt. He would not consent to sink to the level of the Nizam and he believed that he was destined by the English to the fate of a pensioned Nawab.

Tipu was completely outmanoeuvred and out-generalled. He had no allies to help him. The Nizam's army did not play much effectual part on the British side and the Peshwa's troops were not there to help the British. But the organisational work was this time very efficient. Tipu was defeated by Stewart at Sedasere and by Harris at Malavally. He was driven to the defences of his capital, of which the siege was begun on 17 April and the assault was made on 4 May, 1799. Tipu fell fighting bravely. His sons surrendered and the rule of the dynasty came to an end.

The Wodiyars, who were nominal rulers in the days of Haider Ali and in the early years of Tipu Sultan's regime, were restored to a portion of the dominions ruled by the Sultan and his father. Besides Kanara, Coimbatore, Wynaad and Dharapuram, the entire sea coast of the kingdom of Mysore was annexed by the British. By Article 8 of the Subsidiary Treaty with the Raja of Mysore the East India Co. was "to undertake the defence and could garrison in whatever manner they may judge proper all fortresses and strong places in the Mysore territory."

Arthur Wellesley, later famous in English history as a soldier and a statesman, first came into prominence as the leader of the Hyderabad contingent in this Anglo-Mysore War and then played a prominent part along with Col. Close, the Resident, and Purnaiya, the old finance minister and now the Diwan, in the establishment of the new order in Mysore. Tipu's family was sent to the fort of Vellore, which was appropriated for their residence. Sir Arthur Wellesley thus summarises the Governor-General's first year's work:

> "Our principal ally, the Nizam, was restored to us, the French State growing in the peninsula of India was destroyed, our formidable native enemy Tipu, the ally of the French, was subdued".

Wilks says that:

> "the decision of history will not be far removed from the observation almost proverbial in Mysore that Haider was born to create an empire, Tipu to lose one. Haider was an improving monarch and exhibited few innovations, Tipu was an innovating monarch and made no improvements".

Civil Administration

In civil administration the first thing to note was the difference in the attitude of the father and Son to the nominal king. Haider never openly assumed the royal title. He maintained an attitude to the old dynasty more or less like that of the Peshwas to the successors of Shivaji. Tipu dethroned the Raja, made him practically a state prisoner and openly assumed the title of Sultan in 1786.

The coins of Haider Ali are remarkable for their conservatism. He exercised the sovereign right of striking coins in his own name for the first time in Bednur which he described as his swarajya and whose name he changed to Haidernagar. None of Haider's coins anywhere exhibit more than the initial letter of his name and in associating his coins with Hindu deities, he showed very remarkable toleration. Tipu had even a new calendar based on the mauludi year. He changed the names of the mint towns as well. Kirkpatrick says in this connection that Tipu's calendar was that in common use in Mysore but he substituted Arabic names for Hindu ones, assigned to the cyclic years and months.

Haider's finance was also characterised by his conservative traditional outlook. He would rent his country in large districts to amildars. His terms were favourable. They paid regularly but succeeded in amassing large sums even after payment of public revenues. Haider's spies would inform him. The amildars would be asked to attend the Durbar, compelled to disgorge their wealth, given a small present and sent to other districts. Tipu changed the institutions of his father and also changed his own pretty often. He wanted to introduce a system of checks and balances. In each area the military were under an officer called Sudur, the civil under an officer called Asaf.

The Killadars were under the former. The Asaf had the tahsildars and head farmers under him. The Sudur and the Asaf had their cutcheries in the same hall. But as has been said:

"all these checks served only to diminish the revenue. All parties soon found that it was wiser to agree and divide the public money than to quarrel and send their complaints to the Sultan. The Asaf and the Sudur with their cutcheries, the tahsildars and their cutcheries and the head farmers and the accountants of villages, all had their respective shares which were as well ascertained as their pay. The whole amounted on an average throughout the extent of Tipu's dominions to above 30 per cent."

The Mysore government under Haider was a very simple and despotic monarchy. Every department, civil and also military, felt the touch of the genius of the great ruler. Justice was impartially administered. Every important officer owed his position to his ability, not to his social position, and most of the trusted men were raised from obscurity. In these circumstances his Government had a vigour unexampled in India. Tipu's great drawback was his restless spirit of innovation and the increasing bigotry of his later years.

Sir Thomas Munro wrote to his father:

"The great blow of the loss of half of his country seems to have confounded him. He never had the talents of his father but he had always till that event paid his army regularly, kept it in good order, gave a good deal of his attention to business and managed his finances tolerably well."

It is no wonder that the dominions of Tipu showed indications of good government that surprised the British invaders. The revenues of Tipu's dominions, according to the terms of the Treaty of 1792 were 2 crores and 37 lakhs of rupees.

Public Works by Haider

In connection with Haider's public works we should specially mention Dariya Daulat and Lalbagh and the establishment of a grand bazar town named Ganjam Sahr. It is relevant to note that in 1774 when the house of Kadimuddin at Seringapatam caught fire, many buildings including a portion of the temple of Rangaswami were destroyed. Haider rebuilt the temple in so short a period as one month. Tipu's most important constructive work was in Malabar. He was the pioneer of Malabar roads. There were no highways in Malabar before him. Tipu projected and constructed an extensive chain of roads there.

The intolerance of Tipu Sultan has been very much exaggerated. The gringeri letters of Tipu Sultan show that Tipu carried on a correspondence with Jagadguru Shri Shankaracharya in a spirit that we can associate only with a very religious prince. The monastery suffered much in 1791 at the hands of Maratha pindaris. The Guru was supplied by Tipu with necessary funds for replacing the displaced image and for necessary ceremonies. In 1793, Tipu wrote to him, "You are the Jagadguru. You are always performing penance in order that the whole world may prosper and the people may be happy".

These letters prove definitely the sincerity of Tipu's tolerance and do not fit in well with the details of persecution with which we are familiar. Political, military and administrative considerations were responsible for some of the measures of persecution of Haider and Tipu—transplantation and forcible conversion of rebels and the formation of Chela battalions of captive converts like the Turkish janissaries. It would be a mistake to regard these measures as indications of their attitude to their Hindu subjects.

Military System of Haider

The efficiency of the military system of Haider Ali and Tipu Sultan cannot be denied. But in this sphere too Tipu departed to a large extent from the principles of his father. In 1767, at the time of the first Anglo-Mysore War Haider had

210 Europeans, 800 excellent Mughal horse, 12,000 other cavalry, 5,000 grenadier sepoys, 8,000 sepoys with European muskets, 1,000 topasses and 4,000 matchlockmen. In 1780, when he entered the Karnataka he had, as has been mentioned, about 90,000 troops with him. At the outbreak of the war in 1790 Tipu's force was 45,000 regular infantry and 20,000 horse, exclusive of irregular peons.

In 1793, after the loss of half of his territory, his army consisted of 30,000 regular infantry, 7,000 regular cavalry, 2,000 artillery and 6,000 irregular horse, besides a large number of peons. Besides the field army Haider and Tipu had to maintain garrisons in times of war at Seringapatam, Sera, Bednur, Sonda, Chik, Ballapur, Dod Ballapur, Kolar, Hoskote, Bangalore, Dindigul, Coimbatore and Mangalore.

In the days of Haider the British army, small in numbers, was composed almost wholly of infantry. Haider was strong in horse, though not strong enough in infantry and artillery. He lost many battles without injury to his affairs because the British were unable to pursue. A single big victory in the field over Sir Eyre Coote would have made him master of almost every place in the Karnataka. But the situation of the British Government with regard to Indian powers changed completely in the days of Tipu. Cornwallis took with him quite a big army and he was helped by the cavalry of the Marathas and the Nizam. But in 1799, the British army was by it self quite strong both in infantry and cavalry, in quality and number.

The superiority was so great that the issue could not be doubtful. Tipu's artillery and infantry showed the effects of intensive training by Frenchmen, but in the altered circumstances this could not avail. It has been said that his grand military mistake was the neglect of his cavalry, a proper use of which would have made his defeat a much more difficult proposition. The organisation of the army showed traces of weakness. His army was overstaffed. He had about 150 general officers for an army, less numerous than what his father took into the Karnataka in 1780 and for which he had only ten generals.

Tipu's army also fell more and more into arrears and when Seringapatam was attacked by the British, it had received only two issues of pay in 14 months. He went on adding to the defences of Seringapatam for which he spent about 12 lakhs of pagodas. After the opening of the campaign he did nothing effective to retard the progress of the British armies. He had seen his father defy his exultant enemies by shutting himself up in his capital until the rains. He perhaps hoped to repeat his father's performance. But circumstances were changed and he also was very much unlike his father "whose equanimity was uniform in every aspect of fortune and who generally extracted some advantage from every discomfiture."

Haider's Naval Force

In connection with the navy of Haider and Tipu it is necessary to note that Haider and Tipu commanded the entire sea board from Sadashivgarh to Cochin. Haider's conquest of Bednur and Sonda in 1763-64 brought the ports of Honavar, Mangalore, Bhatkal, and Sadashivgarh in his possession. He could now have a fleet of his own and in 1765, according to the Portuguese, he had thirty vessels of war and a large number of transport ships. In 1766, his fleet was of very considerable help in the conquest of Malabar. It consisted of 80 vessels, 13 topsail vessels, several mach was of war, besides a great many shibars and small crafts. The conquest of North Malabar and South Malabar completed, Haider had more ports under his control. In 1769, Haider temporarily abandoned Malabar, which he reconquered soon after the Maratha menace was over.

The Moplahs were great navigators and they formed excellent sailors. Haider's fleet had two commanders—Stannett and Latif Ali Beg. In 1768, when the Bombay government sent a squadron of ships to the Malabar coast with European troops and sepoys, Haider's naval power collapsed. The British expedition failed on land but Stannett proved to be a traitor. He joined the British with a part of his fleet. Undaunted by this collapse of his naval power, Haider began another shipbuilding programme. With the help of some Portuguese and Dutch ship-builders he strove to realize an ambitious scheme of ship-building. But he could not realise his plan. Sir Edward Hughes in 1780 entered Mangalore harbour and destroyed the enemy's ships he found there. Thus failed the second attempt of Haider.

Tipu, however, walked in the footsteps of his father. General Mathews on getting possession of some of his seaports in 1783 found 19 large ships, some completely built and others in great forwardness. In 1796, Tipu established a Board of Admiralty and planned the erection of 20 lines of battle ships and 20 frigates. Neither Haider nor Tipu had the necessary respite that alone could have enabled them to equip a fleet strong enough to hold its own against the British on the west coast. Unable to build a strong navy of his own, Haider depended in his campaigns of 1781 and 1782 very much on French naval support and he occupied Porto Novo in order to provide the French with the necessary landing facilities. The French never gave him adequate naval support and in spite of the triumphs of Suffren at sea, there must have been profound distrust in his mind of the French promises and it was perhaps in this mood that he remarked to Purnaiya about the British naval power—"I can ruin their resources by land but I cannot dry up the sea."

5

Country's Condition at the Time

General Literature of the Age

The literary works of Amir Khusrau apart, the general literature of the age, including fiction and poetry, folklore and ballads and the books on the life-history and teachings of *sufi* saints and *bhakti* reformers in Hindi, Urdu and the various *prakrits* or regional languages, constitutes a valuable sources of our information on the social life and condition of the people at large.

The material available in this field is very rich in social content, *albeit* it exists in so many and varied vernacular languages, dialects and scripts, as to make it humanly impossible for any single student of social history to survey even a fraction of it. The author of this study, therefore, needs no apologies to record that, in this respect, he has relied almost exclusively on the researches done already by a galaxy of national and regional scholars of socio-cultural history. Obviously, while making a select use of such material, he has exercised his discretion to re-arrange the facts and give his own interpretation of the socio-cultural phenomenon; a few of the works and the modern authorities thereon, where used, have been referred to in the body of the text.

Foreigners' Accounts

After the death of Harsha Vardhana and loss of its political unity, India, 'barring its coastal regions', was gradually cut off from the other countries. It has rightly been asserted that one of the great achievements of the turkish conquest of northern India 'was the ending of this isolation and the establishment of the international status of India in the then-known world.' We possess a few invaluable travelogues of the foreigners who visited India during the early medieval period these throw a flood of light on the political developments and socio-cultural history of the times.

Ibn Battuta (c. 1304 -78) occupies a premier position among the early travellers; he was an arab adventurer from Morocco who was an expert in Islamic theology and jurisprudence. He left his home in 1325 on a life-long tour of the world, and after passing through the countries of northern Africa and the Arabian peninsula, reached Sindh in 1333; from there he moved on to. Delhi He was extended patronage by Muhammad bin Tughluq who appointed him the *qazi* of Delhi. He held this post for about eight years but, to his misfortune, some cases of corruption and dishonesty were brought forward against him which landed Ibn Battuta into the jail.

However, he secured his release by making a personal appeal to the sultan. The latter despatched Ibn Battuta to China at the head of a diplomatic mission in 1342; on the way his party met with a shipwreck and he had to return to Delhi without completing his assignment. Thereafter, Ibn Battuta bade farewell to Delhi and moved on his sojourn again; after visiting Maldive islands and Ceylon, he returned to southern India and stayed at Madura for a short while. From there he went to Mecca on a *hajj* pilgrimage before his return to his homeland in 1349.

Ibn Battuta received a warm reception from the ruler and the people of Morocco; by this time he had acquired a world-wide fame as philosopher and saint. He enjoyed love and reverence of his countrymen and died at the ripe old age of seventy-three.

Ibn Battuta wrote his travelogue, entitled *Kitab-i-Rehla,* in Arabic, a part of which is devoted to his experience of the Indian life at Delhi and Madura. His book is a primary source of history of the reign of Muhammad bin Tughluq; it throws light on the socio-political condition of his times. *Kitab-i-Rehla* is a very valuable treatise written by a foreigner on the life and conditions of the people of Hindustan during the Tughluq period.

Abdur Razzak, the celebrated author of *Matlaus Saadain wa Majmaul Bahrain.* 'The Rising of the two Fortunate Planets (Jupiter and Venus) and the Junction of the Two Seas', was a Persian scholar. He was born at Herat in 1413; his father Jalaluddin Ishaq was a widely travelled man who held the post of *qazi* of Samarqand towards the fag-end of his life under sultan Shah Rukh of Khurasan.

Abdur Razzak entered the service of the Sultan after the death of his father in 1437. He was sent as an ambassador to the court of Vijayanagara; he stayed in Deccan for about two years (1442-43). He adorned the court of the sultans of Khurasan till his death in 1482; during the last ten years of his life, he was the superintendent of the *khanqah* of the late sultan Shah Rukh.

Abdur Razzak spent his time in literary pursuits; the above-mentioned history of central Asia, in two volumes, is one of his contributions. In the first volume, the author gives, among other things, an account of Amir Timur's invasion of India; in the second volume, he describes the history of Timur's descendants from Shah Rukh (c. 1404) to sultan Hasan Mirza (upto 1470 A.D.); it is in this volume that he gives a detailed account of his journey to and from Vijayanagara court and its working, the personal life-style of the sovereign and his courtiers, and the socio-cultural condition of the people of

Deccan in general. His travelogue is one of the primary sources of history on the cultural achievements of the Vijayanagara kingdom.

A few European travellers, who visited India during the early medieval period have also made some useful references to the land and its people in their travelogues. They include, among others, Marco Polo, Nicolo Conti, Duarte Barbosa and Domingos Paes. Marco Polo, 'the great father of modern geography', was a native of Venice. He set on a sojourn of the world in the company of his father and uncle in 1271, and after passing through many countries, reached the court of Kublai Khan, the mongol emperor of China, in 1274.

Marco Polo entered into the service of the great *khan* and stayed in his court for seventeen long years. Thereafter, he returned to Venice in 1294-95; on his way back, Marco Polo visited the Andaman (Angaman) islands and sailed along the eastern and western sea coasts of India.

In the course of his explortions, he attempted to acquaint himself with 'the natural history' and rich agricultural and industrial products which might become valuable as articles of trade between India and Europe. Marco Polo, in his travelogue, speaks of brisk maritime trade and commerce along the Indian coasts. He describes the life and condition of the common people and gives a vivid account of their dress, food habits, manners and social customs.

More than a century and a half later, yet another Venetian, Nicolo Conti (Nicolo de'Conti), visited southern India under similar conditions. As a young man Nicolo Conti had settled in Damascus as a merchant sometime in the beginning or the fifteenth century. The spirit of adventure and exploration led him to the countries of the East, including India, Ceylon, Sumatra, Java and China.

It is said that, after about twenty five years of wanderings he ultimately returned to his mother country in c. 1444. While in Cairo, he fall into the hands of some arab fanatics; lost his wife and two children, and was compelled to renounce Christianity in order to save his life. On return to Rome, he pleaded for absolution for his apostasy from Pobe Eugene IV.

The latter granted his request on the simple condition that, as a penance, he should narrate his true adventures in the far-off lands. His narrative, which was recorded in Latin by the Pope's secretary (Poggio Bracciolini), constitutes the travelogue of Nicolo Conti.

He had sailed along the coast of Malabar and visited the interior of Deccan in c. 1420 is travelogue gives a few glimpses of the royal court of Vijayanagara and throws light on the socio-economic condition of south India in general Similarly, the description of south India by Duarte Barbosa, a Portuguese official in Cochin during c. 1500-16, is of great geographical and ethnographical significance. So also is the narrative of another Portuguese traveller, Domingos Paes, who visited Vijayanagara kingdom during c. 1500-02.

India was known to the west 'as a great populous country, rich in gold, spices and textiles' since time immemorial. In the middle ages, Constantinople, 'then the chief mart for Indian goods,' conveyed by the northern overland routes, was the centre of attraction for the European merchants. Amongst them, the Ventians enjoyed unrivalled monopoly of the Indian trade through Egypt in the first half of the fifteenth century; they worked in collaboration with their Indian and Arabian counterparts who shipped the Indian goods to Egypt through the Arabian Sea.

The Turkish occupation of Constantinople (1453 A.D.) and the subsequent spread of the Ottoman sway in northern Africa, including Egypt, gave a serious set-back to the trade relationships between India and Europe. Portugal, under the leadership of Henry the Navigator, was the first European country to undertake the task of opening up direct trade with

India. After the discovery of the sea-route to India via the Cape of Good Hope by Vasco de Gama (1497 A.D.), the Portuguese established and zealously maintained their monopoly of eastern trade for ever a century until they received an effective challenge from the Dutch, the French and the English.

Revival of European contacts with India through the sea-route opened the flood gates of the subcontinent to the merchants, Christian missionaries, travellers and adventurers. It is impossible to estimate even approximately the number of Europeans who visited India during the period of the imperial mughals. The mughal authority was well established over a vast portion of the country in the seventeenth century while the peripheral territories were governed by the local rulers, most of whom recognised, explicitly or implicitly, the paramountcy of the mughal crown.

The imperial mughals enjoyed fame for their wealth, prowess and princely qualities; they meted out a liberal treatment towards the foreigners and gave complete freedom to the christian missionaries to carry on the propagation of their faith through peaceful means. The European visitors usually enjoyed the 'oriental hospitality' of the mughal monarchs and their bureaucracy in abundant measures.

That is why the Europeans of all shades and hues continued to swarm the land like honey bees, many of them ventured to the imperial court just to have a glimpse of the Grand Mogor or Mogul. Of course, at the initial stages, they 'approached India in a mood of childlike wonder without the least sense of racial superiority; until the whole of the country was traversed and laid open by European travellers, India remained a part of those regions where everything was gorgeous and splendid.'

Soon after, there followed a rat race among them to acquire whatever they could from this 'wonderland'. In the words of a modern historiographer of pre-independence era,

> "To the Portuguese, India seemed a second Peru, where diadems might be torn from the brows of the princes-nay, another new world for conquest and conversion to the Dutch, she looked like a large market which afforded favourable field for ambitious enterprise to the French, she was a big theatre for lucrative intrigue where they could reap a rich harvest of gains and fame; to the English she was an emporium which offered untold trade facilities... In the scramble that followed among these four European rivals, the English, whose methods were less showy but more sure and successful; proved to be the fittest, and therefore, survived the remaining three."

No wonder, quite a few of these Europeans have left valuable descriptions of their observations and experiences in the land of the Grand Moguls, in the form of diaries and travelogues. personal letters and communications addressed to their friends and relations in Europe, official papers and account books of their trade, religious or political activities, and reports of such missions to the courts of the mughal emperors, their provincial governors and other local rulers.

The historical value of these differs from document to document, depending upon the objectives and intellectual standard of the writers. Some of these documents contain mere street gossip or deliberate distortion of facts, while many others reflect the racial, religious and national prejudices, borne by the writers towards India and its people. Nevertheless, taken as a whole, these accounts comprise a unique category of the primary source material which throws a flood of light on the contemporary history of the-mughal period.

Broadly speaking, it can be classified into three categories records of the European factories, travelogues of the merchants and adventurers, and the accounts of the christian missionaries. The Hakluyt Society of Great Britain, named after Richard Hakluyt (1552-1616), a famous English traveller, has made a great contribution towards the advancement of historical research by publishing the accounts of many such travellers and adventurers who visited India during the mughal period.

They include Richard Hakluyt, William Hawkins, Sir Thomas Roe, Sir James Lancaster, William Hedges, Peter Mundy, John Jourdain, Pietro della Valle and many others.

Akbar's interest in religious and spiritual matters brought him in contact with the christian missionaries. In response to his invitation, three Jesuit missions from the Portuguese settlement at Goa visited the imperial court from 1580 to 1605 and stayed there long enough, as state guests, to explain the principles and practices of their religion. Their personnel comprised among others, Fr. Anthony Monserrate, Fr. Jerome Xavier and Fr. Emmanuel Pinheiro. The Jesuits continued to enjoy influence at the court of Jahangir as well.

Their reports, though highly prejudicial, are of immense value to the modern historiographers of the mughal age. The first known Englishman to reach India during -the mughal period was Fr. Thomas Stevens who joined the Society of Jesus at Goa and remained there for forty long years (1579-1619) as a missionary. Ralph Fitch was the first English merchant to visit Fatehpur Sikri and Agra.

Captain William Hawkins was the first Englishman to appear in the mughal court during the reign of Jahangir. He had brought a gift of 25,000 gold coins and a letter from James I of England for securing trade facilities. Hawkins was well received by Jahangir (April 1609) in spite of the opposition of the Jesuit Fr. Pinheiro who represented the Portuguese interests at the mughal court. About Hawkins's trade mission to India, Lane-Poole observes:

> "It was a singular situation for a bluff sea captain to find himself in an unknown land, called upon to meet a great Emperor about whom absolutely nothing was known in England. There was nothing to suggest the

most distant dream that in two centuries and a half the slight introduction Hawkins was then effecting between England and India would culminate in the sovereignty of a British queen over the whole empire where the Light of the World (Nur Jahan) and her imperial husband then reigned."

The second English merchant of note to appear at the court of Jahangir was Paul Canning who visited Agra in 1612. William Edwards brought (1615 A.D.) yet another letter from king James to the mughal emperor, *albeit* the most renowned English agent to visit the court of Jahangir was Sir Thomas Roe. He and his chaplain Terry stayed in India for over three years (September 1615-February 1619) and went about with 'Jahangir in his southern tour of Maridu and Ahmadabad; their mission was a failure *albeit* their accounts are of invaluable historical importance for the reconstruction of socio-cultural history of Jahangir's times.

William Foster, in his book, entitled, *Earl Travels in India,* has edited and published the diaries of John Mildenhall (1603-5), Ralph Fitch (1583-89), William Hawkins (1603-13), William Finch (1608-11), Nicholas Withington (1612-16) and Thomas Cory at (1614-17). The diaries of many other European travellers to India such as Francois Bernier, J. B. Tavernier, J. A. Mandeslo Manucci, Edward Terry, Rebert Coverte, Sir Thomas Herbert, and Alexander Hamilton, have also been published. De laet's, *Description of India and Fragment of Indian History* (1625 A.D.), has been found to be 'a complete gazetteer of Jahangir's India,' compiled faithfully by the writer.

Various Archaeological Sources

The archaeological sources, including the inscriptions, coins, monuments and other antiquities, are of immense value in the reconstruction of the socio-cultural history of medieval India. Edward Thomas was the first among the modern historiographers of medieval India to make extensive use of numismatics for the preparation of his book entitled, *The Chronicles of the Pathan Kings of Delhi;* his work has been supplemented by the catalogue of coins in various museums of India and England.

The Archaeological Survey of India has brought many new sources to light. These sources are particularly of great value to the historiographers of regional history of southern India and some Hindu states for the period during which they remained outside the pale of muslim domination. The inscriptions have been published mostly in the, *Epigraphia Indo-Moslemica, Epigraphia Indica* and other antiquarian journals.

A collection of all the inscriptions published in the, *Epigraphia Indo Moslemica* (1907-38), chronologically arranged with summaries, is given by V.S. Bendrey in, *A Study of Muslim Inscriptions.* The researches done by Johan Marshall, Percy Brown, Burgess, Fergusson, Havell, Cousens, and a host of other specialists in art and architecture give us an insight into the cultural trends of the times.

They are a living testimony to the intermingling and synthesis of the hindu and muslim architectural traditions and structural designs, and reveal, in unambiguous terms, the living conditions, faiths and beliefs as well as the socio-cultural outlook of the Grand Mughals and the upper strata of the medieval Indian society.

Bibliography

Ahmad, M.B. : *The Administration of Justice in Medieval India*, Aligarh, 1941.

Akbar, Muhammad : *The Punjab under the Mughals*, Lahore, 1948.

Ali, Athar : *The Mughal Nobility under Aurangzeb*, New Delhi, 1966.

Ali, M. : *The Mughal Nobility under Akbar*, Dept. of History, Aligarh Muslim University, 1966.

Aziz, Abdul : *The Mansabdari System and the Mughal Army*, Lahore, 1954.

Banerjee, A.C. : *Rajput Studies*, Calcutta, 1944.

Banerjee, S.K. : *Humayun Badshah*, Calcutta, 1938.

Barth, A. : *The Religions of India*, London, 1521.

Behere, N.K. : *The Background of the Maratha Renaissance in the 17th Century*, Bangalore, 1946.

Beni Prasad : *History of Jahangir*, London, 1922.

Bhargava, V.S. : *Marwar and the Mughal Emperors, 1526-1748*, Delhi, 1966.

Bhattacharya, S.N. : *A History of Mughal North-East Frontier Policy*, Calcutta, 1929.

Blumhardt, J.F. : *Catalogue of Hindi, Punjabi and Hindusthani Manuscripts in the Library of the British Museum*, London, 1899.

Brij Narayan and Sri Ram Sharma : *A Contemporary Dutch Chronicle of Mughal India*, Calcutta, 1957.

Burn, Sir Richard : *The Cambridge History of India*, Cambridge, 1937.

Caldecott, R.M. : *Life of Babar*, London, 1844.

Carpenter, J.E. : *Theism in Medieval India*, London, 1926.

Chablani, H.L. : *The Economic Condition of India during the Sixteenth Century*, Delhi, 1929.

Chand, Tara : *Influence of Islam on Indian Culture*, Allahabad, 1943.

———— : *Society and State in the Mughal Period*, Delhi, 1961.

Chatterjee, Anjali : *Bengal in the Reign of Aurangzeb*, Calcutta, 1967.

Chicherov, A.I. : *India, Economic Development in the 16th-18th Centuries*, Moscow, 1971.

Chopra, P.N. : *Social Life under the Mughals*, Agra, 1963.

———— : *Society and Culture during the Mughal Age*, Agra, 1963.

Danvers, F.C. : *The Portuguese in India*, London, 1894.

Das, H.H. : *The Norris Embassy to Aurangzeb*, Calcutta, 1959.

De Laet, Joannes : *The Empire of the Great Mogol*, Bombay, 1928.

De Tassy : *Grachin Histoare de la Litterature Hindonie et Hindoustanie*, Paris, 1870.

De, U.N. : *Some Aspects of Medieval Indian History*, New Delhi, 1971.

————: *The Mughal Government, A.D. 1500-1707*, New Delhi, 1970.

Duff, Grant : *A History of the Mahrattas*, London, 1826.

Edward Barlow : *Barlow's Journal, 1670-97*, London 1934.

Edwardes, S.M. and H.L.O. Garrett : *Mughal Rule in India*, Delhi, 1962.

Elliot, H.M. : *Memoirs on the Races of North-Western Provinces of India*, London, 1869.

Erskine, W.A. : *History of India under Babur and Humayun*, London, 1854.

Fanshawe, N.C. : *Delhi : Past and Present*, London, 1902.

Farquhar, J.H. : *Modern Religious Movements in India*, London, 1924.

Faruki, M. : *Aurangzeb and his Times*, Bombay, 1935.

Fergusson, J. : *History of Indian and Eastern Architecture*, London, 1910.

Francois, Bernier : *Travels in the Mogul Empire, 1656-68*, London, 1916.

Frazer, R.W. : *Literary History of India*, London, 1898.

Ghauri, I.A. : *War of Succession between the sons of Shah Jahan, 1657-58*, Lahore, 1964.

Ghauri, Iftikar Ahmad : *War of Succession between the Sons of Shah Jahan, 1657-1658*, Lahore, 1964.

Gladwin, F. : *Reign of Jahangir*, Calcutta, 1788.

Glamann, K. : *Dutch-Asiatic Trade, 1620-1740*, The Hague, 1958.

Gode, P.K. : *Studies in Indian Literary History*, Bombay, 1956.

Goswami, B.N. and J.S. Grewal : *The Mughal and Sikh Rulers and the Vaishnavas of Pindori*, Simla, 1969.

Grewal, J.S. : *From Guru Nanak to Maharaja Ranjit Singh*, Essays in Sikh History, Amritsar, 1972.

——— : *Guru Nanak in History*, Chandigarh, 1969.

——— : *Muslim Rule in India*, Calcutta, 1970.

Habib, Irfan : *The Agrarian System of Mughal India*, Bombay, 1963.

Haig, W. : *Historic Lanamarks of the Deccan*, Allahabad, 1907.

Hasan, Hadi : *Moghul Poetry : its Culture and Historical Value*, Madras, 1952.

Hasan, Ibn : *The Central Structure of the Mughal Empire and its Practical Working up to the year 1657*, Oxford, 1936.

Hasan, Mohibbul : *Historians of Medieval India*, Meerut, 1968.

Hastings, J. : *Encyclopaedia of Religion and Ethics*, Edinburgh, 1915.

Havell, E.B. : *Handbook to Agra and the Taj*, Agra, 1912.

Hearn, H.C. : *The Seven Cities of Delhi*, London, 1906.

Hodivala, S.H. : *Historical Studies in Mughal Numismatics*, Calcutta, 1923.

Hopkins, E.W. : *The Religions of India*, Boston, 1895.

Husain, A.B.M. : *Fatehpur Sikri and its Architecture*, Dacca, 1970.

Husain, Wahid : *The Administration of Justice during the Muslim Rule in India*, Calcutta, 1934.

Husain, Yusuf : *Glimpses of Medieval Indian Culture*, Bombay, 1957.

Irvine, W. : *Army of the Indian Moguls*, London, 1903.

———— : *Later Mughals*, Calcutta, 1921-22.

————: *The Army of the Indian Moghuls : Its Organization and Administration*, London, 1903.

Irwin, John and P.R. Schwartz : *Indo-European Textile History*, Ahmedabad, 1960.

Jafar, S.M. : *Education in Muslim India*, Peshawar, 1936.

———— : *Some Cultural Aspects of Muslim Rule in India*, Peshawar, 1938.

Karim, Abdul : *Dacca, the Mughal Capital*, Dacca, 1964.

Keene, H.G. : *Handbook to Delhi*, Calcutta, 1906.

———— : *The Fall of the Moghul Empire*, Delhi, 1971.

Kennedy, Pringle : *History of the Great Moghuls*, Calcutta, 1968.

Khan, Iqtidar Alam : *Mirza Kamran*, Dept. of History, Aligarh Muslim University, 1964.

Khosla, R.P. : *Mughal Kingship and Nobility*, Allahabad, 1934.

Krishnamurti, R. : *Akbar : The Religious Aspect*, Baroda, 1961.

Kulkarni, A.R. : *Maharashtra in the Age of Shivaji*, Poona, 1969.

Kulshreshtha, S.S. : *The Development of Trade and Industry under the Mughals, 1526-1707*, Allahabad, 1964.

Lal, K.S. : *Studies in Medieval Indian History*, Delhi, 1966.

Latif, S.M. : *Agra, Historical and Descriptive*, Calcutta, 1896.

Law, N.N. : *Promotion of Learning during Muhammedan Rule*, London, 1916.

Levy, R. : *The Social Structure of Islam*, Cambridge, 1957.

Macdonald, D.B. : *Development of Muslim Theology, Jurisprudence and Constitutional Theory*, New York, 1903.

Maclagan, Sir E. : *The Jesuits and the Great Mogul*, London, 1932.

Mahaley, K.L. : *Shivaji the Pragmatist*, Nagpur, 1969.

Mahalingam, T.V. : *Administration and Social Life under Vijayanagar*, Madras, 1939.

Majid, K. : *The Law of War and Peace in Islam*, Luzac, London, 1941.

Malgaonkar, M. : *Chhatrapatis of Kolhapur*, Bombay, 1971.

———— : *Kanhaji Angrey, Maratha Admiral; an account of his life and his battles with the English*, Bombay, 1959.

Malleson, G.B. : *Akbar*, London, 1890.

Manucci, N. : *Memoirs of the Mogul Court*, Michael Edwardes, London, 1957.

Modi, J.J. : *Parsees at the Court of Akbar*, Bombay, 1903.

Moin-ud-Din, Muhammad : *History of the Taj*, Agra, 1905.

Monserrate, Fr. A. : *Commentary on his Journey to the Court of Akbar*, Cuttack, 1922.

Moreland, W.H. : *From Akbar to Aurangzeb*, London, 1923.

———— : *India at the Death of Akbar*, London, 1920.

———— : *The Agrarian System of Moslem India*, Cambridge, 1929.

Nadkarni, R.V. : *The Rise and Fall of the Maratha Empire*, Bombay, 1966.

Narang, G.C. : *Glorious History of Sikhism*, New Delhi, 1972.

Nicholo Manucci : *Storia do Mogol, 1653-1708*, London, 1907 08.

Nijjar, B.S. : *Punjab under the Great Mughals*, Bombay, 1968.

Nizami., K.A. : *Medieval India, a Miscellany*, Dept. of History, Aligarh Muslim University, 1969.

———— : *Studies in Medieval Indian History and Culture*, Allahabad, 1966.

Orme, Robert : *Historical Fragments of the Mogul Empire*, London, 1805.

Pandey, A.B. : *Society and Government in Medieval India*, Allahabad, 1965.

Pant, D. : *The Commercial Policy of the Moguls*, Bombay, 1930.

Poole, Stanley : *Aurangzeb and the Decay of the Mughal Empire*, Delhi.

————: *Medieval India under Mohammedan Rule*, Delhi, 1963.

Prasad, Ishwari : *The Life and Times of Humayun*, Calcutta, 1955.

———— : *History of Medieval India*, Allahabad, 1940.

Qadir, A.S. : *Memoirs of Chand Bibi : The Princess of Ahmadnagar*, Hyderabad, 1937.

Qanungo, K. : *Dara Shukoh*, Calcutta, 1952.

Qanungo, K.R. : *History of the Jats*, Calcutta, 1925.

———— : *Sher Shah and his Times*, Bombay, 1965.

Qureshi, I.H. : *The Administration of the Mughal Empire*, Karachi, 1966.

Rahim, M.A. : *History of the Afghans in India, 1545-1631*, Karachi, 1961.

Ranade, M.G. : *Rise of the Maratha Power and other Essays*, Bombay, 1961.

Rawlinson, H.G. : *Shivaji the Maratha : his Life and Limes*, Oxford, Clarendon, 1915.

Ray, Nihar Ranjan : *The Sikh Gurus and Sikh Society; a Study in Social Analysis*, Patiala, 1970.

Ray, Sukumar : *Humayun in Persia*, Calcutta, 1948.

Rizvi, S.A.A. : *Muslim Revivalist Movements in Northern India in the Sixteenth and Seventeenth Centuries*, Agra, 1965.

Rosenthal, E.I.J. : *Political Thought in Medieval Islam*, Cambridge, 1958.

Roy, N.B. : *The Successors of Sher Shah*, Dacca, 1934.

Saksena, B.P. : *History of Shah Jahan of Delhi*, Allahabad, 1932.

Saletore, B.A. : *Social and Political Life in the Vijayanagara Empire*, Madras, 1934.

Sangar, S.P. : *Crime and Punishment in Mughal India*, Delhi, 1967.

Santanam, K. : *An Anthology of Indian Literatures*, New Delhi, 1969.

Saran, P. : *Studies in Medieval Indian History*, Delhi, 1952.

————: *The Provincial Government of the Mughals, 1526-1658*, Allahabad, 1941.

Saraswati, S.K. : *Glimpses of Mughal Architecture*, Calcutta, 1930.

Sardesai, G.S. : *Anecdotes of Aurangzeb*, Calcutta, 1925.

Sardesai, G.S. : *History of Aurangzeb*, Calcutta, 1912.

———— : *House of Shivaji*, Calcutta, 1955.

———— : *India of Aurangzeb*, Calcutta, 1901.

———— : *Studies in Aurangzeb's Reign*, Calcutta, 1933.

———— : *Studies in Mughal India*, Calcutta, 1919.

Sarkar, J.N. : *History of Aurangzeb*, Calcutta, 1915.

———— : *Mughal Administration*, Calcutta, 1952.

———— : *Studies in Mughal India*, Calcutta, 1919.

———— : *History of Aurangzeb*, Calcutta, 1925.

Sen, Kshitimohan : *Medieval Mysticism in India*, London, 1936.

Sen, S.N. : *Foreign Biographies of Shivaji*, Calcutta, 1927.

———— : *The Military System of the Marathas*, Bombay, 1958.

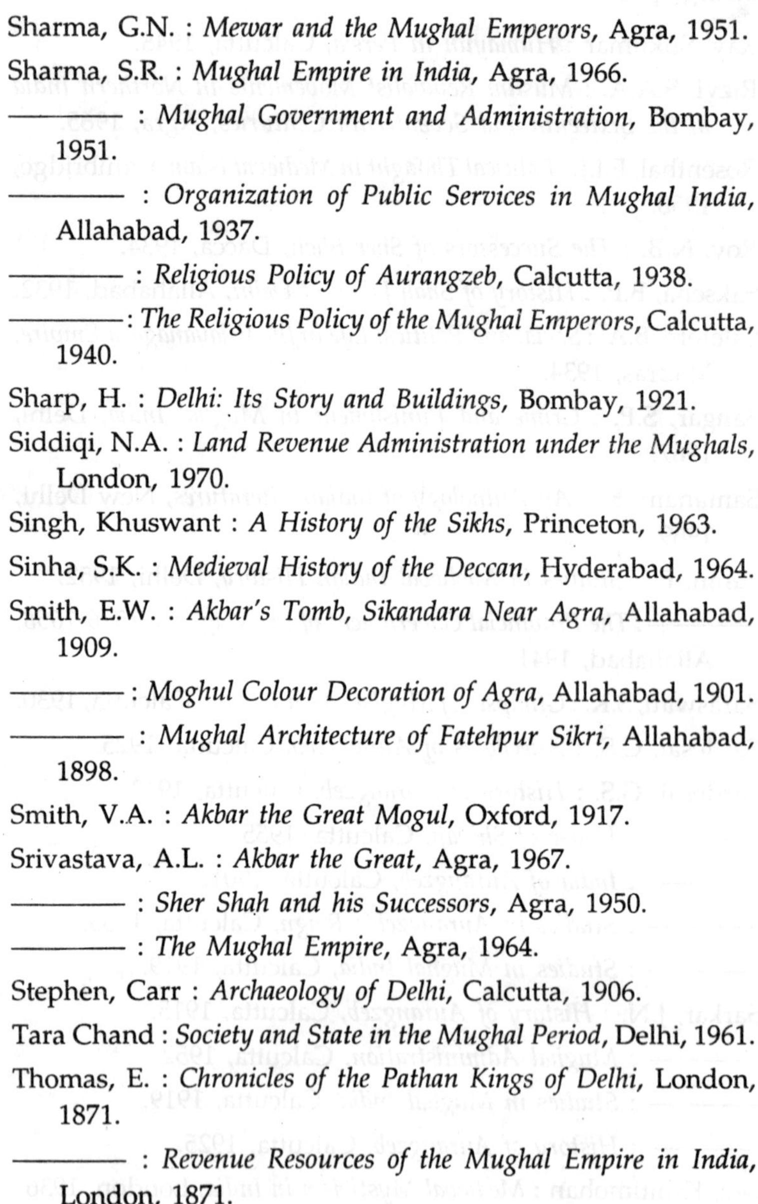

Sharma, G.N. : *Mewar and the Mughal Emperors,* Agra, 1951.

Sharma, S.R. : *Mughal Empire in India,* Agra, 1966.

——— : *Mughal Government and Administration,* Bombay, 1951.

——— : *Organization of Public Services in Mughal India,* Allahabad, 1937.

——— : *Religious Policy of Aurangzeb,* Calcutta, 1938.

———: *The Religious Policy of the Mughal Emperors,* Calcutta, 1940.

Sharp, H. : *Delhi: Its Story and Buildings,* Bombay, 1921.

Siddiqi, N.A. : *Land Revenue Administration under the Mughals,* London, 1970.

Singh, Khuswant : *A History of the Sikhs,* Princeton, 1963.

Sinha, S.K. : *Medieval History of the Deccan,* Hyderabad, 1964.

Smith, E.W. : *Akbar's Tomb, Sikandara Near Agra,* Allahabad, 1909.

———: *Moghul Colour Decoration of Agra,* Allahabad, 1901.

——— : *Mughal Architecture of Fatehpur Sikri,* Allahabad, 1898.

Smith, V.A. : *Akbar the Great Mogul,* Oxford, 1917.

Srivastava, A.L. : *Akbar the Great,* Agra, 1967.

——— : *Sher Shaḥ and his Successors,* Agra, 1950.

——— : *The Mughal Empire,* Agra, 1964.

Stephen, Carr : *Archaeology of Delhi,* Calcutta, 1906.

Tara Chand : *Society and State in the Mughal Period,* Delhi, 1961.

Thomas, E. : *Chronicles of the Pathan Kings of Delhi,* London, 1871.

——— : *Revenue Resources of the Mughal Empire in India,* London, 1871.

Tod, James : *Annals and Antiquities of Rajasthan,* Popular, London, 1914.

Tripathi, R.P. : *Rise and Fall of the Mughal Empire*, Allahabad, 1956.

Varma, R.C. : *Foreign Policy of the Great Mughals*, Agra, 1967.

Villiers-Stuart, G.H. : *Gardens of the Great Mughals*, London, 1913.

Wellesz, Emmy : *Akbar's Religious Thought Reflected in Mogul Painting*, London, 1952.

Williams, L. F. Rushbrook : *An Empire Builder of the Sixteenth Century*, London, 1918.

Winternitz, M. : *History of Indian Literature*, Calcutta, 1927.

Xavier S.J. : *Muslims of the Mughal Empire; Controversial and Missionary Activity*, Schoneck, 1957.

Yazdani, G. : *Bidar, Its History and Monuments*, Oxford, 1947.

Zaheer, Sajjad : *Urdu, Hindi, Hindusthani*, Bombay, 1947.

Zimmer H. : *Philosophies of India*, London, 1953.

Index

D

E

F

G

H

I

J

K

L

M

N

O

P

Q

R

S

T

U

V

W

Y

Z

❑❑❑